consumers and citizens

Cultural Studies of the Americas

Edited by George Yúdice, Jean Franco, and Juan Flores

Cultural Studies of the Americas   Volume 6

Néstor García Canclini

consumers and citizens

GLOBALIZATION AND MULTICULTURAL CONFLICTS

Translated and with an Introduction by George Yúdice

University of Minnesota Press

Minneapolis • London

The University of Minnesota Press gratefully acknowledges the assistance provided for the publication of this book by the McKnight Foundation.

Published by the University of Minnesota Press
111 Third Avenue South, Suite 290
Minneapolis, MN 55401-2520
http://www.upress.umn.edu

Library of Congress Cataloging-in-Publication Data
García Canclini, Néstor.
    [Consumidores y ciudadanos. English]
    Consumers and citizens : globalization and multicultural conflicts /
Néstor García Canclini ; translated by George Yúdice.
        p.   cm.
    Includes bibliographical references and index.
    ISBN 0-8166-2986-2 (hard: alk. paper) — ISBN 0-8166-2987-0
(pbk.: alk. paper)
    1. Mexico—Civilization—20th century.   2. Mexico—Relations—
Foreign countries.   3. Popular culture—Mexico.   4. Communication
and traffic—Social aspects—Mexico.   5. Technology—Social aspects—
Mexico.   6. Consumers—Mexico—Attitudes.   7. Nationalism—
Mexico.   I. Title.   II. Series.
F1234.G22713 2001
972.08'3—dc21   00-012031

Printed in the United States of America on acid-free paper

The University of Minnesota is an equal-opportunity educator and employer.

11 10 09 08 07 06 05 04 03 02 01   10 9 8 7 6 5 4 3 2 1

For Sandra

Contents

Translator's Introduction

From Hybridity to Policy

For a Purposeful Cultural Studies

Néstor García Canclini, an Argentine with a doctorate from the University of Paris, has been a professor of anthropology at the Universidad Autónoma Metropolitana—Iztapalapa since the early 1990s, where he heads the Program for the Study of Urban Cultures. He is undoubtedly the best-known and the most innovative cultural studies scholar in Latin America. His work straddles the disciplines of anthropology, sociology, art and literary studies, and cultural policy studies. Among his many books, *Cortázar, una antropología poética* (Cortázar, a poetic anthropology, 1968), on the noted Argentine "Boom" novelist and short-story writer, and *La producción simbólica* (Symbolic production, 1979), on the relationship of politics and avant-garde art in Argentina, reveal the range and originality of García Canclini's early work.[1] In the late 1970s, he began to conduct work on changes in the "popular" or folk cultures in Mexico, where he resettled as a consequence of the inhospitable atmosphere, particularly for progressive intellectuals like himself, created by the military dictatorship in Argentina.[2] This work led him to the creation of a rich and very serviceable methodology for studying the intersection of, on the one hand, mass, popular (or "folk," in U.S. parlance), and high culture, and, on the other hand, modernization in the spheres of communications and the economy. His *Las culturas populares en el capitalismo* (1982) (*Transforming Modernity: Popular Culture in Mexico* [1993]), which won the prestigious Casa de las Américas prize for best "essay," was an important corrective to both the clientelist subordination of indigenous cultures under the Mexican state and to romantic portrayals of these cultures as pure and innocent, although he also denounced their oppression.[3] It was also a book that resonated among those Latinamericanists familiar with cultural studies as it was practiced by Raymond Williams and Stuart Hall, among others. *Culturas híbridas: estrategias para entrar y salir de la modernidad* (1990) (*Hybrid Cultures: Strategies for Entering and Leaving Modernity* [1995]) further elaborated the critique of museum-bound views of culture, demonstrating that the dividing line between all three varieties (popular, mass, and high) blurs quite frequently and, in most cases, one is the supplement or constitutive exclusion of the other.[4] Rather than posit a postmodern Latin American condition, he registered, with the detail characteristic of the ethnographer and the art or literary critic, the ways in which artists, intellectuals, and popular communities engaged the pressures of modernization in a changing political context. *Consumidores y ciudadanos: conflictos multiculturales de la globalización* (1995) (*Consumers and Citizens: Globalization and Multicultural Conflicts* [2001]) maps the effects of urban sprawl and global media and commodity markets on citizens, critically, and yet shows that the complex results offer not only a shrinkage of certain traditional rights (particularly those of the welfare or clientelist state) but also openings for expanding citizenship.[5] Although in García Canclini's opinion consumers are not cultural dupes, he also does not hold to the voluntarist view that consumer choice is the same as a viable politics. This book includes a range of specific policy recommendations for a Latin American cultural space that can hold its own against the juggernaut of Hollywood and "Americanism" more generally. His recently published edited volumes, *La ciudad de los viajeros* (1997) (The city of travelers) and *Cultura y comunicación en la ciudad de México* (1998) (Culture and communication in Mexico City), focus on how the residents of Mexico City experience the built and broadcast environment;[6] *Las industrias culturales en la integración latinoamericana* (1999) (The culture industries in the integration of Latin America) consists of state-of-the-art sectorial analyses of the culture industries for the purposes of making concrete policy interventions in the creation of the Latin American cultural space that he proposed in *Consumers and Citizens*.[7] As I write this Introduction in August 1999, García Canclini has just completed his latest book, *La globalización imaginada* (Imagined globalization), in which he addresses many of the issues dealt with in prior books—multi- or interculturalism, migration, urban expansion, and cultural studies—in the context of globalization.[8] In this book he also gives a critical twist to relations between Latin Americans and North Americans (and especially Latinos) in the context of a U.S. projection of multiculturalism.

Conditions of Reception: The Currency of Hybridity

García Canclini is best known in the English-speaking world for *Hybrid Cultures: Strategies for Entering and Leaving Modernity*. First published in Mexico in 1990, this book has been widely read in cultural studies circles, in part because of the currency of theories of hybridity since the 1980s. This is both serendipitous and troublesome. The nearly two decades–long discussion among U.S. cultural studies scholars concerning flexible and multiple identities has provided a receptive context for García Canclini's proposal that in late modernity all identities straddle borders, whether geopolitical, cultural, or epistemological.[9] For the purposes of these introductory comments, I am taking a very broad view of cultural studies, a field that examines multiple, contending forces and power relations and that includes popular culture analysis, feminism, postcolonialism, deconstruction, Chicano and other minority discourses, discussions of border culture, queer studies, and so on. For conjunctural reasons that I shall elucidate subsequently, cultural studies rather than anthropology or sociology proper is the multifarious field in which García Canclini's work on hybridity resonates. Cultural studies as a political and intellectual project has been in an ongoing process of opening itself to revisions from the above-mentioned critical initiatives, as exemplified by the impetus provided by the work of the Marxist Literary Group since the late 1970s and the transformations of journals such as *Social Text* over this same period. Years before *Social Text*'s groundbreaking critique of postcolonialism,[10] the postcolonial framework had already been put to the test in the journal in the spate of commentaries on Fredric Jameson's proposal that all third-world texts are necessarily national allegories.[11] Indeed, the publication of Jameson's essay was accompanied by an account of the critical reception it encountered when delivered in Havana in 1985.[12] A subsequent issue carried Aijaz Ahmad's trenchant critique of Jameson's own national (U.S.), gendered (male), and racial (white) positioning, and suggested that the neat divide between third and first worlds was not viable precisely because of the effects of the new strategies of global capitalism and the struggles against them.[13]

The theories of hybridity that received the greatest receptivity at that time in this comprehensive definition of cultural studies were those associated with postcolonialism and minority cultures. Most exemplary is Homi Bhabha's proposal that the colonial situation and its legacy in postcolonialism introduced an incommensurability in the very heart of national projects. Colonial mimicry, which Bhabha considers subversive of European models, for example, both opened up and supplemented the neat divide between colonizer and colonized. With the intensification of transnational phenomena in the postcolonial era, this undermining of stable identities was magnified, introducing more numerous temporalities into the processes of identification. Rather than national coherence, Bhabha refers to a cultural difference that ensues from the split between a national pedagogy that takes the "people" as its historical objects and the performative work by which heterogeneous practices are transformed into the signs of a national culture while carrying with them the traces of difference. As such, hybridity is characterized by Bhabha as "the perplexity of the living as it interrupts the representation of the fullness of life."[14] Although expressed in a very different language, reflecting regional and disciplinary differences, García Canclini also characterized hybrid cultures as being fundamentally liminal, borders where struggles and negotiations confront "rigid wires and fallen wires."[15] In such sites, power is not defined by "confrontations and vertical actions," but, following Foucault, by "interwoven relations," whose cultural and political effectiveness is not explained by the imposition of power, but by the play of differences in the fabric of social life: "What gives [hybrid cultures] their efficacy is the obliqueness that is established in the fabric. How can we discern where ethnic power ends and where family power begins, or the borders between political power and economic power?"[16] As in Bhabha's reflection on colonial situations, García Canclini understands Latin American societies as constituted in the "intersection of different historical temporalities" ensuing from the multiple positions that they occupy in the symbolic as well as the political and financial world economies. As such, the multitemporal hybridity of Latin American societies is a function of a multiple relation to modernization. Some have celebrated this heterogeneity as proof that Latin America invented postmodernism before it ever gave signs of life in Europe and the United States.[17] García Canclini's interest, however, is to demonstrate the power of culture in political and economic projects and to analyze the effects of modernization in the periphery in order to help devise proposals for bettering life chances for the majority who barely survive. As we shall see, there is a significant difference in García Canclini's approach when compared with Bhabha's. Whether or not hybridity can discursively subvert Western reason is less important than its usefulness in pointing to practices that help democratize hierarchical and authoritarian societies both culturally and economically.

Toward the end of "DissemiNation," Bhabha focuses his discussion of the slippage between historical pedagogy and cultural performance on the foreignness that inheres therein. His emphasis is on the aporia that drives the narration of the nation to posit the "cultural condition for the enunciation of the mother-tongue,"[18] on the one hand, and the multiplication of borders that trouble the interior of national space, on the other. "What is...significant...is the emergence of a hybrid national narrative that turns the nostalgic past into the disruptive 'anterior' and displaces the historical present—opens it up to other histories and incommensurable narrative subjects."[19] We might ask what exactly is Bhabha's own investment in this incommensurable liminality? The answer, it seems, is a form of empowerment that comes from the condition of estrangement that inheres in liminality: "From this splitting of time and narrative emerges a strange, empowering knowledge for the migrant that is at once schizoid and subversive."[20] The agency of that empowerment is the minority subject. We might inquire into the nature of the empowerment wrought by liminality: how does it articulate with a politics? Bhabha argues that the aesthetics of interstiality serves to empower the marginalized insofar as it is nonessentialist and nonintegrationist,[21] and to foster new modes of cultural identification across the divides that modernity has drawn throughout the world.[22] It is as if Bhabha expected estrangement—or the unhomely—to be redeemed by an aesthetic practice that relies for its effectiveness on the autonomy of the institution of art rather than a politics that would struggle to open the institution into encounters and conflicts (he says little, indeed, about institutions).

In order to appear as material or empirical reality, the historical or social process must pass through an "aesthetic" alienation, or "privatization" of its public visibility. The discourse of "the social" then finds its means of representation in a kind of *unconsciousness* that obscures the immediacy of meaning, darkens the public event with an "unhomely" glow. There

is, I want to hazard, an incommunicability that shapes the public moment; a psychic obscurity that is formative for public memory.[23]

To argue that classic aesthetic distancing (whose counterparts are
the Russian Formalist *Ostranienie* and the Freudian *Verfremdungseffekt*)
is the means by which colonized or subaltern "otherness" makes itself
present—Bhabha writes "begins its presencing," an allusion to Heidegger's notion of "unveiling"—is to misunderstand how two orders of sociality (aesthetics and politics) interact. Literary theory and cultural studies are rife with these assimilations of social problems to philosophical
and aesthetic categories: Heidegger's homelessness versus homeless people; Kristeva's abjects vis-à-vis social "deviants"; Freud's uncanny vis-à-
vis parent-to-child power differentials; French feminists' play of the sig-
nifier vis-à-vis women's sexuality; and so on. It is only by a sleight of hand,
I would argue, that the aesthetic can be made to redeem the "disadvan-
taged" side of this dubious equation. As we shall see, this dichotomy is
evident in various statements from the Latin American Subaltern Studies
Group, who on the one hand is concerned about the exclusion of subalterns from national consolidations and state-oriented cultural critique,
and yet abstracts away the lived presence of subalterns by construing
them as a force of negation (the "unveiling" or rejection of Eurocentrism).
      This is indeed a familiar move within a broadly conceived U.S. cul-
tural studies framework: the contention that the most effective struggle
vis-à-vis power is the supplementation that the "weak" introduce into
the hegemonic discourses of the powerful. In a 1985 text, Bhabha had
proposed the "colonial hybrid" as the paradoxical instance in which the
authority invested in the colonists' identity was subverted by the mim-
etism of their colonized others.[24] In another influential text from 1985,
Donna Haraway embraced the myth of the cyborg to characterize the
agency that troubled the organic wholeness of identity.[25] "[C]ommit-
ted to partiality, irony, intimacy and perversity" (151), the "cyborg myth
is about transgressed boundaries, potent fusions, and dangerous possibilities which progressive people might explore as one part of needed
political work" (154). Like Bhabha, Haraway drew on the experience of
minoritized people to characterize her quintessential hybrids and cyborgs. "Women of color," and in particular Chicanas such as Chela San-
doval and Cherríe Moraga, who respectively brandished an "oppositional
consciousness" (157) and a mestizo delegitimation of purity and origins
(175), taught Haraway about "the power of the margins" and "liminal
transformation." As hybrids and members of a "bastard race," in Har-

away's words, they are identified as the demolishers of Western identity and dualisms that are inherent to the "logics and practices of domination of women, people of color, nature, workers, animals—in short, domination of all constituted as others, whose task is to mirror the self" (177).

García Canclini also senses the utopian potential in the critique of a normative Western subjectivism on the part of "new (or not so new) social actors, who are no longer exclusively white, Western, and male." Focusing on Latin American artists—whether of high, popular, or mass culture—who produce "hybrid" work, García Canclini attributes to them an "interrogative relationship with societies, or fragments of them, where they think they see living sociocultural movements and practicable utopias."[26] But the critique of the aesthetics of hybridity expressed by artists and writers from Tijuana, that most hybrid of border towns, is instructive of the pitfalls of the knee-jerk assumption that subaltern cultural practices ensuing from a given social situation are necessarily subversive. These Tijuana artists and writers took performance artist Guillermo Gómez-Peña to task for celebrating the hybrid border as the expression of a more "multifocal and tolerant" culture. They reminded him and other postmodern celebrants that hybridity results from having to satisfy basic needs by participating in a system of production and consumption not of one's choosing. These Tijuanans "reject the celebration of the migrations often caused by poverty in the place from which people migrate, and which is repeated in their new destination." They resent, moreover, those ubiquitous theorists and artists from metropolitan centers in Mexico or the United States who "want to discover us and tell us who we are."[27] There is a resentment in these words, for the Tijuanans suspect that Gómez-Peña and his artistic and theoretical kin were accumulating cultural capital useful in museological or academic struggles by claiming to have an experiential knowledge of the aesthetic of the day—appropriation, pastiche, impurity, sampling, and so on—drawn from the experience of the subaltern on the other side of the border. The Tijuanans understood this as a legitimation strategy that necessarily traded on the migrants' or *maquiladora* workers' experience of hardship.

Although García Canclini understands that hybridity undermines such dualisms as North/South, European/indigenous, folk/mass—"[c]ultures are no longer grouped in fixed and stable wholes, and therefore the possibility disappears of being cultured by knowing the repertory of 'the great works,' or of being popular because one manages the meaning of the objects and messages produced by a more or less closed community (an ethnic group, a neighborhood, a class)"—he also eschews, for the very same reason, the voluntarism that proclaims the "epistemic privilege" of the oppressed. Between representation and its undoing by hybridity, García Canclini, unlike Bhabha or Haraway, concentrates on the mediation of institutions that never permit one or the other to prevail completely. "The artistic market and the reorganization of urban visuality generated by the culture industry and the fatigue of political voluntarism are combined to make unrealistic any attempt at making of high art or folklore the proclamation of the inaugural power of the artist or of prominent social actors."[28] I would go a little further and elaborate this insight: neither the representations disseminated by government agencies, the media, labor and consumer markets, or academic disciplines such as anthropology nor the scrambling of these representations through the intersection of these institutions or other contingencies provide a foundation for the epistemic privilege of any one individual or collective subject.

Some U.S. cultural studies critics, including Latinamericanists, are troubled by García Canclini's reticence in "taking the side" of the subaltern. It goes without saying, of course, that he does not side with the dominant classes, capital, or the culture industries. García Canclini reminds his critics that not all subalterns are struggling for inclusion in a democratic society:

> My principal aim is to understand under what conditions and in what direction the processes of deterritorialization, opening and hybridization of traditional heritages are contributing to democratization in this *fin de siècle,* while many reterritorializations—like that of Sendero Luminoso...—have the effect of reinforcing authoritarianism, dogmatism and fundamentalism (which in Latin America, Eastern Europe and other areas are obstacles to democratic reconstruction and the resolution of the basic problems of the inhabitants).[29]

This reminder flies in the face of John Beverley's criticism that García Canclini is reformist rather than radical for not seeking to contribute to a historical bloc in which the subaltern will have a protagonist role in the struggle for hegemony.[30] From García Canclini's point of view, Beverley's aspirations appear quite voluntarist. In his more recent work, including *Consumers and Citizens,* written after this statement, García Canclini has devoted most of his energies to discover viable practices that enable scholar-activists to contribute to this endeavor. His increasing involvement in cultural policy as a complement of research is one direction that I comment on subsequently. I argue that such involvement in cultural policy is not simply accommodationist reformism, as Beverley has alleged.

At heart, Beverley is skeptical that a traditional intellectual (i.e., not from the subaltern classes) can effectively espouse the cause of the subaltern. Consequently, he assimilates in knee-jerk fashion García Canclini's position to that of neo-Arielist arguments according to which analytic authority should remain among traditional or "critical" intellectuals.[31] Neo-Arielism, for Beverley, "is a variant of Néstor García Canclini's claim that with modernity the category of subalternity itself is no longer relevant, since it depends for its functional efficacy on traditional, premodern culture that has been overtaken by modernity and urbanization."[32] Beverley engages in a willful oversight here, disregarding the target of García Canclini's critique, which is the ways in which discourses of the "popular" have been manipulated and hybridized. For example, in *Transforming Modernity* he takes to task critics "influenced by a Gramscian analytical framework" because they draw a Manichaean opposition between elites and popular masses that enables them to posit too easily "anesthetizing" or "contestatory" qualities to elite or popular cultural products and practices, without examining the complex mediations (religious beliefs, bureaucratic agencies, markets, media, tourism) that have their own impact on those products and practices.[33] García Canclini goes on, however, to provide his own neo-Gramscian framework that emphasizes the cross-class and transnational industrial articulations that complicate the Manichaean schema.

In *Hybrid Cultures* García Canclini extends his critique of neo-Gramscians' reliance on

> superparadigms and generat[ing] popular strategies to which they attempt to subordinate the totality of the facts: all that is not hegemonic is subaltern, or the inverse. The descriptions then omit ambiguous processes of interpenetration and mixing in which the symbolic movements of different classes engender other processes that cannot be ordered under the classifications of hegemonic and subaltern, modern and traditional.[34]

This may indeed be the case among the Latin American Gramscians whom he takes to task. It should be pointed out, however, that by the time he began his research on *Transforming Modernity* in the late 1970s, the work of Hall, Williams, and especially Laclau, which made the same criticisms as García Canclini and in some cases went significantly beyond his, had already been published. In 1977, each published a major

xviii   Translator's Introduction

theoretical piece. Williams elaborated a quite workable concept of mediations that accounts for ideological processes better than the base–superstructure dichotomy and raised the question of residual, dominant, and emergent formations that complicate the notion of ideology within the hegemonic process; Hall recognized Gramsci's understanding of tradition as something reworked within given conjunctures and elaborated on the dialogic and ongoing contestation within knowledge and in and across institutions; and Laclau proposed the oft-cited notion of articulation as the fusion of nonclass elements within the contradictions or power blocs, which enabled the insight that (reworked) traditions may be continuous from one power bloc to another, "in contrast to the historical discontinuities which characterize class structures."[35]

The "Popular"

The criticism that can legitimately be leveled at García Canclini is that he throws out the baby of the subaltern with the bathwater of the popular. This is because of a kind of transcultural and translational parallax that makes it difficult to understand how a concept developed in one geocultural region is applied in another. This problem of parallax is also at work in the misreadings by several cultural studies critics of García Canclini's work, particularly their refusal to understand why he proceeds with caution whenever intellectuals invoke the popular. The popular and the subaltern are, of course, kindred concepts, both passing through a foundational theoretical turning point in the work of Antonio Gramsci, on whom García Canclini, despite his critiques of neo-Gramscians, has taken inspiration, particularly in *Transforming Modernity*. Before delving into the use of the notion of the popular in Latin America, of which García Canclini is one of the most astute critics, it will be worthwhile to give a brief history of the term in Gramsci.

The notion of the popular was used by Gramsci in his diagnosis of the rise of fascism in 1920s Italy and as part of his program for moving Italian politics in a more revolutionary direction. In his estimation, progressive Italian intellectuals were out of touch with the social forces, particularly the "popular masses," necessary for the construction of a "national-popular" consciousness or "collective will" that in turn were necessary for revolution.[36] In France, the Jacobins ushered in a national-popular bloc by creating an alliance with the "popular masses," in particular the peasantry, which enabled the creation of a modern state (131–32). But the legacy of quasi-feudal "economic-corporate" domination in

Italy, characterized by autonomous city-states, dependent regions, and a mechanical bloc of social groups, was not conducive to national unification until the Risorgimento in the mid-nineteenth century, and then only "inorganically" under the leadership of Cavour and the Moderate Party, without significant involvement of popular classes. Indeed, the absence of popular elements enabled the Moderate Party to absorb the more liberal-democratic intellectuals of the Action Party of Mazzini and Garibaldi, thus serving the interests of northern (Piedmontese) capitalists (204). Gramsci calls this northern dominance a "dictatorship without hegemony," in which Piedmont stood in for but did not properly function as a "leading" social group (106). The northern bourgeoisie did not show the "inflexible will to become the 'leading' party," as did the Jacobins (80). Instead, the Piedmontese state "'led' the group which should have been 'leading.'" This state loosely held together ruling-class "nuclei" throughout Italy, but these nuclei "did not seek to 'lead' anybody, i.e., they did not wish to concord their interests and aspirations with the interests and aspirations of other groups" (104–5). The result was the failure to achieve a "national-popular collective will," particularly without a "*simultaneous* burst into political life" of the "great mass of peasant farmers" (132).

The construction of a national-popular will in Latin American societies faced similar challenges to those outlined by Gramsci. Juan Carlos Portantiero, for example, considered Gramsci's analysis of "Caesarism" and "Bonapartism" applicable to Latin American nationalist populisms, particularly Varguismo in Brazil, Cardenismo in Mexico, Peronismo in Argentina, and Aprismo in Peru.[37] This situation results when a potentially catastrophic contention between social forces is intervened in by a third actor, for example, the military, which brings into play an array of "auxiliary [often popular] forces directed by, or subjected to, their hegemonic influence," and "succeeds in permeating the State with its interests, up to a certain point, and in replacing a part of the leading personnel."[38] In this case, the popular forces do not, obviously, take power, but some of their agendas, particularly those that have been articulated into the third actor's ideological offensive against dominant forces, are incorporated into state policies. The history of the relationship between the left and popular masses has not been a felicitous one in Latin America, for leftist intellectuals and indeed revolutionaries (e.g., Che in Bolivia or the Sandinistas regarding the Misquitos) have not understood the specificity of popular subjects' historical, geocultural, and ideological formations. Because these formations are rooted in social, political, and cultural struggles on a national or regional scale, socialist or revolutionary strategy must permit the development of cultural policies in which popular groups participate. This has not often been the case. In any event, the above-mentioned populisms have left deep marks, which are only now, under neoliberalism, being scuffed into oblivion.

A proper understanding of the hybridization of modernity and tradition, foregrounded in García Canclini's work since at least *Transforming Modernity*, would require an account of populism in Latin America from the 1920s to the 1960s, which the scope of this Introduction does not permit. Suffice it to say that culturally, and literarily in particular, the experience of populism was accompanied by a series of aesthetics of hybridity that expressed the struggles, incorporation, co-optation, and resistance of popular masses.[39] These masses resisted and negotiated the means of incorporation into modernizing projects in the aftermath of World War I, a process that was intensified as the leading economies permitted developing countries to strengthen import-substitution industrialization. But these historical circumstances that enabled the rise of this classic Latin American populism changed in the 1960s. Import-substitution industrialization was no longer viable in the world economy and power blocs were reunited under the control of transnational capitalism. Leftist articulations of populism, transmuted into guerrilla movements in many contexts, were energetically countered by new military dictatorships (Southern Cone) or authoritarian governments (Mexico). U.S. anti-insurgency policies were an important intervention in these circumstances, offering the carrot of aid for development (e.g., the Alliance for Progress) and the stick of military intervention (e.g., the Chilean coup) and training (e.g., the School of the Americas). Analytically, as the dominant classes could no longer transform and neutralize these radicalized populisms, outright coercion (torture, massacres, disappearances) became the prescribed instruments to rein in the threats. At the same time, new media industries, especially television, whose reorganization under conglomerates such as Mexico's Televisa and Brazil's Globo was facilitated by these repressive governments, began to transform the *popular* into the *mass*. The mass media, of course, have a longer history in Latin America than this turning point in the 1960s; they became significant players in modernization and education as early as the beginning of the century in some countries.

According to Renato Ortiz, the 1960s represent the crystallization of a common cultural consciousness among so-called popular sectors and leftist intellectuals with the potential to create an alternative hegemony that might change the "equilibrium" between political and civil society within the state. In countries like those of the Southern Cone, Brazil, and Mexico, it is not possible to speak of hegemony as an equilibrium between political and civil society. Ortiz, for example, writes of the "precariousness of the very idea of hegemony among us."[40] Instead, what characterized countries such as Argentina, Brazil, and Mexico was a pact between state-aligned elites who promoted import-substitution industrialization and an equally state-aligned popular nationalism that sought state welfare, delivered in corporatist forms since the 1920s and 1930s. The origins of "popular culture" in Latin America can be traced to this paradoxical state, which re-created those institutions most responsible for supporting that culture: education, radio, film, museums, and anthropological institutions. It is through these institutions that a good deal of "people's culture" was disseminated, not outside of the market but squarely within the culture industries. The most salient examples are samba and carnival in Brazil and *rancheras* on radio and in film in Mexico. The nationalization of samba, for example, involved the intervention of the Vargas regime in the 1930s, the radio broadcasting and recording industries, as well as various social institutions, such as carnival, and "popular" networks.[41] The shift that takes place in the 1960s is the incipient accommodation of Brazilian and Mexican media to international standards. This mass-mediated internationalization, often considered "Americanization," has significant consequences for the rearticulation of the "national popular," which García Canclini addresses in *Transforming Modernity* and subsequent books.

By the time the dictatorships gave way to a new phase of democratization under a neoliberal consensus, the media and a host of new civil society forms of organization articulated the new logic under which popular antagonisms would be negotiated. This does not mean that the racialized popular mass of the population ceased to be a force to contend with; it did mean that the possibility of radicalizing their demands in socialist terms became increasingly unlikely. Neoliberal populisms in the 1980s and 1990s in Argentina (Menem), Brazil (Collor), and Peru (Fujimori) revealed the degree to which the form of incorporating popular classes had changed. Furthermore, the defeat of the Central American revolutions, the utter marginalization of Cuba, particularly after the demise of the Soviet Union, and the "fundamentalization" or criminalization of several guerrilla struggles, especially in Peru and Colombia, signaled the unworkability of change by means of armed insurrection. Indeed, many "national liberation fronts" (e.g., the Sandinistas and the Salvadoran FMLN) transformed themselves into civil society organizations after more than a decade of struggle, as did the neo-Zapatistas almost immediately. I have argued elsewhere that the recourse to civil society (succored by U.S. foundations and European and global nongovernmental organizations) is fully compatible with neoliberalism.[42] As state budgets for social programs are cut, it makes sense to free-market advocates to have civil society "organize itself," a turn of events examined by the Mexican intellectual Carlos Monsiváis in *Entrada libre: crónicas de la sociedad que se organiza* (Free entry: chronicles of a society that organizes itself).[43] It is in this context that García Canclini has made the clarion call to rethink how we understand popular movements.

Rethinking the Popular

The rethinking of the popular comes with an exuberant rejection of its incorporation into a national discourse. This is no doubt because of the fear that a radicalization of populism will engender those forces to which the dictatorships reacted. It is also due to the recognition that globalization has altered the circumstances under which it was politically viable to appeal to the popular for progressive ends. Without progressive potential, the popular—and the claims that it serves as the ground for opposition to imperialism—becomes a fetishized symbol of Latin America's hybrid temporality, caught between the magic of the traditional and the indigenous or African and the realist "rationality" of modernity. For example, José Joaquín Brunner, one of the most influential intellectuals of the transition to democracy in Chile, reviles the national-popular as an outdated myth:

> The national-popular preserves the old desire to give culture a unifying ground, be it a class, racial, historical, or ideological one. When culture begins to deterritorialize, when it becomes more complex and varied, assumes all the heterogeneities of society, is industrialized and massified, loses its center and is filled with "lite" and transitory expressions, is structured on the basis of a plurality of the modern—when all this takes place, the unifying desire becomes reductionist and dangerously totalitarian or simply rhetorical.[44]

Echoing García Canclini's recognition of the hybridization of popular traditions with the market and mass culture, Brunner breathes a sigh of relief as the national-popular subject recedes into insignificance:

Today the national and the popular are in the public plaza but also in the market, in rural traditions but also in transitory urban styles, in the mass media, and in educational institutions, in global communications and the flows that traverse them, and so on. National and (modern) popular are television (whether it transmits an opera plain and simple or a soap opera); the school, that forms, filters, and selects; Catholicism, elections and their rituals, rock music in various languages, and Bata sandals.

In other words, Macondo has been nothing but a nostalgic sentiment for quite some time, an illusion and a myth of the national-popular, just like protest song, political painting, the novel of social content, radical clubs, and Citroneta.

Today it no longer makes any sense to speak of the national-popular as we did twenty years or half a century ago.[45]

This dismissive reaction follows in part from the other problematic attitude concerning the popular: its romantic heroization, to the point of finding in the Sendero Luminoso or the Colombian guerrillas the true manifestation of a national-popular. The oscillation between dismissal and heroization has had its effect on how the history of popular agency is conceived.

Taking the Mexican Revolution as an example, the accounts of the 1920s and 1930s portrayed an agrarian revolution in which "the people" broke with feudal oppression. These accounts took on epic proportions, as Gilbert Joseph and Daniel Nugent remind us, in the hands of foreign admirers (e.g., Frank Tannenbaum and John Steinbeck) and partisans of the new revolutionary state (José Valadés, Jesús Silva Herzog, etc.).[46] Revisionist histories, conditioned by the crisis of the Mexican state in 1968, in contrast, focused on state domination and management, largely leaving aside popular participation. Indeed, there seemed to be no popular agency. More recent work, particularly that which is inspired in Gramsci's accounts of the hegemonic process, provides a fine-grained historical account of the "articulation of distinctive forms of social consciousness and experience" that constitute the popular as well as inform the state.[47] Perhaps the most exemplary study in this regard is Florencia Mallon's *Peasant and Nation: The Making of Postcolonial Mexico and Peru*.[48] Mallon proposes an expanded notion of both the popular and the intellectual, giving historical flesh to Gramsci's insight that consciousness and identity are an achievement of collective everyday practices in a context of unequal power relations. As such, her work does not merit the criticism leveled by John Beverley that she simply sought to find the popular elements left out of official histories or demonstrate that "peasant communities actually did have a decisive role in the formation of the state in Peru and Mexico."[49] Far from assuming that subalterns can simply be represented in history, Mallon reconstructs a network of relations in which the meaning of actions (e.g., resistance, influence, and negotiation) can be discerned. She focuses on practices within the shifting relations in rural communities—family members of different generations and gender identities, local intellectuals such as teachers, justices of the peace, local commissioners of public instruction, and so on—and of these with regional and national officials. Her account of agrarian reform, education, and local government in the sierra de Puebla shows that identities and forms of knowledge were fashioned in the complexly negotiated processes of partial integration in and resistance to national policies and discourses that left a sedimented memory that enabled the Mexican state to achieve hegemony in the twentieth century because it could tap into these discourses. This memory, moreover, enabled popular actors in the 1910s to rework already established agendas and alliances, even if they were subsequently suppressed. Mallon's point is that this harking back to the past "does not constitute the reactivation of atavistic peasant communities but rather the reorganization of already sophisticated political alliances and discourses in a new context."[50] The objective is not so much to argue for the protagonism of peasants in the construction of hegemony as to demonstrate that they articulated a historical memory grounded in resistance and negotiation and that could be used and projected beyond their particular situation in given historical conjunctures.

This is a view of popular culture already present in García Canclini's *Transforming Modernity*. He focuses on handicrafts and fiestas not to recuperate archaic practices or to criticize their accommodation to the state, the culture industries, and tourism. Beyond the anthropological view that fiestas are those moments when a collectivity "goes into its deepest self, that part that normally escapes it, in order to understand and restore itself," García Canclini sees them as the means to negotiate deficiencies in the agrarian structure, fulfill their consumption needs, earn tourist dollars, and enjoy state sponsorship.[51] A skeptical reader following García Canclini's arguments will assume that Indians simply adapt their practices to the incentives provided externally, inserting mass produced nonindigenous music into their fiestas or representations of modern objects (e.g., airplanes) into their pottery for the benefit of tourists and foreign consumers. Despite such commercialization and the state's intervention to reproduce an ethnic sense of difference and national identity, García Canclini concludes that the fiesta provides "a degree of ceremonial readaptation, a new state for a torn community that finds in the fiesta a means to reassert those elements of its identity that come from the past and, in changes, a way to update the representation of its hardships and inequalities as well as its historical cohesion."[52] We have here an early formulation of the insight in *Consumers and Citizens* that identity is a coproduction.

These convergences notwithstanding, one gets a sense that García Canclini focuses primarily on the changes wrought *on* indigenous culture by modernization while Mallon (re)constructs the ways in which popular groups resist and shape the practices of those who would transform them. In *Hybrid Cultures,* García Canclini has an almost allergic reaction to the emphasis that some neo-Gramscians put on domination and resistance: "There is no folklore belonging only to the oppressed classes; nor are the only possible types of inter-folkloric relations those of domination, submission, or rebellion."[53] There may be a disciplinary and conjunctural difference at work here. García Canclini conducts ethnographic research in the context of transculturation with the consumer, culture, and tourism industries; Mallon examines negotiations between popular sectors and officialdom in an era of incipient modernization, before these other mediating institutions further complicated the scenarios in which the popular classes had, perhaps, a more direct opportunity to enact their will. The question to ask about popular culture is not whether or not there is a popular will, but under what circumstances and in what relations with what other groups it manifests itself and gains cultural and political space. And if the circumstances do not favor this possibility, then the task of the scholar-intellectual might be to shed some light on the means to transform the disadvantages. Here Mallon and García Canclini point in different, although not contrary, directions. For Mallon, the recovery of "embedded memory and practice" may "allow us to imagine more clearly how subaltern peoples might, after conquering the space to do so, create their own alternative polities."[54] For García Canclini, recovery is treacherous terrain and even if it were not, it is not, in itself, enough. "Indians and urban popular classes [must] manage to convert those 'remnants' [i.e., identity symbols] from the past into 'emergent,' challenging expressions."[55]

This transformation is what García Canclini considers the "*construction of a counterhegemonic project,*" but it does not depend only on recovery or knowledge. For him, there are other steps to be taken and it is probably mistaken to assume that a particular collective actor can do this on its own. "[P]opular sectors [must] organize themselves into cooperatives and unions from which they can begin to regain ownership of the means of production and distribution" as well as "appropriat[e] the symbolic meaning of their work." This is achieved not by "reintegrat[ing] into an Indian context" (already carried out by state institutions and tourism), but by "formulat[ing] a strategy for gradual control over spaces and mechanisms of circulation."[56] Furthermore, policy recommendations for popular self-determination have to be conjunctural; what enables participation in one historical context may hinder it in another. Indeed, García Canclini's work has increasingly focused on the policy considerations for enhancing a democratic culture in tandem with his broadening of the examination of the interaction of popular traditions with transnational culture industries, particularly in the large urban centers of Latin America. This orientation marks the shift from the focus on handicrafts and fiestas in *Transforming Modernity,* written in the late 1970s and early 1980s, to *Consumers and Citizens,* written in the 1990s, with the pivotal work on cultural reconversion in *Hybrid Cultures* (1990) about midway. This latter work gives a wealth of examples from art, literature, music, handicrafts, and urban culture to demonstrate that traditions have not been rendered obsolete, as Brunner seems to imply in his well-placed yet perhaps overly emphatic repudiation of *Macondismo* (i.e., Latin American magical realism), but that they have been resignified in the context of the overall restructuring of society, politics, and the economy. "Instead of the death of traditional cultural forms, we now discover that tradition is in transition, and articulated to modern processes. Reconversion prolongs their existence."[57]

Citizenship in the Age of the "International Popular" and Fragmented Politics

Throughout the 1980s, García Canclini's interests developed gradually from policies that presume that popular groups can take control of the production and consumption process to a more mediated understanding of how appropriation works in fragmented urban settings in the context of an increasing tendency to consume "international popular" culture.[58] "Consider that today no 'national' cinema can recoup investment in a film from ticket sales within its own borders. It has to target multiple sales venues: satellite and cable TV, networks of video and laser disk rental outlets. All of these systems, structured transnationally, facilitate the 'defolklorization' of messages they put into circulation" (chapter 5 of this volume). These conditions foster a collective memory made from the fragments of different nations, making it difficult for that memory to be distilled from any one particular group,[59] although "American" references may predominate. We are reminded here of Appadurai's suggestion that supranational cultural formations (e.g., the Indian diaspora or Latinoness in the United States) emerge from processes of deterritorialization of peoples, commodities, money, images, and ideologies.[60] Under these conditions, of what some have considered a "global ecumene" and others Armageddon, the familiar "national-popular" constructions of medium-scale nations ("Spain," "Yugoslavia," "Britain," "Italy") obviously founder and give way to a range of smaller nationalisms ("Catalonian," "Basque," "Serbian," "Albanian," "Scottish," "Padanian") and supranational federations (the European Union) and trade agreements in search of a supranational cultural cement (the Southern Common Market or MERCOSUR).

The "popular" has also given way to a social movement framework, at first associated with opposition to dictatorships and subsequently to democratization in the context of the postdictatorial and postauthoritarian transition. In this latter context and under the sway of neoliberalizing economies and polities, social movements have tended to accommodate to a civil society paradigm, according to which citizens engage in voluntary associations, often organized as nongovernmental organizations (predominant in Latin America) or nonprofit organizations (typical of the United States), to perform a myriad of social services, including cultural activities. Fiscal and juridical forms of organization have begun to take precedence over the local political bosses who integrated "popular sectors" into clientelist networks. NGOs and civil society networks are flexible and nomadic, capable of producing a sense of participation, if not always meeting the needs of the population. There are, of course, many situations in which this model does not seem to correspond to the antagonisms brought forth by subordinated groups. The Colombian guerrillas and Sendero Luminoso in Peru certainly are not good examples of democratic organizations. There is, however, no theory of civil society that can easily exclude those associations that manifest undemocratic behavior. García Canclini recognizes the paradox that the effort to institute democracy may already be tainted by the inclusion of nondemocratic groups. "How can a program that is democratic and respectful of a group's structures be established if the structures in question are paternalistic, authoritarian, and based on bonds of blood rather than affinity? Moreover, what if the state that promotes democratization is also racked by these same nondemocratic characteristics?" (chapter 9 of this volume). One might, following David Ronfeldt, characterize these as manifestations of "uncivil society," which are just as likely as democratizing social movements to emerge in a polity in which state authority is undervalued and a premium is put on difference, decentralization, and voluntary association.[61] The focus of attention, however, has been on those mobilizations that further the democratization of national societies, such as the previously mentioned neo-Zapatistas or the Brazilian movement of the landless (the Movimento dos Sem Terra). Although the latter two seem to have maintained a certain autonomy from the state and capital, most civil society organizations are permeable by institutions of the corporate sector, the government, and the "globalized civil society" of international NGOs. The supposed autonomy of social movements—their particularly social, as opposed to political, agendas—does not obtain independently of channeling by capital and the state.

Drawing on earlier arguments, we can characterize the historical conjuncture in which these civil society organizations arise as consisting of the following features: (1) the eradication of revolutionary populism by the Southern Cone dictatorships and counterrevolutionary Central American military regimes of the 1960s, 1970s, and 1980s, or the authoritarian-paternalistic rule characteristic of countries such as Mexico; (2) the emergence of social movements that could not appeal directly to politics, yet stretched the significance of the cultural and the personal to the point of having political effects; (3) (re)democratization and incorporation of social movements under the international hegemony of neoliberalism in the 1980s and 1990s; (4) the demise of socialism, which left little opposition to the legitimacy claimed by neoliberals in their program to transform (through structural adjustment, privatization, and downsizing of the public sector) the legacy of the national-popular or national-populist state (a process that is still taking place); (5) the increasing dispersion of so-called popular sectors as a result of urbanization and urban sprawl, to the point, as García Canclini argues in *Consumers and Citizens,* that there is little communication across difficult-to-reach sections of the megalopolis, thus making it impossible to produce coherent narratives of the popular (chapter 4 of this volume); (6) the abandonment of public spaces for traditional forms of congregation, again the result of urban sprawl, but more significantly of a preference for home-delivery of entertainment via TV, video, and cable; (7) the concomitant transnationalization of publicness due to various forms of supranational linkages, from migrant circuits to multinational networks and supranational regional integration agreements such as NAFTA (North American Free Trade Agreement) and MERCOSUR that are rearticulating the imagined community.

Rather than take all of these transformations as bad news, García Canclini remains optimistic when he recommends urban cultural policies that respect and disseminate the differences that characterize the fragmentation of urban sprawl (chapter 3 of this volume). "The diversification of tastes might have something to do with the cultural formation of a democratic citizenship" (chapter 7 of this volume). But democracy is much more complicated than the wishful dreams of liberal theorists. "Hence the paradox: those who sought to bring democracy to the locality soon learned that they had to make pacts with neighborhood bosses in order to gain access to the dwellers and to insert themselves into local sociocultural structures" (chapter 9 of this volume). And to further complicate the dream of democracy, we might remember Foucault's critique of civil society, which defends itself by identifying and purging those who are construed as "other" or abject; that is, civil society reproduces itself by segregating those to be eliminated, and generates a host of institutions (e.g., prisons, psychiatric asylums, schools) that both serve this purpose and conceal it by establishing "rehabilitation" as their mission. This is a view of civil society that flies in the face of the notion of hegemony that Gramsci had put forth. Gramsci had written that

> [o]f the many meanings of democracy, the most realistic and concrete one in my view can be worked out in relation to the concept of "hegemony." In the hegemonic system, there exists democracy between the "leading" group and the groups which are "led," in so far as the development of the economy and thus the legislation which expresses such development favour the (molecular) passage from the "led" groups to the "leading" group.[62]

With economic development, there is a fusion of the "ethical" or disciplinary state (in the hands of intellectuals) and the "interventionist" or regulatory state (in the hands of politicians and technocrats), which protects the economic interests of the national bourgeoisies, as well as " 'protect[s]' the working classes against the excesses of capitalism."[63] The result is a civil society that presumably regulates itself. Foucault, however, took a skeptical view of the regulatory society, whose history has been told predominantly by focusing only on two of the three tactical instruments that ensure hegemony (national consciousness and its attendant historical, cultural, linguistic, and philological discourses; and class struggle, with its attendant discourse of political economy). The third instrument, which, according to Foucault, has received scant attention, is the security or welfare state. This security state declared war on the internal dangers of the polity by means of "bioregulation."[64] Elsewhere I have argued that "bioregulation" by the modern state has been augmented by an expansion of "cultural regulation" in the neoliberal postmodern state.[65] This insight should lead us to view the formulation of cultural policies with caution.

Subalternity: Negation or Negotiation?

Any theory of democracy, liberal or radical, has to deal with these complicating factors: criminality as a form of (un)civil society and abjectification by a society that "defends itself." They also have to be taken into consideration by those who have most criticized García Canclini: Latin American subalternists. In the early 1990s, a group of Latin American subaltern scholars was formed in the United States to rethink the crisis of the left. Although the crisis was generated by the failure of communism and popular revolutionary struggles in Central America and the Andean countries, this problem was largely an academic one among U.S. scholars. Many of these scholars had been involved to some extent as fellow travelers and in some cases participants in these struggles. As those struggles were defeated, so too were the foundations of the very beliefs of these academics. Did "the people" turn against the Sandinistas? And if so, where had the Sandinistas—aside from confronting the U.S. juggernaut—gone wrong? According to John Beverley, neither the Cuban nor the Nicaraguan revolutions radicalized sufficiently the relation between the dominant and the subaltern. Even when they sought to empower "the people," the protagonism of vanguard politicians and intellectuals continued to have "counterproductive effects."[66] The implication is of a neat progressive politics with no complicating factors, if only the bourgeoisie and intellectuals had opened a space for the subaltern. As we shall see, the subalternists' very conception of the subaltern does not make this a workable proposition.

There was already a proclivity to attend to the subaltern in the incorporation of *testimonio* into the U.S. academy. But the very genre raised serious problems about representation: Who speaks for whom?

Can the subaltern speak? How are voice and perspective mediated? What is left of the subaltern in this process of mediation? And so on. These very questions raised problems for the academics who wrote about *testimonio*.[67] Many derived legitimacy within an institution in transformation (i.e., undergoing multiculturalization) by becoming experts on the genre and linking their own subjectivity to that of the testimonial informants. A scholarship that engages in advocacy is, of course, an important contribution of the new social movements to cultural studies. It would indeed be foolish to pretend that there is not already a politics conditioning research agendas. But the subalternists seemed to be rather unreflexive about their own stake in the cause of the subaltern.

The adoption of Ranajit Guha's definition of the subaltern—as the constitutive exclusion that enables the writing of a historiography that fails to make the nation "come to its own"[68]—permitted the Latin American subalternists to turn from the question of representation of subalterns or of their transactions with colonial or national power brokers to one of their constitutive absence or refusal to engage in coloniality. The questions that Latin American subalternists asked, then, had to do with the force of the subaltern as a negation of colonialist power and its manifestation in historiography and other forms of writing. Academically, this adoption allowed them to have their cake and eat it too. They could accuse García Canclini of reformism by seeking to create a democratic space within the already existing system of oppression, and at the same time not have to engage in a representational politics that would put them in a similar situation. In other words, their double use of subalternity (as the oppressed and as negation) is similar to the assimilation of political categories to aesthetico-philosophical ones that I discussed earlier in considering the sleight of hand that Bhabha and Kristeva, respectively, operate in moving from hybrid subjects to hybridity as a condition of interstiality or from abjects to abjection.

Latin American subalternists deride García Canclini's empirical fieldwork on popular cultures as one more instance of the ethnographic impulse to know the other. Instead, the subalternists' preferred mode of practice is textual analysis, for there is where the constitutive exclusion of absent signification best manifests itself. It thus boggles the mind to consider that subalternists have no properly subaltern politics. When it comes to taking a stance, they are no different from your garden variety identity politicians: they promote "ethnic, nationalist, or regionalist demands, the struggle of women for equality, and the resentment or 'negativity' that generally characterizes subaltern identities."[69] Subalternists

put a premium on colonial history and have little to say about the engagement of subalterns with media and consumption. They view strategies of representation with suspicion because they are subject to channeling in consumerist and media circuits that render them ineffective
as means of empowerment. Consequently, the Latin American subaltern
studies group has emphasized the negativity that inheres in the conception of the subaltern by the South Asian group.

This insight puts the onus on them not only to come up with an
analysis of this crisis of representation, but also to devise an effective
politics. Predictably, this is their quagmire. They claim to summon the
subaltern directly:

> We're disconnected, by virtue of being in an elite position, from subal-
> tern culture, but now we have a series of techniques that allow us to ac-
> cess the subaltern directly, instead of depending on the native informant
> of classical anthropology, who just told us what we wanted to know in
> the first place. The native informant lent himself or herself to imperial-
> ist, colonialist, racist, Eurocentric designs and conceptions. We have got
> around the native informant problem, we can hook directly into the sub-
> altern now, "boot it up," so to speak.[70]

Despite this note of self-irony, John Beverley remains optimistic that
"our work [can] incorporate th[e] negativity [of subaltern people who
reject representation], and thus become a part of the agency of the subaltern in its struggle against domination."[71] When asked how exactly
that negativity can be incorporated as part of a political project, Beverley is forced to acknowledge that it is perhaps a one-way street between
subalterns and the institution of the university. Academic subalternists
can devise new ways of detecting the inadequacy of historical texts for
any political or social project, or more generally, transform into conceptual terms the practices that resist institutionalization. (Here Beverley
confesses to a "knee-jerk rejection of institutionality.")[72] But it seems
as if the question of what an academic might do for subalterns cannot
even be asked. Subalternity, it turns out, is the will to refusal, and as
such it does not constitute the entirety of the psychopolitical makeup
of social and historical "actors." There are, in fact, no "actors" in subalternity. Instead, there is the will to refusal. Subalternity, then, is a kind
of will to power, understood as "relation(s) without relata" that cannot be
represented. As such, it offers the academy a different way of knowing,
setting "aside the dominating visual [or representational] metaphorics of
traditional epistemology." Like the will to power, it is a "self-consuming

concept."[73] The question remains: what can a self-consuming concept offer politics and the "outside" of institutionality? Beverley's argument that a politics based on the pivotal position of the subaltern can lead to the creation of a new historical bloc, while well-intentioned and properly utopian, seems quite voluntarist, particularly for an academic whose involvement with subalterns is largely textual.

Ironically, the very possibility of a hegemonic historical bloc seems foreclosed by the postmodern historical turn that Beverley and other subalternists acknowledge. This is Alberto Moreiras's argument, himself a onetime member and certainly the most self-reflexive of the group. The struggle for hegemony as the practice of ideological rearticulation through the institutions of civil society is, according to Moreiras, already a given form of counterhegemony, one that is functional to contemporary capitalism. "One must understand politics beyond [the space provided by] articulation, because articulation, that fundamentally populist device, as Laclau and Mouffe have taught us, is already the place of a pseudopolitics."[74] The proper space of politics is, for Moreiras, subalternity understood as the confrontation with the necessary incompleteness of articulation, of what defies it. "The subalternist notion of historic failure points to the identification and study of indigestible blockages in non-European transculturation, and purports to find in them a critical possibility for the operational release of modes of cultural-historical interpretation that counter the necessarily teleological bent of 'historical transition' or mode of production narratives."[75] A viable politics can then only be negative in a deconstructionist sense, and the subaltern is that instance of what enables a politics that cannot be captured by the social. The properly political can then only function as posthegemonic, "not as a substitute for or as the defeat of the theory of hegemony but rather as its effective supplement, that difficult place from which to think of [society's] constitutive exterior."[76] Multiculturalism, as the most recent and "successful" form of articulation is, thus, "consistent with the cultural logic of multinational capitalism," writes Moreiras, citing Slavoj Žižek approvingly.[77]

To the degree that democracy understood as multicultural equity is consistent with multinational capitalism, García Canclini's objective is to create a supranational cultural space that may be beyond the parameters of the hegemonic at the same time that it is not outside of contemporary capitalism, global yet strategically rooted in the local. To this end, García Canclini's political strategy in *Consumers and Citizens* is to view consumption as "means of thinking" that creates new ways of being citizens. However, the mediated public sphere, particularly in the context of globalization and regional integration, overflows the classic sphere of political interactions. The public nowadays is the mediation by which social institutions (re)present multiple aspects of social life to their audiences. In this regard, traditional and even recent progressive thinking on the expansion of citizenship to the "popular" (or "subaltern") sectors is outdated, particularly insofar as it holds to the national frame as the proscenium of action and a "Gutenbergian" conception of how to negotiate the public sphere. García Canclini advocates rethinking politics in relation to consumption, although not necessarily the U.S. model. Globalization has transformed the traditional sentimental-educational terrain of citizenship formation. National patrimonies, folklore, and the high arts are losing viewers and users, or their functions have shifted. Consumption, then, has to be rethought in relation to the culture industries. But in Latin America, this means confronting the problem of "Americanization."

The political problem that García Canclini tackles is also posthegemonic in the sense that it cannot be resolved at the national level, which was the frame in which Gramsci conceived of the hegemonic process. This is precisely why García Canclini considers it important that alliances of states and civil society groups have an important role in brokering a supranational cultural space, particularly in setting regulatory policies so that the affective aspects of cultural interpellation—identity formation—are not so overwhelmingly articulated by national elites or by U.S.-identified transnational corporations. For García Canclini, neoliberalism and privatization are not the answers; these just enable transnational corporations to gain greater control in Latin America. He argues that since experience has shown that privatization has not made utilities function any better, the state should get back into the public interest, helping to create better systems of cultural intermediation (chapter 8 of this volume). In this regard, the activities of the "grassroots explosion" of the new social movements, which must form part of this Latin American cultural space, cannot substitute for the conventional responsibilities of states in providing resources and incentives in education, health, social, and cultural services, leaving the administration of these services, however, to local communities. More specifically, García Canclini's own model of a culturally integrated supranational federalism is premised on a range of specific policies: the creation of a Latin American media space; the creation of book, magazine, film, TV, video common markets in the region; setting quotas of 50 percent Latin American production and distribution in movie theaters, video outlets, radio broadcasts, television programming, and so on; the creation of a Foundation for the Production and Distribution of Latin American Media; the regulation of foreign capital, and policies to strengthen Latin American economies; the development of citizenship by giving greater attention to a politics of recognition in keeping with the multiplication of claims by all sectors of society (chapter 8 of this volume).

I would propose that García Canclini's view of negotiation might offer a better opportunity for a radical politics than the subalternists' deconstructivist negation. The only form of agency available to subalterns in this politics of negation is refusal, which in any case never comes in pure form. García Canclini's empirical work registers acts of negotiation in most spheres of activity, even those that are most culturally precious. It is the intellectual who sloughs off the transactional qualities from resistance, as if they were not entwined in action. Mikhail Bakhtin's insights are useful here. According to him, there is no such thing as an absolute "one's own," but rather a socially worked-out negotiation (or mismanagement) of the constraints and leeways available. Insofar as "one's own" language or voice is "populated" with others' value-laden voices, it cannot pass "easily and freely into the private property of the speaker's intentions."[78] Taking as his point of departure a similar insight about identity and even will as a "coproduction," García Canclini argues:

> The culturally hybrid features resulting from cross-class interaction force us to recognize that alongside struggle there is also negotiation. And negotiation does not appear as a process external to the constitution of the actors, to which they might resort on occasion for political convenience. It is a mode of existence, something intrinsic to the groups that take part in the social drama. Negotiation is located within collective subjectivity, in the most unconscious culture of politics and daily life. Its hybrid character, which in Latin America derives from a long history of mixtures and syncretisms, is accentuated in contemporary societies through complex interactions between the traditional and the modern, the popular and the elite, the subaltern and the hegemonic. (Chapter 9 of this volume)

García Canclini does not endeavor to tell subalterns how to negotiate. Rather, he and his fellow researchers listen to and accompany people as they negotiate the complex and fragmented world at the century's end. The aim of his work is to help scholars, policy makers, and other interested parties to understand how they might help out in these processes of negotiation that underlie even some of the most fundamentalist of movements. García Canclini could, of course, be more reflexive about this aspect of his work. At times, he tends to speak of a bipolar divide between negotiation and fundamentalism. This is most evident in his recent work on comparative multiculturalisms in Latin America and the United States, to which I turn.

The Incommensurability of Latin American and U.S. Identities

García Canclini is one of a handful of Latin American scholars who have endeavored to seriously engage the reciprocal impact of Latin American and U.S. societies on each other. Because much of the interest in his work has come from the transdiscipline of cultural studies as well as Chicano studies, in both of which representations of identity have a central role, García Canclini has addressed several recent studies to the difficulty in using the same term—identity—on different sides of the border. Generally, he exhibits a pronounced distaste for identity politics as it is practiced in the United States. Although he understands the historical reasons for the contemporary need to base political advantage on clearly defined communities, he feels that this leads to a disabling separatism. In the Preface to the English-language edition of this volume, he states that whereas "in Latin America [what] has been called cultural pluralism or heterogeneity is conceived as part of the nation, . . . in the U.S. debate, as various authors explain, 'multiculturalism means separatism.'" In *La globalización imaginada* (Imagined globalization), García Canclini points to certain lexical and semantic gaps when comparing Latin America and the United States that, in his estimation, are convincing evidence of the impossibility of translating deep-rooted cultural concepts across borders. Why, for example, doesn't English have an equivalent for the Spanish *mestizo,* the Portuguese *mestiço,* or the French *métis?* (109). English-language approximations, like creolization, belong to a different domain, a linguistic one in this case. And those terms that do refer to the mixture of races—half-caste, half-breed, mixed-blood, and so on—are generally pejorative and even scandalous, whereas in Latin America *mestizo* has had positive connotations since the 1920s in some countries (113). Even taking into account that blacks and indigenous peoples have been the "others" of the normative demographic profile in both contexts, blacks (in Brazil) and Indians (in Mexico) have been imagined as the very epitome of the national subject, at least in their mixed or *mestizo* variants (116).

Although García Canclini notes that racism is just as rooted in Latin America as it is in the United States, he wants to emphasize the relative plasticity of identity in Latin American contexts that give people a certain leeway in negotiating identity. In the United States, he writes, "identities tend to be autonomous unities ... while in Brazil the subject preserves the possibility of various different affiliations, circulating among identities and mixing them" (117).[79] While acknowledging the significant difference between U.S. and Latin American forms of identification, it seems to me that García Canclini does not go far enough in his critique of the situation of blacks and Indians who have less leeway in negotiating away from the stigma of race. Not for nothing does the concept of "bettering the race" (*mejorar la raza; melhorar a raça*) or "whitening" (*emblanquecer; emblanquecimento*) exist in Spanish America and Brazil. Latin America does in fact allow for a racially more diverse melting pot than the United States, but "unmixed" blacks and Indians are generally excluded. Recognizing this fact does not mean, however, that the identity politics generated and bolstered by affirmative action in the United States will work in Latin America. According to García Canclini, affirmative action contributes to hard-and-fast separations in the United States. But one can imagine that millions of Brazilians and Mexicans could easily claim to be of Afro and indigenous descent if that were to give them educational and employment advantages. That would simply be an expression of the plasticity of identity rather than a fixed essentialism.

García Canclini's view of U.S. identity politics also suffers a bit from cultural parallax. His view of U.S. separate identities is only partial and somewhat stereotypical. In fact, there has been a major overhaul of racial identification in the United States since the 1960s. Civil-rights legislation and judicial action on that basis, a move to decentralize and democratize American culture, the revision of census categories, and the emergence of media and consumer niche marketing have all conspired to refashion American demography into five categories, all of which are melting pots: whites or European-Americans, blacks or African-Americans, Hispanics/Latinos, Asian-Pacific Americans, and Native Americans. To these five panethnicities, women and gay men and lesbians should also be added, for the category of protected groups will include those who have suffered past discrimination on the basis of race, color, gender, and sexuality. This emerging ethnoracial and identity system also has an implicit premise that there is no one overriding American normativity, a belief among many liberals and progressives that is deeply Americocentric. The very system itself is normative, and exercises significant force, such as when students are routed into classes depending on their ethnicity, or when it is expected that members of a given group will behave in a particular way. Panethnicization has also eroded the salience of "WASP" normativity, to which García Canclini continues to refer. Instead, there is an implicit "Anglo-conformity" that characterizes the descendants of Italians, Poles, Greeks, and Jews just as much as the Daughters of the American Revolution.

The shift to a discussion of normativity should make it evident that *mestizaje* is analogous to "Anglo-conformity." Although it is still true that whiteness is valued in Latin American societies, the *mestizo* or mixed-race person is normative in most Latin American societies, so long as the mixture does not shade too dark. Venezuelans, for example, refer to themselves as *criollos,* irrespective of race, except for indigenous tribes and blacks from neighboring Guyana, who are considered to be "truly black." It is this *mestizo* normativity that has in large part stymied the efforts of black movements to gain significant empowerment. And not only blacks. There are various constituencies (e.g., regional groups, such as the *nordestinos* of northeastern Brazil) that do not feel integrally part of the normative nation as it has been projected from the dominant centers of national polities (e.g., São Paulo or Rio de Janeiro). This is a point that García Canclini himself emphasizes in *Consumers and Citizens,* and it is for this very reason that his Latin American cultural space would be a preferable alternative to national cultural policies that have reified folkloric or high-art norms. Furthermore, as he points out both in *Consumers and Citizens* and *La globalización imaginada,* supranational trade agreements and transnational migrations are making the national norm an outdated and unworkable framework for identity. The crux of the matter, however, is whether or not the U.S. way of negotiating the increasingly multicultural character of societies will take precedence. Not so much against this possibility but in the hope of reconverting it, García Canclini's recent efforts have been aimed at including Latin American agendas in the creation of a democratic multicultural ethos and politics.

consumers and citizens

The North–South Dialogue on Cultural Studies

One way of introducing this book is to say that it examines globalization as a process of fragmentation and recomposition; rather than homogenize the world, globalization reorders differences and inequalities without eliminating them. Hence, the rise of multicultural societies should be seen in connection with globalizing movements.

The research projects presented here take Latin American cities and culture industries as their basic objects of study. Although this book may be understood as having been written from the specific locale of Latin America, its perspective should not be considered to be outside the reach of globalization, nor as a difference that leads directly to radical alternatives, that is, to a totally different society. What is the meaning of our thoughts and actions when we acknowledge that they necessarily take place within globalization processes, that is, within the hegemonic tendencies of urbanization and the industrialization of culture? Some interpret this fact as the triumph of "one way of thinking" and as the end of ideological diversity. I prefer to consider this situation as a framing horizon, albeit an open and relatively undetermined one. To get beyond the binarism of local versus global it is necessary to focus on the concrete conditions in which cultural practices develop in different countries, on the interaction of globalizing projects and the specific multicultural social arrangements obtaining in given regions.

It is now a commonplace of history that Latin America was "invented" by Europe. Initiated by Spain and Portugal through conquest and colonization, this invention was reelaborated through the interventions of France, England, and other metropolitan nations. The ensuing relations of dependency, characterized in each period by conflicts and hybridizations, were succeeded in the twentieth century by new linkages with the United States. This displacment cannot be seen, however, as the simple replacement of one master for another. The transition from dependency on Europe to subordination to the United States was paralleled by changes in agricultural, industrial, and financial markets, transformations in the production, circulation, and consumption of technology and culture, and an upsurge in demographic flows of migrants, tourists, and exiles. All this altered the structure of dependency.

The changes in the four areas examined in the following pages—cities, markets, technology-culture connections, demographic displacements—rendered obsolete past characterizations that helped explain the relations between Latin America, on the one hand, and Europe and the United States, on the other. The connections that now make us dependent on the United States and on global powers cannot be explained as relations of *coloniality,* which imply the occupation of a subordinated territory, or as *imperialist* relations, which entail a linear domination by the imperial center over the subaltern nations. Only if we focus on the exception of Puerto Rico can one discern a colonial condition; but all other Latin American countries ceased to be colonies one or two centuries ago. However, U.S. imperialism relegated these countries to dependency and a peripheral position within the world system of unequal and uneven exchanges.

Another clarification is in order. Sometimes the displacement of dependency from Europe to the United States is interpreted as the passage from a sociopolitical subordination to a socioeconomic submission. We Latin Americans presumably learned to be citizens through our relationship to Europe; our relationship to the United States will, however, reduce us to consumers. France, England, Germany, and to a degree the United States inspired our constitutions, the construction of republican regimes, and the participation of our citizens in political parties, labor unions, and social movements. These liberal influences were reelaborated in the circumstances of our multiethnic social composition and the peculiar evolution of our democratic regimes.

In the past few decades, the intensification of economic and cultural relations with the United States has encouraged a model of society in which many state functions have disappeared or been assumed by private corporations, and in which social participation is organized through consumption rather than through the exercise of citizenship. This new metropolitan model has compounded the already existing problems of the inadequate development and instability of our democracies, and the stranglehold on representative institutions by the dictatorships of the 1970s and 1980s; the resulting synergy has a greater capacity to transform Latin American civil societies into atomized ensembles of consumers.

This book attempts to understand why the argument that relations with the United States have intensified a new mode of dependency is inadequate for explaining the current transformations in our citizen and consumer roles. The relation between citizens and consumers has been altered throughout the world due to economic, technological, and cultural changes that have impeded the constitution of identities through national symbols. Now they are shaped by the programming of, say, Hollywood, Televisa, and MTV. For many men and women, especially youth, the questions specific to citizenship, such as how we inform ourselves and who represents our interests, are answered more often than not through private consumption of commodities and media offerings than through the abstract rules of democracy or through participation in discredited political organizations. This process could be understood as loss or depoliticization from the perspective of the ideals of liberal or enlightened democracy. But we may also posit, as do James Holston and Arjun Appadurai, that the political notion of citizenship is expanded by including rights to housing, health, education, and the access to other goods through consumption.[1] It is in this sense that I propose reconceptualizaing consumption, not as a mere setting for useless expenditures and irrational impulses, but as a site that is good for thinking, where a good part of economic, sociopolitical, and psychological rationality is organized in all societies.

Cities

Recognizing these transformations does not mean endorsing the dissolution of the city in consumption, nor nations in globalization. Nor do I believe that this is what is happening. In order to understand the shift from "classic" identities (nations, classes, ethnicities) that no longer con-

tain us to new global structures that satisfy in different ways our interests and desires, we must take into consideration the recomposition of
social relations and the obstacles to satisfaction today. These obstacles
may well be an expression of the zeitgeist and of the universal crisis in
paradigms and certainties, as we read in much postmodern theory. But
they may also be studied empirically as they accommodate to different
contexts. Both Anglo-American humanities and *cultural studies* traditions, more in keeping with the first approach, as well as the predominantly social-scientific Latin American approaches to the study of culture, are legitimate.[2] My own focus on *narratives* of multicultural crisis
in an age of globalization as well as my *empirical research* on how multiculturalism plays out in cities and communications processes speak
to the relevance of working in both modalities.

This desire for a dialogue between Latin American and Anglo-
American thought, between the social sciences and the humanities (without accepting any necessary correspondence between both pairings),
was motivated by preoccupations about how globalization processes, led
but not governed by U.S. culture, might affect the future of Latin culture. This concern was not all that evident to me while I was writing,
but two years after the Spanish-language edition was published, I realized (with the help of reviews in Latin American and Anglo-American
forums) that it guided my explorations of changes in communications
industries and their publics in Latin America and my interest in comparing these with European audiovisual industries and publics. Somewhat less obviously, this concern also guided my analysis of the decomposition and transformations of large Latin American cities.

The passage from a Latin-European origin to a North American
"destiny" has modified not only Latin American societies, but also the
social sciences, the arts, and sources of authority and prestige in mass
culture. In less than fifty years, the capital cities that set the trends of
our thought and aesthetics ceased to be Paris, London, and to a lesser
extent Madrid, Milan, and Berlin; their places within the regional imaginary came to be occupied by New York for intellectual elites; by Miami
and Los Angeles for middle-class tourists; and by California, Texas, New
York, and Chicago for migrant workers.

A revealing indicator of the waning importance of the European
conception of the city as a center of civic, commerial, academic, and
artistic life is that the U.S. metropoles preferred by many Latin Americans are not even cities. Academics prefer Stanford, Duke, or Iowa (a
campus without a city) over the great urban centers. The middle classes
yearn to realize their fantasies in Disneyland or Disney World, as well

as in shopping centers that, even when they are in the middle of a city, require one to move in a deurbanized manner, according to European standards of urban life. There are very few European-style cities like New York or San Francisco in the United States.

What does this have to do with the disintegration of Latin American megacities (and many medium-size cities) such as Mexico City, São Paulo, Caracas, Lima, and Bogotá? It is obvious that we are not dealing with imperialist impositions here, nor with mere degraded copies of U.S. urbanism. This book contains analyses of certain Latin American megalopolises as global cities; however, the transformations that grip them are generated intrinsically by processes of unequal development and contradictions internal to them: mass migrations; the contraction of labor markets; flawed urban and housing policies; social services inadequate for an expanding population and urban sprawl; interethnic conflicts; the deterioration of the quality of life and an alarming increase in crime. The large cities of our continent, imagined by governments and migrants until very recently as the avant-garde of our modernization, are today the chaotic scenes of informal markets where hordes of people try to survive under the most archaic forms of exploitation, or by having recourse to networks of solidarity or violence.

All of this is internally driven but at the same time related to new modes of subordination of peripheral economies and to transnational restructuring of markets for material and communicational commodities. Just as in the cities of the first world, many Latin American cities serve as laboratories for degraded multicultural encounters and simultaneously develop as strategic centers for commercial, informational, and financial innovation, dynamizing the local market as it is incorporated into transnational circuits. For this reason, Mexico City and São Paulo are as revealing as New York or London for research that explores the rearticulations between the global and the local, between the flows of deterritorialization and reterritorialization. This research also introduces some "heterodox" issues into the debates on urbanism and globalization, or perhaps it only accentuates contradictions that are also visible in metropolitan multicultural centers.

Communications

The increasing dialogue among cultural studies scholars in the United States and Latin America is usually carried out in the domain of discursive analyses, especially those oriented toward literary or artistic production. Although, to their credit, they have provided legitimacy for *testimonios,*[3] popular texts, and other discourses excluded from the canon, their scope is usually limited to nonindustrialized culture, and their critical discussion circumscribed within academic institutions. There is little place within this academic discussion for what takes place in the mass media, except when the latter is legitimized in relation to issues of importance in the educated sphere. The vast expansion of communications research in the United States and Latin America, and particularly hard data concerning investment, the industrial restructuring of symbolic production, and mass consumption, is rarely incorporated into cultural studies. The "encyclopedia" *Cultural Studies,* edited by Lawrence Grossberg, Cary Nelson, and Paula Treichler, offers almost no data, tables, or other empirical materials in its eight hundred pages, although several essays deal with communications, consumption, and the commercialization of culture.[4] It is remarkable that a few of the contributors, Grossberg among them, do demonstrate an acute understanding of mass culture in other research not necessarily published under the rubric of "cultural studies."[5]

For more than half a century, the cultural exchanges between the United States and Latin America have taken place less in literature, the visual arts, or traditional culture than in communications industries. But even the "high" arts undergo industrialization in keeping with market criteria and the search for mass audiences, and this massification is certainly a key dimension in the meaning of exhibitions such as the New York Metropolitan Museum of Art's blockbuster *Mexico: The Splendors of Thirty Centuries,* or of the novels of such best-selling authors as Isabel Allende, Laura Esquivel, and Gabriel García Márquez. Something similar takes place in the use of historical patrimony in the tourist industry and in the circulation of ethnic or national musics in world music, all of which contribute to the reproduction and renewal of North and South American imaginaries. But it is in the competition and mergers among communications corporations dealing with TV, informatics, and even magazine publishing that we see the greatest ferment in inter- and multicultural activity.

This book, like others written in recent years by the likes of Jesús Martín Barbero, Renato Ortiz, and Beatriz Sarlo,[6] tries to relocate the theory and debates on identity, heterogeneity, and hybridization within the context of competing claims to audiovisual space among the United States, Europe, and Latin America. Beyond the struggles over the expansion of communications, which reproduce and recontextualize Latin Americans' concerns about their "Latinity" and their "Americanness,"

conceptual analysis and empirical research on the differences and coincidences in this interregional triangle are crucial for rethinking cultural
policies. We academics must come to grips with the fact that state policies have become outdated, be they for the preservation of monumental and folkloric patrimonies or for the promotion of high culture with
ever-diminishing resources. The effects of the U.S. preference to consider radio, TV, and other communications media as nothing but business enterprises, a view being taken up in Europe and Latin America,
should provoke us to reexamine questions of property among these
media, be they state- or privately owned. These effects should compel
us researchers to conduct careful analyses of the reconstitution of public
spaces and the mechanisms, whether defunct or re-created, by which
the multiple voices present in each society are recognized or excluded.

The criticisms of this book by a few European specialists lead me
to think that I have overidealized the exemplary value of European audiovisual space. The privatization of communications media in Spain and
France since the late 1990s forces us to be less optimistic about the ability of the European Union to protect the mediated public sphere from
the pressures of the international market. Nevertheless, I think that the
general description of the cultural policy options that I offer here, and
the analysis of their significance for multicultural societies, are still pertinent for the discussion that is only now getting under way in Latin
American studies of culture and in U.S. cultural studies. Perhaps this is
an area where it would be appropriate to take into consideration the
contributions of British *cultural studies,* which are more sensitive to the
importance of examining the industrialization of culture, and whose
vitality and remodeling I had the opportunity to witness in the interventions of scholars such as Stuart Hall and Philip Schlesinger, among
others, at a meeting of European and Latin American media specialists
in October 1996 organized by the University of Stirling.[7]

In British research we also find a greater concern with the role of
the state, owing to its function in Britain as a representative of the public sphere and as a regulator of private interests. The state's role in cultural
matters in Britain is historically more important than in the United
States.

Multiculturalism(s)

If the Anglo-American and Latin American worlds experience globalization differently it is because of the different ways in which they con-

ceptualize their multicultural character. This is something that was not completely clear to me when I wrote this book. In my presentation at the Stirling conference I suggested that the key difference between the Latin American study of culture and *cultural studies* might be summarized as follows: What in Latin America has been called cultural pluralism or heterogeneity is conceived as part of the nation, whereas in the U.S. debate, as various authors explain, "multiculturalism means separatism" (Hughes, Taylor, Walzer).[8] We know that in the United States it is convenient, as Peter McLaren notes, to distinguish between conservative, liberal, and leftist multiculturalisms. The first one subordinates ethnic separatism to the hegemony of WASPs and their canon, which stipulates what should be read and learned in order to be culturally correct. Liberal multiculturalism postulates the natural equality and cognitive equivalence of all races. Leftist multiculturalism explains the breaches in equality as the result of unequal access to resources. But only a few writers, like McLaren, advocate the need to "legitimize multiple traditions of knowledge" and to prioritize the construction of solidarities over the demands of each group. That is why thinkers such as Michael Walzer express their concern that "the sharp conflict today in North American life is not the opposition of multiculturalism to hegemony or singularity," or to "a vigorous and independent North American identity"; it is, rather, the antagonism of a "multitude of groups to a multitude of individuals." "Equally strong voices and varied intonations do not produce harmony—contrary to the ancient image of pluralism as a symphony in which each group played a part (although one might ask who wrote the music?)—but cacophony."[9]

The Latin American canon, or what we might construe as such, owes a lot to Europe. Throughout the the twentieth century, however, it combined influences from different European countries and articulated them in a heterodox manner with diverse national traditions. One can see the traces of German expressionists, French surrealists, Czech, Italian, and Irish novelists in the works of authors such as Jorge Luis Borges and Carlos Fuentes. All of these authors were unknown to each other, but writers from peripheral countries "can handle" them "irreverently and without superstition," as Borges liked to say, not without some exaggeration. Although Borges and Fuentes might be considered extreme cases, I find that Latin American humanities and social-science scholars, and more generally cultural producers, make a critical appropriation of metropolitan canons and reconvert them, so to speak, responding to different national motivations. Moreover, Latin American societies are not structured by a multiplicity of ethnocommunitarian groupings, but—as I suggested earlier—more in keeping with French models of secular republicanism and Jacobin individualism. These models, of course, are rendered more open and flexible as they come into contact with the multicultural realities of Latin America.

On account of this different history, the tendency to resolve multicultural conflicts in Latin America through affirmative-action policies has not been prevalent. This is not to say that in Latin America there have not been nationalist and ethnicist fundamentalisms, promoting exclusivist self-affirmations and resisting hybridization by constructing a single absolutist patrimony that illusorily casts itself as pure. There are analogies between, on the one hand, the separatist emphasis that takes self-esteem as a key factor in the rights claims of women and minorities in the United States, and, on the other hand, some Latin American indigenous and nationalist movements that interpret history in a Manichaean manner, reserving all virtues for themselves and blaming others for the problems of development. However, this has not been the dominant tendency in our history. And much less in this era of globalization in which it becomes more obvious that ethnic and national identities are hybrid constructions, asymmetrically interdependent and uneven. Indeed, it is in this unavoidable relation to hybridity that each group must defend its rights. Thus, artistic and intellectual movements that identify with ethnic or regional demands, such as the Zapatistas in Chiapas, construe this particular problem as a matter for debate concerning the nation and how it might be relocated within the framework of international conflicts. It is ultimately a critique of modernity. This is, in fact, the Zapatistas' own strategy. There are, of course, lingering controversies about indigenous autonomy, particularly the ambivalence evident in cultural or political independence as it intersects participation in national and global processes.

Subjects

These reflections imply a question insinuated at the beginning, where I stated that speaking from Latin America does not entail attributing any special prerogative to what might be discovered and critiqued from a peripheral position. The convergences and differences in conceiving multiculturalism in different regions are also evident in the varying enunciative standpoints or observational locations of cultural research. In North America one finds constant questioning of universalist theories that, in the guise of objectivity, have smuggled in colonial, Western, masculine, white, and other biases. The deconstructive criticisms leveled at this objectivism have also been developed in Latin American social sciences and humanities: nationalists, Marxists, and others associated with dependency theory similarly objected to metropolitan social and cultural theories and made creative use, from the 1960s on, of Gramsci and Fanon. It is only recently that U.S. cultural studies scholars—and some Latinamericanists—proposed the latter as novel approaches without any reference to work by Latin Americans who had taken these precedents as a point of departure with similar objectives in mind. However, when it comes to other aspects, such as the contributions of feminist critique to the study of culture, Latin American scholars are quite weak, although the dialogue with the U.S. academy is fluid and helps to make up for this shortcoming (e.g., in the work of Heloísa Buarque de Hollanda and Nelly Richard).[10]

Can one hope for a radical renewal ensuing from the claims of these peripheral or excluded actors? What is the relation between epistemological creativity and social or geopolitical power? Whatever the answer to these questions might be, it is evident that in the wake of the 1960s and 1970s, when it was common to believe that the colonized, the subaltern, workers, and peasants had epistemic privilege, there are not many left who think that there are privileged positions for the legitimation of knowledge. We are discouraged from resorting once again to this belief by the many sound epistemological arguments and many lessons gleaned from the repeated historical failures of the overvaluation of the oppressed as the privileged source of knowledge.

If we are to heed the call to attend to the dangers that fundamentalism posits for conceptions of identity, and examine their self-affirmation as a central concern of research and policy, as David Theo Goldberg recommends in *Multiculturalism,* then we should shift the analytical emphasis to heterogeneity and hybridization. The cultural analyst gains little by studying the world from the vantage point of partial identities. It is not enough to study them only from the metropolis, or from the context of peripheral or postcolonial nations, or even from one isolated discipline, or even a totalizing knowledge. An effective study of culture focuses on the intersections.

Adopting the point of view of the oppressed or excluded can be helpful in the *discovery* stage, as a way of generating hypotheses or counterhypotheses that challenge established knowledges. Adopting this viewpoint also enables us to discern domains of the real that go unattended by hegemonic knowledge. But when it comes to epistemological *justification*, it is better to situate the analysis in the intersections in those zones where narratives encounter and cross each other. Only in these sites of tension, encounter, and conflict is it possible to pass from sectorial (or openly sectarian) narratives to an elaboration of knowledges capable of deconstructing and exercising control over the conditionings of each enunciation.

This also means that we should go beyond cultural studies limited to hermeneutic analysis and open up to a research agenda that combines signification and facts, discourses and their empirical groundings. In sum, we should construct a rationality that can encompass everyone's reasonings as well as the structure of conflicts and negotiations.

To the degree that specialists in the study of culture want to achieve scientifically consistent research, their final objective is not the representation of the voice of the silenced but an understanding and naming of the places where their demands or everyday life enter into conflict with those of others. Contradiction and conflict are categories to be found at the core of this conception of cultural studies. Not to see the world from only one pole of the contradiction but to understand its specific structure as well as its potential dynamics. The utopias of change and justice can, in this sense, articulate with the project of cultural studies, not as a prescription for the selection and organization of data, but rather as a stimulus for exploring under what (real) conditions the real will cease to repeat inequality and discrimination, and become a setting for the recognition of others. I take up here a suggestion made by Paul Ricoeur in his critique of U.S. multiculturalism, that it would be better to emphasize a politics of *recognition* over a politics of identity. "In the notion of identity there is only an idea of the same, while recognition is a concept that directly integrates alterity, that permits a dialectic of same and other. The demands on behalf of identity always contain violence toward the other. The search for recognition, on the other hand, entails reciprocity."[11]

Twenty-first-Century Consumers, Eighteenth-Century Citizens

This book attempts to understand how changes in modes of consumption have altered the possibilities and forms of citizenship. The exercise of citizenship has always been associated with the capacity to appropriate commodities and with ways of using them. It has also been commonplace to assume that the difference in modes of consuming and using commodities is canceled out by equality of abstract rights, actualized in voting, in choosing a political party or a labor union as one's representative. The insolvency of politics and the loss of belief in its institutions have created opportunities for other forms of participation. Men and women increasingly feel that many of the questions proper to citizenship—where do I belong, what rights accrue to me, how can I get information, who represents my interests?—are being answered in the private realm of commodity consumption and the mass media more than in the abstract rules of democracy or collective participation in public spaces.

In these times, when electoral campaigns occupy the television studio more than the convention hall, engage in a contest of images rather than doctrinaire polemics, and rely on the seduction of marketing surveys more than on the power of persuasion, it is all too understandable for us to be brought together as consumers even when we are being addressed as citizens. In a world in which technobureaucratic decision making and an international uniformity imposed by neoliberalism have overridden debates about the future orientation of societies, it seems that planning takes place at global levels beyond the threshold of observation. In these circumstances the only accessible things are the commodities and messages delivered to our homes and which we use "as we see fit."

The Familiar and the Foreign: A Dissolving Dichotomy

We can appreciate the radical character of these changes if we examine the way in which certain commonsense expressions have varied in meaning to the point of losing it. In the middle of this century in some Latin American countries, it was not unusual for discussions between parents and children about what the family could afford to buy or about rivalries with the neighbors to end with the paternal dictum: "No one is satisfied with what they have." This "conclusion" condensed several ideas: satisfaction with the achievements of those who had migrated from the countryside to the city; recognition of the advances ushered in by industrialization; the advent of new forms of comfort in daily life (electric lighting, telephones, radios, even automobiles). All of this made many Latin Americans feel like the privileged inhabitants of modernity. And the dictum was the defensive response of parents to new demands made by sons and daughters who had attained middle and even higher education. They were responding to a proliferation of household appliances, to new markers of status, to radical political ideas, to innovations in art and sensibility, to the adventure of ideas and feelings, all of which were difficult to get used to.

Generational conflicts over what is necessary and desirable are another way to establish identities and construct what distinguishes us. We are leaving behind the era in which identities were defined by ahistorical essences. Today, instead, shaped by consumption, identities depend on what one owns or is capable of attaining. The constant transformations in technologies of production, in the design of objects, in the most extensive and intensive communication among societies—and the concomitant expansion of desires and expectations—have a destabilizing effect on identities traditionally bound to repertoires of goods particular to an ethnic or national community. That political version of being satisfied with what one has, which was the nationalism of the

1960s and 1970s, is now seen as the last attempt of elites who promote economic development, or of the middle classes and some popular movements, to contain within uncertain national borders the global explosion of identities and the consumer commodities that differentiate them.

The expression finally lost its meaning. How can we possibly be satisfied with what we have if we don't even know what it is? In the nineteenth and twentieth centuries, the consolidation of modern nations made it possible to transcend the small-town views of peasants and indigenous peoples at the same time that it kept in check the dissolution of peoples into the boundless dispersion of the world. National cultures seemed to be reasonably apt systems for preserving, within the homogeneity imposed by industrialization, certain differences and a territorial rootedness that coincided, more or less, with the spaces of production and circulation of commodities. To eat like a Spaniard, a Mexican, or a Brazilian was not only a way of maintaining specific traditions but also an act of reproduction with the commodities generated by one's society. These products were within easy reach and less expensive than imported ones. A piece of clothing, a car, or a television program were more accessible if they were nationally produced. The symbolic value of consuming "our" products was, moreover, reinforced by the economic rationality of the times. To seek out foreign commodities and brand names was a way of attaining prestige and sometimes a choice for quality. General Electric or Pierre Cardin: internationalization brought with it symbols of *status*. Kodak, Houston's hospitals, and Visconti represented the kind of industry, medical care, and cinema that our countries did not have. But they were within our reach.

This dualistic, schematic opposition between what is one's own and what is the foreign no longer seems to hold any meaning when we think of a Ford assembled in Spain, with a Canadian windshield, an Italian carburetor, an Austrian radiator, English cylinders and battery, and a French transmission. I turn on my television set, made in Japan, and what I see is a world film, produced in Hollywood, made by a Polish director with French assistants, actors of ten different nationalities, and scenes filmed in four countries that also put up the capital. The large corporations that provide us with food and clothing also have us travel bottlenecked on highways that are the same the world over, and fragment the production process by making component parts of commodities in countries where the labor costs are cheaper. Objects thus lose any necessary tie to territories of origin. Culture becomes a process of multinational assemblage, a flexible articulation of parts, a montage of features that any citizen in any country, of whatever religion or ideology, can read and use.

What distinguishes *internationalization* from *globalization* is that in the days of the internationalization of national cultures, when you were not satisfied with what you had you could find an alternative elsewhere. The majority of messages and commodities that we consumed were made in our own societies, with strict policing of customs offices and laws that protected what each country produced. Nowadays, what is produced in the entire world is right here and it is difficult to know what is our own. Internationalization was an opening of the geographic boundaries of each society for the purpose of bringing in the material and symbolic commodities of all the other societies. Globalization operates according to a functional interaction of dispersed economic and cultural activities, and a multicentric system of production of commodities and services, in which the speed of circulation around the globe is much more important than the geographic sites where decisions are made.

There are two ways of interpreting the discontent wrought by globalization. For certain postmodern writers, the problem is not what is lacking but the obsolescent and fleeting nature of what one has. We shall examine this culture of the ephemeral when we consider the shift from moviegoers who select what films to see on the basis of directors, actors, and their place in film history, to video viewers who are only interested in premieres. Much of what is done in the arts today follows rules of periodic innovation and obsolescence, but not, as in the case of the avant-gardes, by engaging in true experimentation. Instead, cultural expressions are subordinated to the values that "dynamize" markets and fashion: inexhaustible consumption, surprise, and entertainment. For similar reasons, cultural policy becomes erratic: with the decline of emancipatory narratives that construe the present as a part of history or as a search for a renewed future, political and economic decisions are now made according to the seductive immediacy of consumption, or in line with a free-trade ethos stripped of any memory of its errors, or on the basis of the frenzied importation of the latest models. As if past experience did not teach anything, these policies lead to foreign debt and a crisis in the balance of payments.

A more complete understanding of the effects of globalization should also focus on those groups whose unmet needs have multiplied. The neoliberal mode of globalization consists of cutting jobs in order to lower costs. The competition among transnational corporations, whose center of decision making all but escapes detection, renders insignificant the interests of labor and nations. The result is that 40 percent of the population in Latin America is deprived of stable employment and a minimal safety net. Latin Americans are condemned to barely survive the ups and downs of an informal economy that is also globalized, ogling the hodgepodge of merchandise hawked on the street corners: Japanese electronic gadgets and clothes made in Southeast Asia, esoteric herbal remedies, and local crafts. In these immense shantytowns that encroach on the historic centers of large metropolises, there are few reasons for satisfaction when one sees goods from every corner of the earth for the benefit of the haves who buy them and immediately walk off oblivious to their surroundings.

What Doubts Are There?

At the same time that we accept globalization as an irreversible tendency, we want this book to cast doubt on two premises: that the global can stand in for the local, and that neoliberalism is the only way to participate in globalization.

If we consider the diverse ways in which globalization incorporates different nations and different sectors within each nation, it is evident that homogenization is not the way in which it relates to local and regional cultures. Many national particularities persist despite transnationalization. Furthermore, the market's reorganization of production and consumption to maximize and concentrate profits transforms those particularities into inequalities. The question to ask, then, is whether the neoliberal mode of globalization is the only one, or the most desirable one, for carrying out a transnational restructuring of societies.

To answer this question obviously requires a thorough economic analysis of the contradictions of the neoliberal model. But it is also important to discern what is cultural about globalization, the market, and consumption. None of these processes take place or change without human relations and social constructions of meaning. It might be obvious to invoke this principle, but it is a necessary counterbalance to the prevalence of market and consumer analysis conducted solely in the interest of commercial efficiency, or the supposed expediency of globalization as the quickest way to increase sales. The latter are plausible explanations of social relations if we look at society only from the vantage point of business or advertising.

What other outlooks are there today? Not long ago a political perspective was seen as an alternative. The market discredited that position in a curious way: not only by fighting it and showing itself more efficient as a way of organizing societies, but also by cannibalizing it, submitting politics to the rules of commerce and advertising, spectacle and corruption. A better alternative, however, may be found in the social relation at the heart of politics: the exercise of citizenship. But we must approach citizenship without dissociating it from those activities through which we establish our social belonging, our social networks, which in this globalized era are steeped in consumption.

In order to establish the analytic relations between consumption and citizenship, we have to deconstruct those conceptual frameworks that render consumer behavior as predominantly irrational and assess citizen action on the basis of rational ideological principles. Indeed, consumption is usually imagined as the site of the sumptuary and the superfluous, where the primary drives of subjects can be classified and ordered by means of marketing analysis and advertising schemes. On the other hand, citizenship is reduced to a political matter, as if people voted and acted on public issues for only individual reasons or on the basis of the rational debate of ideas. Such a separation is evident even in the latest work by a lucid political theorist such as Jürgen Habermas. His self-critique of his book on the public sphere still seeks to discern "new institutional arrangements that enable opposition to the transformation of the citizen into a client."[1]

When I propose in chapter 1 of this volume that consumption is good for thinking, I am basing my analysis on the hypothesis that when we select goods and appropriate them, we define what we consider publicly valuable, the ways we integrate and distinguish ourselves in society, and the ways to combine pragmatism with pleasure. I then go on to explore how received views of consumption and citizenship can change if they are examined in tandem, employing the analytical tools of economics and political sociology. But these concepts also need to be examined as cultural processes with the aid of anthropological methods suitable for discerning and analyzing diversity and multiculturality. My concerns are thus compatible with studies on cultural citizenship carried out in the United States, in which citizenship is seen not only in relation to rights accorded by state institutions to those born within their territorial jurisdiction, but also as social and cultural practices that confer a sense of belonging, provide a sense of difference, and enable the satisfaction of the needs of those who possess a given language and organize themselves in certain ways.[2]

It should be said, however, that U.S. work on cultural citizenship is aimed at legitimizing minorities, whose practices, based on linguistic, educational, and gender differences, are not sufficiently recognized by the state. I share the interest in opening up a state-designated notion of citizenship to that multicultural diversity, but—in keeping with the importance given in this book to cultural policies—I feel that the affirmation of difference should be joined with efforts to reform the state, not only for it to accept the autonomous development of diverse "communities," but also for it to guarantee equal access to the resources brought by globalization.

In Latin America too the experiences of the social movements have led to a redefinition of what is understood by citizenship, not only in relation to rights of equality but also rights to difference. This entails a desubstantialization of the concept of citizenship traditionally employed by jurists. Rather than abstract values, rights have come to be seen as something constructed and changing in relation to practices and discourses. Citizenship and rights have to do not only with the formal structure of a society; they also refer to the status of the struggle for recognition of others as subjects with "valid interests, relevant values, and legitimate claims." Rights are thus reconceived as "regulatory principles of social practices that define the rules of expected reciprocity in social life in accordance with the agreed upon (and negotiated) mutual attribution of obligations and responsibilities, guarantees and prerogatives of each member." Rights are seen as the expression of a state order and a "civil grammar."[3]

In truth, we are only beginning to achieve this equilibrium between state and society. The rejection of state domination and monolithism led, in the 1970s and 1980s, to an overvaluation of autonomy and the transformative force of the social movements. Once we rethink citizenship as a "political strategy,"[4] we can more easily include emerging practices that have not yet been sanctioned by the juridical order and recognize the role of subjectivities in the renewal of civil society. It thus becomes possible to understand the relative place of these practices within the democratic order and to search for new forms of legitimacy that take a more lasting form in another type of state. Rethinking citizenship also presupposes a recognition of the right to access and belonging to a sociopolitical system, as well as the right to participate in the remaking of the system, that is, to redefine the very arrangement in which we desire to be included.

Redefining citizenship in connection with consumption and political strategy requires a conceptual framework for examining cultural consumption as an ensemble of practices that shape the sphere of citizenship. This framework also enables us to transcend the fragmentation that characterizes renewed analytical interest in this category. The dissatisfaction with the juridical-political sense of citizenship has led to advocacy for a notion of cultural citizenship, as well as forms of citizenship defined by race, gender, and ecology, to which we can add an infinite multiplicity of demands, resulting in a splintered concept.[5] In the past, the state provided the framework (albeit unjust or biased) that contained the variety of forms of participation in public life. Nowadays, the market brings together these forms of participation through the medium of consumption. We need to respond with a strategic concept that can articulate the various strands of citizenship so that they complement each other in the new and the old settings of the state and the market.

This revision of the links between state and society cannot take place unless we take into account the new cultural conditions in which the public and the private have been rearticulated. The public sphere, where citizens discuss and decide matters of collective interest, emerged in the eighteenth century, as is well known, in countries like Germany and France, where it had a limited scope. Communities of readers and participants in enlightened circles established a democratic culture based on rational critique. But the rules and rituals of access to the salons of the democratizing bourgeoisie limited the debate on the common interest to those who could inform themselves as readers and who could understand society in accordance with the communicative rules of writing. Until the middle of the nineteenth century, the vast sectors of the population excluded from the bourgeois public sphere—women, workers, peasants—were considered, in the best of cases, virtual citizens who could be incorporated into deliberations on matters of common interest only insofar as they became literate. That is why leftist parties and social movements that represented the excluded practiced a Gutenbergian political culture rooted in books, magazines, and pamphlets.

Some intellectuals and political activists (e.g., Mikhail Bakhtin, Antonio Gramsci, Raymond Williams, and Richard Hoggart) acknowledged the parallel existence of popular cultures that constituted an informal "plebeian public sphere," organized through the medium of more restricted oral and visual communications. In many cases, they tended to see this sphere—as did Günther Lottes in a not so distant text, from 1979—as "a variant of the bourgeois public sphere," whose "emancipatory potential" and "social presuppositions have been suspended."[6] Some Latin American writers have been working on and providing *cultural* acknowledgment for these diverse modalities of communication. But we have provided scant theoretical frameworks for understanding these popular circuits as forums where there emerge networks for the exchange of information and citizen apprenticeship relating to the consumption of contemporary mass media. In this regard, we have not gotten beyond the facile idealizations of political and communicational populism.[7]

Neither social revolutions, nor the study of popular cultures, not even the exceptional sensibility of certain alternative political and artistic movements, have shown the degree to which the public and the exercise of citizenship have developed since the nineteenth century; it is, rather, the vertiginous growth of audiovisual communications technologies that has made this evident. But these very electronic media that catapulted the masses into the public sphere are responsible for channeling citizen activity toward consumption. They led to the establishment of other means of gaining information, of understanding the communities to which one belongs, of conceiving and exercising rights. Disillusioned with state, party, and union bureaucracies, the publics turn to radio and television to receive what citizen institutions could not deliver: services, justice, reparations, or just attention. Of course, one cannot claim that the mass media, with their call-in programs or live public forums, are any more successful than public institutions, but they fascinate because they listen and people feel that they do not have to

> put up with the long waiting periods, the delays, or the red tape that defer or distance the satisfaction of their needs. . . . The televised scene moves rapidly and is seemingly transparent; the institutional scene is slow and its forms (particularly those forms that make possible the existence of institutions) are complicated, so much so that they take on an opacity engendered by desperation.[8]

It is not, however, as if the old agents—parties, unions, intellectuals—have been displaced by the mass media. The sudden appearance of these media points, more accurately, to a general restructuring of the articulations between the public and the private. One can also detect this in the reordering of urban life, in the decline of nations as structures that rein in the social, and in the reorganization of the functions of traditional political actors. That is why our research on the transformations wrought by the culture industries is preceded in the first section of this book by an overhaul of the ways in which we think of consumption and everyday life in megacities. The changes in communications and technology are interpreted as part of larger restructurings.

The New Sociocultural Scene

We can summarize the sociocultural changes that are occurring in all of these fields in five kinds of processes:

1. A rearrangement of the institutions and circuits for the exercise of public life. Local and national institutions decline in importance as transnational corporate conglomerates benefit.

2. The reformulation of patterns of urban settlement and coexistence. Condominiums rather than neighborhoods, multicentric distribution throughout the urban landscape rather than face-to-face interaction. This is especially the case in large cities, where basic activities (work, study, consumption) often take place far from home and where the time spent in moving through unknown places reduces disposable time for occupying one's own place.

3. The reelaboration of "one's own," as a consequence of the predominance of goods and messages emitted by a globalized economy and culture over goods and messages based in the cities and nations in which one lives.

4. The consequent redefinition of the sense of belonging and identity, ever less shaped by local and national loyalties and more and more by participation in transnational or deterritorialized communities of consumers (youth in relation to rock; TV viewers of CNN, MTV, and other satellite-beamed programs).

5. The shift from the citizen as a representative of public opinion to the consumer interested in enjoying quality of life. One indication of this change is that argumentative and critical forms of participation cede their place to the pleasure taken in electronic media spectacles where narration or the simple accumulation of anecdotes prevails over reasoned solutions to problems. Another indication is the ephemeral exhibition of events instead of a sustained and structural treatment.

Many of these changes got their start with the industrialization of culture in the nineteenth century. *Telenovelas,* for example, have their origins in theater performed in town squares or in serialized romances. The antecedents of radio and television mass audiences go back to the school and the church.[9] All of these constitute the cultural bases of what we now identify as the plebeian public sphere. What is new about the second half of the twentieth century is that these audiovisual and mass modalities for organizing culture have been subordinated to corporate profit criteria, as well as to a global order that deterritorializes their contents and forms of consumption. The combination of deregulatory and privatizing tendencies with the transnational concentration of corporations has decreased the number of public voices, in "high" as well as in popular culture. This restructuring of economic and cultural practices leads to a hermetic concentration of decisions among economic and technological elites, and generates a new order of exclusion of the majorities now incorporated as clients. The diminishing effectiveness of traditional and enlightened forms of citizen participation (parties, unions, grassroots associations) is not offset by the incorporation of masses as consumers or as occasional participants in spectacles that political, technological, and economic power brokers offer in the media.

We might say that as we leave the twentieth century, the societies that organize us as consumers for the twenty-first century return us to the eighteenth as citizens. The global distribution of commodities and information makes it possible for core and peripheral countries to come closer: we purchase transnational products in comparable supermarkets, on television we watch the latest films by Spielberg or Wim Wenders, the Barcelona Olympics, live coverage of the fall of an Asian or Latin American president, or the destruction resulting from the latest Serbian bombing. In Latin American countries, an average of 500,000 hours of television are transmitted yearly, while the countries that compose Latin Europe transmit only 11,000. In Colombia, Panama, Peru, and Venezuela there is one video player for every three households with a television, a higher proportion than in Belgium (26.3 percent) or Italy (16.9 percent).[10] We may be underdeveloped as endogenous producers of electronic media, but not as consumers.

Why isn't this simultaneous access to material and symbolic goods accompanied by a global and more complete exercise of citizenship? The attainment of technological comfort and information from everywhere coexists with the resurgence of fundamentalist ethnocentrisms that isolate entire peoples or that pit them fatally against each other, like the ex-Yugoslavians and the Rwandans. The contradictions are likely to erupt in peripheral countries and in those metropolises where selective globalization results in the exclusion of the unemployed and migrants from basic human rights such as work, health, education, and housing.

The enlightenment project to generalize these rights led many, throughout the nineteenth and twentieth centuries, to seek a home for all in modernity. With the imposition of a neoliberal conception of globalization, according to which rights are necessarily unequal, the novelties of modernity now appear to the majority only as objects of consumption, and for many as little more than a show to be watched. The right of citizenship, which should be to decide how these goods are produced, distributed, and used, is circumscribed to the domain of elites.

However, when we recognize that when we consume we also think, select, and reelaborate social meaning, it becomes necessary to analyze how this mode of appropriation of goods and signs conditions more active forms of participation than those that are grouped under the label of consumption. In other words, we should ask ourselves if consumption does not entail doing something that sustains, nourishes, and to a certain extent constitutes a new mode of being citizens.

If our answer is yes, it becomes necessary to accept the premise that public space overflows the sphere of classic political interactions. " 'Public Space' is the 'mediated' 'mediatory' frame in which the institutional and technological mechanisms endemic to postindustrial societies present the multiple aspects of social life to a 'public.' "[11]

From the People to Civil Society

The study of the restructuring of the relations between consumption and citizenship allows us to explore ways out of the muddle in which the crisis of "the popular" has left us. At demonstrations in Latin American cities, one can still hear expressions such as "If these aren't the people, then where else can one find them?" This was a convincing formula in the 1970s when military dictatorships suppressed parties, unions, and student movements. It is understandable that one or two hundred thousand people gathered in Buenos Aires's Plaza de Mayo, in Santiago de Chile's Alameda, or marching in the streets of São Paulo could feel that their defiant outburst represented those who had lost the possibility to express themselves through political institutions. The restitution of democracy opened up new spaces for making demands. However, in the countries mentioned here, as in the rest of Latin America, the crisis of liberal, populist, and socialist models, the collapse of traditional forms of representation, and the absorption of the public sphere by the mass media rendered these claims questionable. In those nations where voting is noncompulsory, more than half of eligible voters ignore elections. Where it is obligatory, polls show that 30 to 40 percent have not decided for whom to vote as late as one week before the date of the election. If demonstrations in the streets and public squares decrease in size, dispersing into myriad parties and movements of youth, indigenous peoples, feminists, human-rights advocates, and so many others, we are left with the last part of the question: where are the people?

In any event, when those whom we call "the people" vote, another alarming concern arises: Why do leaders who have impoverished their following manage to hold on to the consensus of the mistreated masses? There is not only one single explanation. Explaining this is rather like assembling a jigsaw puzzle. It entails understanding how hegemonic forces manage to position themselves in the strategic settings of the economy and politics, and in communications, precisely the medium in which societies are transformed in this second half of the twentieth century. In contrast, we find that leftist, socialist, or simply democratic movements are incapable of acting in these decisive scenarios. They have spent their time debating where the struggle was not taking place or echoing the arguments of yesteryear. We have already referred to the belated discovery that the discussions on the public interest and the formulation of alternatives should (also) take place in the electronic media that inform the vast majorities.

The problem of speaking in the name of the popular is that it has not encouraged us to radically question the discourse and politics of representation, but rather to substitute that notion with the concept of civil society. In Mexico in the mid-1990s, for example, the claims to enact civil society come just as easily from the opposition parties as from the dozens of movements of urban activists, youth, feminists, religious groups, and the neo-Zapatista guerrilla insurgency. They all question the ability of parties to adequately express social demands. The formula "civil society" has the advantage, at times, that its "spokespersons" can be differentiated from those of the state. However, the diversity of its representatives, the often antagonistic character of its demands, and the almost always minoritarian character of its support end up reproducing problems that the concept of the popular never managed to resolve.

Just as "the popular" increasingly became elusive due to the multiplicity of representations disseminated by folklore, the culture industries, and political populism, so also the concept of civil society is used nowadays to legitimize the most heterogeneous agendas of groups, nongovernmental organizations, private corporations, and even individuals. Despite the various interests and strategies that inspire these sectors, they all coincide in accusing the state of society's problems and in assuming that things would be better if the state ceded its initiatives and power to civil society. But since each understands something different by this vague concept, it can appear as a typical imagined community, in the terms that Benedict Anderson used to define the nation.[12]

When one reads how civil society is written about, it is possible to imagine her as "a lady who understands things very well,[13] knows what she wants, what she has to do; she is good, very good, and of course is the only possible adversary against state perversion."[14] A new source of confidence in this age of uncertainties, civil society appears to be one more totalizing concept destined to overlook the heterogeneous and disintegrated ensemble of voices that circulate throughout nations. Some authors define the modes of interaction that the notion of civil society encompasses as different from those of the economy and the state, although connected to them. The best reformulation is given by Jean L. Cohen and Andrew Arato, who include—and at the same time differentiate—"the intimate sphere (particularly the family), the sphere of associations (especially voluntary associations), the social movements, and forms of public communication,"[15] although their weighty tome gives short shrift to this last modality.

The rapprochement of citizenship, mass communications, and consumption has, among other aims, to give recognition to the scenarios in which the public is constituted. It becomes evident that in order to live in democratic societies it is indispensable to accept that the market of citizens' opinions includes as great a variety and dissonance as the clothing and entertainment markets. Remembering that citizens are also consumers leads to finding in the diversification of tastes one of the aesthetic foundations for the democratic conception of citizenship.

The Reinvention of Politics

If we give due acknowledgment to the shift in the locations where citizenship is practiced—for example, the shift from the people to civil society—and to the restructuring of the relative weight of the local, the national, and the global, then we will also have to acknowledge the changes in the politics of representation of identities. Another, cultural mode of doing politics will have to emerge, as well as other kinds of cultural policies.

The process that we have begun to describe as globalization can be summarized as the passage from modern identities to other forms that might be labeled postmodern, despite the increasingly ill-fitting implications of the term. *Modern identities were territorial and almost always monolinguistic.* They were imposed by subordinating regions and ethnicities within more or less arbitrarily delimited spaces. These were called nations and, defined by the form of their state organization, they were pitted against other nations. Even in multilinguistic zones such as the Andean and Mesoamerican regions, the policies of modernizing homogenization concealed their multiculturality under the domination of the Spanish language and the diversity of modes of production and consumption were contained within national arrangements.

In contrast, *postmodern identities are transterritorial and multilinguistic.* They are structured less by the logic of the state than by that of markets. Instead of basing themselves on oral and written communications that circulated in personalized spaces, characterized by close interaction, these identities take shape in relation to the industrial production of culture, its communications technologies, and the differentiated and segmented consumption of commodities. The classic *sociospatial* definition of identity, limited to a particular territory, needs to be complemented by a *sociocommunicational* definition. Such a theoretical reformulation entails that policies concerning identity (or culture) should deal with historical patrimony and develop strategies regarding the locations of information production and communications that play a role in shaping and renewing identities.[16]

What kind of citizenship is expressed by this new type of identity? In Part I of this book I have sought to think of the contemporary citizen as the inhabitant of the city more than of the nation. This citizen feels rooted in his or her local culture (rather than the national culture that the state and parties speak of). But this urban culture is also the site of intersection of multiple national traditions—those of the migrants that come together in any metropolis. At the same time, these traditions are reorganized by the transnational flow of commodities and messages.

The juridico-political coordinates of the nation thus lose force, formed as they were in an age when identity took shape exclusively in relation to the territory of its inhabitants. Now we see vanish, once and for all, those identities conceived of as the expression of a collective being, of an idiosyncracy, or of an imagined community secured by bonds of territory and blood. National culture is not extinguished, but it is converted into a formula that designates the continuity of an unstable historical memory, continually reconstructed in interaction with transnational cultural referents. That is why passports and national identity papers become multinational (as in the European Union) or coexist with other forms of identification. Millions of inhabitants at the end of this century have several national passports, or they make greater use of the documents that define them as migrants rather than those that tether them to the land of their birth. Or they are simply undocumented. How can they believe themselves to be the citizens of only one country? In contrast to the juridical notion of citizenship, which states attempt to delimit on the basis of the criterion of "sameness," new heterogeneous forms of belonging emerge, and their networks are interwoven with the circuits of consumption: they constitute "a space of struggles, a terrain of different memories, and an encounter of unequal voices."[17]

Free trade and supranational integration agreements (the European Union, the North American Free Trade Agreement, MERCOSUR), which I treat in Part II of this book, provide specific *institutional configurations* to the passage from the national to the global and from the public to the private.[18] The differential study of the changes that these commercial agreements bring about in different sociocultural areas is one way of going beyond the metaphysical preoccupation with the "loss of identity." Almost always trapped in a fundamentalist view of ethnic and national cultures, this view makes it difficult to discern the various effects of globalization. Empirical analysis of these processes, on the other hand, makes evident four sociocultural circuits in which transnationalization and regional integration differentially operate:

- The *historico-territorial* circuit. This is constituted by an ensemble of knowledges, habits, and experiences organized throughout various periods in connection with ethnic, regional, and national territories. They enter into play especially in matters relating to historical patrimony and traditional popular culture.

- The *culture of elites*. This is composed of written and visual symbolic production (literature, visual arts). Historically, this sector formed part of the patrimony according to which each nation defined and elaborated its own sense of collective self. But it is fitting to distinguish it from the first circuit because it encompasses works representative of the upper and middle classes who have a greater level of education. This culture is not known nor appropriated by the entirety of each society, and in recent decades it has been integrated into international markets and circuits of valuation.

- *Mass communications.* This circuit is devoted to the mass spectacles of the entertainment industries (radio, film, television, video).

- *Restricted systems of information and communication.* These are meant for the decision makers, who make use of satellite communications, fax, cellular phones, and computers.

Throughout this book, I shall refer to these four circuits of cultural development in order to distinguish the different levels of integration within supranational development. The restructuring of national cultures does not take place in the same way, nor as deeply, in each of these circuits. Thus, the recomposition of identities will vary according to their participation in any one of them.

The competency of national states and their cultural policies diminishes when we move from the first circuit to the last one. Conversely, the younger the inhabitants, the more their actions correspond to the third and fourth circuits, as studies of cultural consumption have shown. In the younger generations, identities are organized less in keeping with historico-territorial symbols—for example, those of national memory—and more in tune with those of Hollywood, Televisa, or Benetton. Analogously, the historic centers of large cities lose importance as neighborhoods spread out, providing meeting places for youth. These places are not organizational nodes so much as "margins where youth can invent themselves." Rather than the core of a hypothetical interiority contained and defined by the family, the neighborhood, the city, the nation, or any of these waning frames, identity comes to be experienced as a "focal point for a shattered repertoire of miniroles."[19] Under these conditions, is it possible for identities to be the object of politics and policy?

There are forms of national and transnational political solidarity, evident in the ecological movement and in nongovernmental organizations, that can be adapted for the practice of citizenship in a globalized world. But the masses, and even the politicized sectors, are little attracted by these international structures. This is borne out by the low voter turnout in the European Parliament elections in 1994 and the limited resonance of Latin American integration initiatives in the agendas of social movements and the platforms of national political parties.

In our analysis of the place of culture in these supranational and free trade agreements in Europe, between the United States, Mexico, and Canada, and among some Latin American countries, we come to suspect that these may be nothing more than agreements among corpo-

rate executives. What possible effectiveness can cultural integration policies have if they are limited to the preservation of monuments and folklore patrimonies, or to the high arts that are, in any case, losing their
audience? These observations are not a minor matter. They must pose
a challenge to globalization. We must ask whether free trade agreements
can also serve the purpose of developing endogenous culture industries
(film, television, video), for these constitute the terrain where mass tastes
and citizenship are shaped. Or are we condemned to continue to be
the suburbs of North America? It should be acknowledged that if this
tendency wins out it will not be due exclusively to unilateral cultural
policies. Our study of the increasing "Americanization" of consumer
tastes in film and video verifies that it is also a matter of the preferences of civil society.

I am not sure if the expression "Americanization" (it might be more
accurate to speak of North Americanization) is adequate, but I cannot
find a better one. It should be noted at the outset that I am not only
referring to the hegemony of U.S. capital and corporations. They are,
without a doubt, a key factor in the confusion of an expanding globalization with the worldwide export of one country's film, television, and
food styles to the entire planet. Our analysis of the changes in the supply of cultural commodities and in the tastes of audiences indicates
that the economic control wielded by the United States is linked to the
rise of certain aesthetic and cultural features that are not exclusive to
that country. They find in it, however, an exemplary representative: the
predominance of spectacular action over more reflexive and intimate
forms of narration; the fascination with a memoryless present; and the
reduction of differences among societies to a standardized multiculturalism where conflicts, if admitted, are "resolved" according to very Western and pragmatic modalities.

We insist on asking about the meaning of the imposition of an aesthetics of action in the context of an epoch whose phase of political hero-
ics has ended. Where are we being led, imprisoned in the present and
in this culture of premieres, when it all coexists with the reawakening
of fundamentalisms in certain premodern traditions? What is the function of the culture industries that not only homogenize but also treat
differences in such a simplistic manner, while electronic communications,
migrations, and the globalization of markets become more complex as
people come together? These questions suffice to realize that the multiple
connections between consumption and citizenship are neither mechan-

ical nor easily reducible to the coherence of economic paradigms or political sociology.

Research as Essay

This book stands halfway between a research study and a collection of
essays. The first three chapters are outgrowths of empirical studies of
cultural consumption in Mexico City. These research projects provided
the points of departure for the current reflection on the transformations
in culture in the Mexican capital and other Latin American cities.[20]

The texts included in this book represent my personal position on
various polemics that have been raging in the area of studies of urban
cultures. I advocate, for example, the need to go beyond the opposition between an anthropology that wraps itself in the mantle of community autonomy and a sociology or a communications approach that
can only make general statements about cities and culture industries.
Working with anthropologists, sociologists, communications analysts,
and art historians afforded me the chance to gain new and multifocal
information on microsocial interaction in everyday life and on the
macrotendencies projected by censuses and surveys. Coordinating the
contributions of all of these researchers was more than an administra-
tive task or an academic routine; it was a stimulating challenge posed
by their discrepancies. I would like my references to their work to be
interpreted as my acknowledgment in this more expansive sense. I would
also hope that the crafting of the written word in these essays demonstrates that the city and the culture industries attract me not only as objects of knowledge but also as places where one imagines and narrates.

The four chapters of Part II, which deal with the restructuring of
identities in this era of the industrialization of culture, supranational
integration, and free trade, are based on personal documentary explorations as well as collective research that I coordinated on the changes
in habits and tastes of film, television, and video viewers in four Mexican cities.[21]

I have tried to use only those data from these studies that are necessary to substantiate the theoretical-methodological and cultural policy arguments with which this book deals. Those who would like more
information on the changes in Mexico City or on audiovisual industries and their audiences can consult the above-mentioned books. I
would like to emphasize that those studies on consumption were ques-

tioned anew from the perspective of the transformation in citizenship. Nevertheless, this latter issue requires further research. There is a special need for more analyses of social movements, to which I give some attention only in the chapter on the negotiations among popular classes.

I would like this book to be read like a conversation with anthropologists, sociologists, and communications specialists, as well as with artists, writers, and art and literary critics, on the meaning of citizens and consumers in the midst of cultural changes that alter the relation between the public and the private. Likewise, this is also a continuation of an ongoing dialogue with those responsible for cultural policies and with participants in consumer and citizen movements. With them I have discussed many of the issues dealt with in these pages. The essay format of this book corresponds to the open character of these conversations and the fragmentary perspectives with which we engage in debates on these matters.

I would like to thank various readers—Juan Flores, Jean Franco, Aníbal Ford, Sandra Lorenzano, Jesús Martín Barbero, Eduardo Nivón, Renato Rosaldo, Ana Rosas Mantecón, and George Yúdice—for their comprehensive commentary on the essays gathered in this book. The list of those who have made valuable observations at symposia or after publication of some of the essays in journals would be too long to enumerate. In some cases, the references to their published works do them at least a little justice. I should make special mention of the financial support provided by various Mexican institutions: the Consejo Nacional para la Cultura y las Artes, the Departamento del Distrito Federal, and the Instituto Mexicano de Cinematografía. Likewise, the Organization of American States and the Rockefeller Foundation contributed so that these essays could have a firm foundation in empirical research on Mexico City and the culture industries. I would like to acknowledge the Universidad Autónoma Metropolitana, especially the Anthropology Department, for its material support, for the fruitful academic exchange that colleagues and students provided. Above all, I would like to thank the members of the Program in Urban Cultural Studies who accompanied me in these anthropological research projects, ever open to the insights and uncertainties of dialogue with other social sciences.

Part I
Cities in Globalization

Chapter 1

Consumption Is Good for Thinking

Proof that common sense does not coincide with "good sense" can be obtained by focusing one's research on consumption. In everyday language, consumption is usually associated with useless expenditures and irrational compulsions. This moral and intellectual disqualification is based on other commonplaces regarding the omnipotence of the mass media, which presumably incite the masses to gorge themselves unthinkingly with commodities.

There are still some who fault the poor for buying televisions, video players, and cars when they don't even own a home. How can one make sense of families who squander their Christmas bonuses on parties and presents when they don't have enough to eat and dress themselves throughout the year? Don't these media addicts know that newscasters lie and that *telenovelas* distort real life?

Rather than responding to these questions, one can inquire into the way in which they are formulated. Nowadays we see consumption as more complex than the simple relation between manipulative media and docile audiences. It is well known that numerous mass communications studies have shown that cultural hegemony is achieved by dominators who corner their audiences. Between them there are *intermediaries* like the family, the neighborhood, and their fellow workers.[1] These studies no longer posit the relation between senders and receivers as one of domination. Communication is not effective if it does not include *collaboration and transaction* between both parties.

To make headway in this area of work, it is necessary to situate communication processes in a larger conceptual framework that emerges from theories and research on consumption. What does it mean to consume? What is the rationality—for producers and consumers—of an incessant expansion and renewal of consumption?

Toward a Multidisciplinary Theory

It is not easy to answer these questions. Research on consumption may have proliferated in recent years, but it continues to reproduce the compartmentalization and disconnection characteristic of the social sciences. There are economic, sociological, psychoanalytic, psychosocial, and anthropological theories on what takes place when we consume. There are literary theories on reception and aesthetic theories on the critical fate of artworks. But there is not a *sociocultural* theory of consumption. I attempt to bring together here the main lines of interpretation and to indicate their points of convergence with the goal of contributing to a global conceptualization of consumption that includes the communication and reception of symbolic commodities.

Let me begin with a definition: *consumption is the ensemble of sociocultural processes in which the appropriation and use of products takes place.* This characterization leads us to understand our acts of consumption as something more than the exercise of tastes, whims, and unreflexive purchases, as is presumed by moralistic judgment, and as something that goes beyond individual attitudes explored in market surveys.

In this view, consumption is understood according to its *economic rationality.* Various trends within this framework posit consumption as a moment in the cycle of social production and reproduction. It is the site of completion of the process initiated when commodities are produced. It is where the expansion of capital and the reproduction of the labor force are realized. From this point of view, needs and individual tastes are not what determine who consumes what, and in what manner. The planning of the distribution of commodities depends, rather, on the administration of capital. In its organization for the provision of food, housing, transport, and entertainment to the members of a society, the economic system "thinks" about how to reproduce the labor force and increase profit on commodities. We may not agree with this strategy, that is, with the selection of who will consume more or less, but it is undeniable that the supply of goods and the inducement through advertising to buy them are not arbitrary acts.

Nevertheless, the macrosocial considerations of large-scale economic agents are not rationalities that shape consumption. Marxist studies of consumption, as well as earlier mass communications research (from 1950 to 1970), exaggerated the determining force of corporations on consumers and audiences.[2] A more complex theory of the interaction of producers and consumers, senders and receivers, as developed in certain currents of urban anthropology and sociology, shows that consumption is also motivated by an *interactive sociopolitical rationality.* When we examine, from the perspective of consumer movements and their demands, the proliferation of commodities and brands, of communications and consumer networks, we see the contribution to these processes of the rules and motivations of group distinction, educational expansion, technological innovations, and fashion. "Consumption," Manuel Castells has written, "is the site where class conflict, rooted in unequal participation in production, continues in the distribution and appropriation of commodities."[3] To consume is to participate in an arena of competing claims for what society produces and the ways of using it. The importance of demands for increased consumption and for a social wage in organized labor initiatives, and the critical perspectives developed by consumer groups, are evidence of how popular sectors think about consumption. If consumption was once a site of more or less unilateral decisions, it is today a space of interaction where producers and senders no longer simply seduce their audiences; they also have to justify themselves rationally.

The political importance of consumption can also be appreciated, for example, in the arguments of the politicians who curbed hyperinflation in Argentina, Brazil, and Mexico. They based their electoral strategies on the increased indebtedness that a change in economic policy might have on those who bought cars or appliances on credit. "If you don't want a return to inflation and higher taxes, which will make it impossible to pay off what you bought, you should vote for me again," said Carlos Menem in seeking reelection as president of Argentina. A formula used in his electoral campaign—the "layaway vote"—demonstrates the complicity of consumption and citizenship nowadays.

A third line of research, the study of consumption as a marker of difference and distinction between classes and groups, has led to a focus on the *symbolic and aesthetic aspects of the rationality of consumption*. There is a logic to the construction of *status* markers and in the ways of communicating them. Books by Pierre Bourdieu, Arjun Appadurai, and Stuart Ewen, among others, show that in contemporary societies a significant aspect of the rationality of social relations is constructed less in the struggle for the means of production and satisfaction of material needs than in the appropriation of the means of symbolic distinction.[4] There is a coherence to the places where the members of a class, and even class fractions, eat, study, live, and take vacations. This also goes for what they read and enjoy, how they inform themselves, and what they transmit to other groups. This coherence comes into view when socioanthropological research seeks to understand these arenas synergistically. The logic that drives the appropriation of commodities as objects of distinction is not the same as the logic involved in the satisfaction of needs. It is defined, rather, by the scarcity of those commodities and the impossibility that others should have them.

This said, this research model's shortcoming is that it tends to understand consumption as primarily a means of creating divisions. If the members of a society did not share the meanings of commodities, if these were meaningful only for the elites or the minorities that use them, they would not serve the purposes of differentiation. An imported car or a computer with new features distinguishes its few owners because those who do not possess them know their sociocultural meaning. Conversely, a handicraft or an indigenous feast—whose mythic sense is possessed by the ethnic group that generated it—become elements of distinction or discrimination when other sectors of the same society take interest in them and understand their significance in some measure. Consequently, we should acknowledge that consumption contributes to the *integrative and communicative rationality of a society.*

Is There a Postmodern Rationality?

Some currents of postmodern thought have drawn attention—in the opposite direction to the one we endorse—to the dissemination of meaning, the dispersion of signs, and the difficulty of establishing stable and shared codes. The scenarios of consumption are invoked by postmodern writers as the most compelling evidence for the crisis in modern rationality and its effects on some of the principles that had governed cultural development.

Jean-François Lyotard is no doubt correct in pointing out that the metanarratives that organized modern historical rationality have been exhausted. But one cannot deduce from the demise of certain totalizing narratives that the global has disappeared as a horizon. Postmodern critique has served the purpose of rethinking the condensed forms of organization of the social that modernity introduced (nations, classes, etc.). But is it legitimate to extend this questioning to the extreme of a supposed postmodern disorder, to a dispersion of subjects that has its paradigmatic manifestation in free markets? It is odd that in this era of planetary concentration wrought by markets so much influence should be attributed to uncritical celebrations of individual dissemination and visions of societies as erratic coincidences of drives and desires.

It is also surprising that postmodern thought should be constituted almost exclusively by philosophical reflections, even when it deals with such concrete objects as architectural design, the organization of the culture industry, and social interrelations. When we try to verify hypotheses in our empirical research, we observe that no society or group can support too much erratic eruption of desires, nor the concomitant uncertainty of meanings. In other words, we need structures by means of which to think and give order to what we desire.

It is useful to remember here several anthropological studies on ritual that touch on the questions relating to the supposed irrationality of consumers that we raised at the beginning of this chapter. How can we distinguish forms of expenditure that contribute to social reproduction from those that dissipate and fragment it? Is the "squandering" of money in the consumption of popular groups a self-sabotage of the poor, a simple demonstration of the incapacity to organize themselves for progress?

A clue in answering these questions is the frequency with which these sumptuary, "excessive" expenditures are associated with rituals and celebrations. A birthday or the anniversary of a patron saint may justify the expense on the basis of morality or religion. However, the expense also makes possible an event through which the given society consecrates a rationality that gives it order and security.

Through rituals, according to Mary Douglas and Baron Isherwood, groups select and pin down—in keeping with collective agreements— the meanings that regulate their lives. Rituals "serve to contain the drift of meanings" and to make visible public definitions of what is judged valuable by general consensus. Rituals are effective when they make use of material things to establish meanings and practices that preserve them.

The costlier these things, the stronger the affective investment and the ritualization that fixes the meanings associated with it. Douglas and Isherwood define many of the things consumed as "ritual trappings" and see consumption as a ritual process whose primary function is "to make sense of the inchoate flux of events."[5]

Anxious or obsessive behavior around consumption may have a profound dissatisfaction at its origin, according to many psychologists. But consumption is otherwise associated, in a more radical sense, with a dissatisfaction that generates an erratic flow of meanings. Buying objects, wearing them on the body, or distributing them throughout the home, assigning them a place within an order, endowing them with functions in one's communication with others, are resources for thinking one's own body, the unstable social order, and uncertain interaction with others. To consume is to make more sense of a world where all that is solid melts into air. That is why, aside from their usefulness in expanding the market and reproducing the labor force, insofar as they distinguish us from others and help us communicate with them, "commodities are good for thinking," in Douglas and Isherwood's words.[6]

Through this play of desires and structures, commodities and consumption also serve to give political order to each society. Consumption is a process in which desires are converted into demands and socially regulated acts. Why do indigenous artisans or popular merchants who become rich because of the felicitous reception of their work, or many politicians and union leaders who accumulate wealth through corruption, continue to live in working-class neighborhoods, control their expenses, and try not to "stand out"? Why do they prefer to continue belonging to their original groups (sometimes holding on to power) than to show off their prosperity?

Alfred Gell's study of the Muria Gond people of India proposes a subtle approach to explain this regulatory aspect of consumption.[7] Thanks to changes in the tribal economy in the last century, the Muria got richer than their neighbors, yet maintained a modest lifestyle that Appadurai, turning Veblen on his head, calls "conspicuous stinginess."[8] They spend quite prodigally on certain commodities so long as they correspond to shared values and do not alter the sumptuous homogeneity.

In indigenous villages in Mexico, I observed the acceptance of external—modern—objects, so long as they can be assimilated to communitarian logic. The growth of income, the expansion and variety of consumer items, as well as the technical capacity to appropriate new commodities and messages owing to higher levels of education, do not have enough power to drive members of the group to abandon themselves to the novelties. The desire to possess "the new" does not operate as something irrational or independent of the collective culture to which these people belong.

Even in totally modern situations, consumption is not something "private, atomized and passive," argues Appadurai, but "eminently social, correlative and active," subordinated to a certain political control by elites. The tastes of the hegemonic sectors have something like a "funneling" function, for they condition the selection of external offerings and provide politico-cultural models for the administration of the tension between what is one's own and what comes from afar.

In the studies on cultural consumption in Mexico, to which I will refer later, we found that popular sectors' lack of interest in experimental art exhibitions, theater, or film is due not only to the weak symbolic capital they draw on for the appreciation of those forms of communication, but also to group loyalty to their communities. Within the urban setting, it is their family context, their neighborhood, and their jobs that maintain the homogeneity of their consumption and control the deviations in their tastes and patterns of spending. On a larger scale, what is understood as national culture continues to serve as the context of selection for what comes from outside.

Transnational Consumer Communities

These communities of belonging and control, however, are undergoing restructuring. What group do we belong to when we participate in a sociality constructed primarily in relation to globalized processes of consumption? We live in a time of fractures and heterogeneity, of segmentations within each nation, and of fluid communication with transnational orders of information, fashion, and knowledge. In the midst of this heterogeneity, we find codes that unite us, or at least permit us to understand each other. But those shared codes refer ever less to the ethnicity, class, and nation into which we were born. Those old units, insofar as they endure, seem to be reformulated as *mobile pacts for the interpretation* of commodities and messages. The definition of a nation, for example, is given less at this stage by its territorial limits or its political history. It survives, rather, as an *interpretive community of consumers,* whose traditional—alimentary, linguistic—habits induce them to relate in a peculiar way with the objects and information that circulate in international networks. At the same time, we find international communities of consumers—we already gave the examples of youth and television viewers—that provide a sense of belonging where national loyalties have eroded.

Since the agreements among producers, institutions, markets, and publics—which constitute the interpretive pacts and renew them periodically—are struck in these international networks, it turns out that the hegemonic sector of one nation has more in common with the elites of another than with the subaltern sectors of its own nation. Twenty years ago, the adherents of dependency theory reacted to the first signs of this process by accusing the bourgeoisie of a lack of loyalty to national interests. And, of course, the national character of these interests was defined by the "authentic" traditions of the people. Today we know that this authenticity is illusory, for the sense of one's own repertoire of objects is arbitrarily delimited and reinterpreted in historical hybrid processes. We can also see an analogous hybrid process in the mixture of "autochthonous" and "foreign" ingredients in consumption by popular sectors, in the peasant artisans who adapt their archaic knowledges in order to interact with tourists, in workers who manage to adapt their work culture to new technologies while maintaining their ancient and local beliefs. Several decades of transnational symbolic construction have created what Renato Ortiz has labeled an "international popular culture," with a collective memory made from fragments of different nations.[9] Although their psyches might continue to harbor a national memory, consumers from the popular classes are nevertheless capable of reading the quotations of a multilocalized imaginary assembled by television and advertising: Hollywood and pop stars, jeans and credit-card logos, sports heroes from various countries, and national sports figures that play in other countries, all constitute a constantly available repertoire of signs. Marilyn Monroe and Jurassic animals, Che Guevara and the fall of the Berlin Wall, the most-consumed soft drink, and *Tiny Toon* can be cited or alluded to by any international advertising designer, confident that his or her message will have meaning even for those who have never traveled outside of their country.

It is necessary, therefore, to find out how identities and alliances are restructured when a national community wanes or when segmented participation in consumption—which becomes the principal criterion of identification—creates solidarity among elites from each country within one transnational circuit and solidarity among popular sectors within another. In our study of cultural consumption in Mexico, we found that the separation among hegemonic and subaltern groups is no longer presented as the opposition between one's own and imports, or between the traditional and the modern, but by a differential affiliation with cultural subsystems with a different complexity and capacity for innovation.[10] While some follow Brahms, Sting, and Carlos Fuentes, others prefer Julio Iglesias, Alejandra Guzmán, and Venezuelan *telenovelas*.

This split is operative not only in the consumption of entertainment. It also segments social sectors via strategic commodities that position them in the contemporary world and enable them to have decision-making capacity. While technological modernization in industry and services requires greater work skills, there is a concomitant increase in school absenteeism and ever lesser access to innovative information by middle sectors (and still less by popular sectors). The knowledge to use data and instruments that enable people to act autonomously and creatively is limited to those who can afford to subscribe to information services and exclusive television networks (on satellite dishes and retransmitters of metropolitan channels). The rest are offered mass communications, concentrated in large monopolies, that carry standard North American programming, plus repetitive *lite* entertainment shows produced in each country.

The characterization of consumption as an unreflexive site of useless expenditure can be criticized as follows. The majority of people are turned away from the most creative trends in contemporary culture as a result of the reorganization of transnational symbolic systems, which takes place according to neoliberal rules of maximum profitability of mass commodities and the concentration of culture among select, decision-making elites. Cultural leveling and depoliticization do not follow from the structure of the medium (television, radio, or video). The possibilities for interaction and critical reflection, on the contrary, have been demonstrated many times, albeit in small-scale experiments that do not translate into higher effectivity among mass publics. Similarly, the deepening of political apathy should not be attributed only to the contraction of public life and the retreat of families to home delivery of electronic entertainment. Nevertheless, this transformation in the relations between public and private in everyday cultural consumption marks a fundamental change in the conditions for the practice of a new type of civic responsibility.

If consumption has become a site from which it is difficult to think, this is the result of its capitulation to a supposedly free, or better yet ferocious, game of market laws. If consumption is to articulate with a reflexive exercise of citizenship, it would have to meet the following requirements: *(a)* a vast and diversified supply of commodities and messages representative of the international variety of markets, with easy and equal access for the majority; *(b)* multidirectional and reliable information on the quality of products, with effective consumer control and the capacity to refute the pretensions and seductions of advertising; *(c)* democratic participation by the principal sectors of civil society in material, symbolic, juridical, and political decisions that organize consumption, such as health standards relating to foodstuffs, concessions of radio and television frequencies, prosecution of speculators who hoard the most necessary products, and management of crucial information for decision making.

These *political* actions, which elevate consumers to citizens, entail a conception of the market as not only a place for the exchange of commodities, but as part of more complex sociocultural interactions. Similarly, consumption is seen not so much as the individual possession of isolated objects, but rather as the collective appropriation, within relations of solidarity with and distinction from others, of commodities that provide biological and symbolic needs, and that serve to transmit and receive messages. The theories of consumption reviewed in this chapter suggest that, when considered complementarily, commercial value is not something contained "naturally" in objects but is rather the result of sociocultural interaction among the people who use them. The abstract character of commercial exchanges, accentuated nowadays by the spatial and technological distance between producers and consumers, led to the belief in the autonomy of commodities and in the inexorable character, extraneous to the things themselves, of the objective laws that presumably regulate the relations between supply and demand. The encounter of modern and "archaic" societies permits us to see that commodities have functions in all societies, and that the commercial aspect is only one of them. Humans exchange objects to satisfy culturally defined needs, to integrate with and distinguish ourselves from others, to fulfill our desires and to map out our situation in the world, to control the erratic flux of desires and to give them stability or security through institutions and rituals.

Within this multiplicity of actions and interactions, objects have a complex life. In one phase, they are only "candidates for commodity status."[11] Then they go through another, properly commercial phase. Finally, they lose this aspect and take on another. For example, masks made by indigenous peoples for ceremonies are sold to a modern consumer and ultimately are put on display in urban apartments or in museums, where their economic value is forgotten. Another example is that of the song produced for exclusively aesthetic reasons, which, once it is recorded, attains mass appeal and profits. Then it is appropriated and modified by a political movement and becomes a resource of identification and collective mobilization. These changing biographies of objects and messages suggest that the commercial aspect of commodities is their opportunity and their risk. We can act as consumers by situating ourselves in only one of these processes of interaction—say, that which regulates the market. As citizens, we can also take more time for reflection and experimentation, taking into consideration the multiple potentialities of objects and taking advantage of their "semiotic virtuosity"[12] in the varied contexts where people might encounter one another.

To pose these questions implies relocating the pubic. The discrediting of states as administrators of the basic sectors of production and information, and the lack of credibility of political parties (including those of the opposition), have contracted the spaces where it was possible to look after the public interest, and where it should be possible to limit and manage the otherwise savage struggle of private commercial powers. In some countries we can detect the emergence of nonpartisan and nongovernmental institutions—such as the ombudsman, human-rights commissions, and independent news groups—that make it possible to uncouple the need to value the public sphere from the province of corrupt state bureaucracies. Some consumers want to be citizens.

After the 1980s, the "lost decade" of economic growth in Latin America, during which states surrendered part of their control of society to private corporations, it has become clear where privatization at any cost leads: to national decapitalization, underconsumption by majorities, unemployment, and impoverishment of cultural offerings. The articulation of consumption and citizenship requires a relocation of the market within society, the imaginative reconquest of public spaces, and interest in the public. Consumption can be a site of cognitive value; it can be good for thinking and acting in a meaningful way that renews social life.

Chapter 2

Mexico

Cultural Globalization in a Disintegrating City

R esearch on cultural consumption in a large city places us at the intersection of debates in the social sciences. There are three inter-
connected problems that demonstrate this linkage between the crisis of
megacities and the crisis in social knowledge:

1. Can one still speak of the city and of urban life in a megalopolis with
   more than ten million inhabitants?

2. To what degree can urban cultures defined by local traditions survive
   in an era in which culture is deterritorialized and cities reordered to
   form transnational systems of information, communication, commerce, and tourism?

3. How can we study urban issues using the existing tools of the social sciences? Which discipline is most relevant for understanding new urban
   cultural processes: sociology, anthropology, or communications studies?

Sociologists versus Anthropologists

What is the difference between an urban sociologist and an urban an-
thropolist? It has been said that the former studies the city while the

latter studies *in* the city.[1] Sociology constructs broad maps of behavior on the basis of census data and statistics, whereas extended field studies enable dense readings of social interaction.

A number of anthropologists have rebelled against the retreat of their discipline to small-scale causes and their effects. Why should we confine ourselves to speak only about the neighborhood while remaining silent about the city? Why should we adopt an approach proper to the study of a village for our work in large urban centers? Some scholars think that the narrow scope of anthropology does not permit an examination of what is essentially urban. The formation and life of the city escape us if we cannot show to what degree the narrow relationships we document in case studies are conditioned by the broad structures of society.[2]

Other scholars argue that anthropology is distinguished not by its object but by its method of study. While sociologists speak of the city, anthropologists let the city speak: their detailed observations and in-depth interviews, their customary residence with people, are ways of trying to listen to what the city has to say. This dedication to the eloquence of everyday acts has been methodologically rich and ethically generous. Nonetheless, questions arise from an epistemological point of view. How reliable is what inhabitants say about their way of life? Who is speaking when subjects interpret their experience: the individual, the neighborhood, or the class to which the individual belongs?

Any urban problem—transportation, pollution, or street vendors—presents us with such a diversity of opinions, and even studies, on the basis of which it is difficult to distinguish the real from the imaginary. Perhaps there is no place where epistemological critiques of common sense and ordinary language are more justified than in large cities: we should exercise caution when recording the divergent voices of our informants and endeavor to discern whether they *know* what they are talking about. The intensity of experience overshadows the unconscious motivations for people's actions, making it possible to edit the sequence of events so as to construct personally advantageous versions of the truth. An uncritical study of the fragmentation and discourses of the city has two drawbacks: it reproduces urban fragmentation through monographic description without explaining it, or it simulates an integration of the fragments, often drawing on the "explanations" given by the least insightful informants. The methodological populism of anthropology thus becomes the "scientific" ally of political populism.

The postmodern debate over anthropological texts has also led us to suspect that we anthropologists too do not really know what we are doing when we conduct ethnographic studies. Malinowski (1922) thought he was describing the Trobrianders exactly as they were, but his *Diaries* also reveal a repugnance for their culture coincident with his passion for the "animality" of their bodies. The debates between Robert Redfield and Oscar Lewis about Tepoztlán suggest that perhaps they were not speaking about the same locality, or that their writings were more than testimony to "having been there" and, instead, as Geertz suspects, were a jockeying for place among those who "are here" in universities and symposia.[3]

With the development of anthropological hermeneutics and ethnopsychoanalysis, interpretive procedures for recording the various layers of meaning concealed beneath the appearance of acts and discourses have become more sophisticated.[4] It remains nonetheless difficult to articulate the various meanings that subjects attribute to their practices and the social and cultural conditioning by which the city provides meanings for each act, often unbeknownst to the actors themselves.

Babel

The problems of what is said and left unsaid by urban subjects, of what sociology says about them and what anthropology hears from them, are joined by an additional difficulty recently discerned in megacities such as Mexico City. This difficulty complicates all of the preceding ones: What happens when one cannot understand what a city is saying, when it turns into a Babel and the chaotic poliphony of its voices, its dismembered space, and the scattered experiences of its inhabitants dissolve the meaning of global discourses?

In Mexico City there are 263,000 indigenous Mexicans belonging to more than thirty ethnic groups who speak a corresponding number of languages.[5] They more or less continue to organize their homes, neighborhoods, and support networks, work out their disputes, and conduct their transactions with the state and their *compadres* just as they did when they lived in Puebla, Oaxaca, or Guerrero. But one does not have to be an indigenous migrant to lose touch with one's language or to have only a fragmentary experience of the city. We all experience this, at least since the 1940s. At that time, the Federal District had one and a half million inhabitants. Now, with sixteen million, the urban perimeter spreads over a territory that no one can apprehend and in which there are no longer any encompassing parameters of organization. The 9.1 square kilometers of Mexico City's territory at the end of the last century do not comprise even 1 percent of the metropolitan area of today.[6] That century-old city continues to exist as the so-called historic downtown, but demographic, industrial, and commercial expansion has created many other urban areas on the periphery that overlap with other cities.

When we began to study the consumption of culture in Mexico City five years ago, we surveyed 1,500 homes with the hope of creating a map of behaviors.[7] We were surprised by the low use of public cultural infrastructure: 41.2 percent reported not going to the movies for more than a year; 62.5 percent of those who claimed to like theater had not seen one play in this period; 89.2 percent had not attended concerts. Nor did popular spectacles and local neighborhood festivals manage to attract in a consistent way more than 10 percent of the population.

What do people do on weekdays, after work or school? According to the survey, the majority of the inhabitants of Mexico City prefer to stay at home rather than use the city in their free time; 24.7 percent say that their principal activity is watching television; 16.3 percent just rest, sleep, or do housework.

On weekends, the majority of the population spend their "free" time in the seclusion of their home life. About 20.5 percent regularly leave the city; they include people in middle and high income brackets with weekend homes in the nearby towns that surround Mexico City, as well as those who travel to Puebla, Toluca, and environs to visit family and friends. In both cases, their trips are planned in keeping with the desire to put distance between themselves and the city, in search of a "different environment," one less polluted and "closer to nature."

Whether they seek to escape the hubbub of the city, confine themselves to domestic life and electronic amusements, or make use of parks and shopping centers, all the interviewees referred to the hostile environment of the city. Because it is difficult on workdays to avoid long commutes, danger, and smog, free time is experienced as such when one is liberated from the pressures of the city and the tensions of public transport. From Monday to Saturday, the crowds on the street necessarily make pragmatic use of urban space, going to and from work and engaging in the basic activities of consumption. But it is precisely the three million vehicles that traverse the city and the 22.5 million person-trips that the city endures every day, their noise and their fury, that discourage recreational and cultural uses of the city.[8]

Why does the general public attend shows so infrequently? One explanation, consistent with international trends, is that participation in public cultural facilities (movie houses, theaters, dance spaces) is declining, while home delivery of culture (radio, television, video) is on the rise. Our survey, which revealed sparse attendance at shows involving collective use of urban space, also found that 95 percent of Mexico City's population regularly watches television, 87 percent listens to radio, and 52 percent of the city's families have videocassette players.

There is another explanation for declining attendance at public shows, which ensues from the territorial and demographic growth of the city. In addition to economic and educational inequalities, which in every society limit the access of majorities to many cultural goods, the irregular and complex urban development of Mexico City and the unequal geographic distribution of facilities make it difficult for people to attend public shows. Almost all of the "classical" cultural venues (libraries, museums, theaters, movie houses, concert and dance halls) are concentrated in the central and southern zones of the city. Consequently, residential segregation reinforces income and educational inequality.

Radio and televison, which are more evenly distributed throughout the entirety of the city, disseminate information and entertainment to all sectors better than the spatially based public venues, access to which has become more difficult as the historic downtown area loses residents to disconnected towns of the periphery.

Our research team had lengthy discussions relating to what these precarious data included or excluded. Communications specialists and some anthropologists emphasized the retreat to domestically consumed culture, the replacement of theaters by radio, of movie houses by home video, and of attendance at stadiums by televised sports events. From the macrosocial perspective of our survey, anarchic urban growth goes hand in hand with the expansion of the electronic media. Industrialization and migration, which over the past fifty years increased the city's population from one and a half million to sixteen million, are part of the same policy of modernization that locates cultural development in the expansion of the media. The imbalance generated by irrational and speculative urbanization is "compensated" for by the effectiveness of communication in technological networks. Territorial expansion and massification of the city, which reduced interneighborhood interaction, took place simultaneously with the reinvention of social and cultural bonds via radio and television. Today these media—with their vertical and anonymous logic—sketch out the new and invisible links of the city.

From a more specifically anthropological perspective, some scholars interpreted the survey data in terms of the multiple uses that people still make of public spaces. During long periods of cohabitation with neighborhood residents, we made a number of discoveries about public interaction: the amount of time women spend conversing while shopping; the value that neighborhood parties have for those who attend; what youths learn by traversing the city on their way to work or to dance *danzón* or rock at night; the constant renewal of city life while waiting for the bus, buying tortillas, talking on the phone, making necessary or chance trips through the cityscape. It is difficult to capture the significance of these occasional activities with surveys, or to quantify their persistence in individual memory or in discussions among family members or friends.

The telescopic gaze of these surveys and the close-up gaze of fieldwork yield different and partially legitimate ways of naming the same ungraspable city.

We extended the reach of our study by carrying out a series of investigations on particular aspects of urban life that combined qualitative and quantitative techniques. We administered our general survey in a shantytown to serve as a reference point that would allow us to determine the similarities and discrepancies between the general structure of consumption in the city and in the local culture; we studied the main areas of Coyoacán (its historic downtown area, its multifamily dwellings, and its squatter settlements); we sought to understand the specificity of cultural reception in the Museum of the Templo Mayor and the Museum of Popular Cultures, and the pleasures of buying handicrafts.[9]

I should like to elaborate on the implications of these approaches to the different kinds of cultural activities in Mexico City, drawing on the research we conducted on the Second Festival of Mexico City in August of 1990.[10] We studied the behavior of the audiences at a representative sample of the nearly three hundred shows included in the festival (we selected thirty-three events, including plays, dance, opera, rock, and other kinds of music, performed in theaters, dance halls, parks, and plazas). Since this festival was the most important cultural event of the city, in terms of both the diversity of the art and shows presented and the size of the audiences that it attracted, it enabled us to discover how different sectors of the city related to art and culture.

This was not simply an audience survey. We explored the relation of the festival to the city and the mass media; we examined the areas from which the audiences came and how they found out about the various events, whether the festival's unusual cultural program had modified their usual cultural behavior, and whether and to what degree the critical evaluations of the public and the press coincided or diverged.[11]

The behavior of the spectators was more easily interpreted against the backdrop of ordinary patterns of reception of mass-mediated fare and relations to cultural institutions and urban space, as they were registered in our survey of 1,500 homes. Inversely, the study of the festival provided greater detail about some tendencies found in the general survey on consumption in Mexico City. Combined attendance at all events of the festival, which failed to reach two hundred thousand, constituted—both in volume and the range of social sectors represented by the participants—more or less 10 percent of the residents who claim to regularly attend public cultural institutions and events.

Four groups alone accounted for almost three-fourths of the audience: students (20.91 percent), office workers (19.90 percent), professionals (17.78 percent), and arts workers (14.18 percent). Workers comprised 2.14 percent, artisans 1.37 percent, while the retired and unemployed did not reach even 1 percent of the audience. As for level of education, those who had completed primary and secondary school comprised 20.02 percent, while 78.54 had attended preparatory high school and higher education. The Mexico City Festival reproduced the segmentations and segregation in the general population ensuing from inequality of income, education, and residential distribution of the city's inhabitants.

The surveys and, especially, the interviews and ethnographic observations revealed a vast diversity in those who attended the festival. Not even those spectators who are characterized as "popular" formed a homogeneous group. An enormous gap divides those who listen in rapt near immobility to the "romantic music" of Marco Antonio Muñiz from those who would rather dance the *danzón* with Pepe Arévalo, and from those who seek generational identity in Santa Sabina's rock music. These demographic segments do not always encounter each other peacefully: we found that adherents of popular and high culture viewed each other with indifference or disdain; this was the case even within the popular sector, divided between rock fans and *bolero* enthusiasts.

One finding that revealed the degree of heterogeneity and segregation of the spectators is that most of them did not even realize that the show they were watching was part of the festival, and only 12 percent demonstrated any knowledge of the festival's other activities. Even at those events that had better informed and educated audiences, only 32 percent could mention other festival activities. Responses to questions about how they found out about a given program varied according to the audiences: those who attended performances of classical music, dance, and theater generally found out through the press; those who attended rock concerts had seen fliers and posters or had received recommendations from friends; those who went to dance halls found out through the electronic media and attendance at previous events. In sum, the reality of the premise that a festival or a city can count on a homogeneous public, on whose basis publicity can be indiscriminately designed, existed only in the minds of the organizers. The majority of the public could not have cared less that the event they attended was part of a festival, and even less about knowing who sponsored it. On reading our research report, one of the organizers acknowledged that "we officials are the only ones who attribute any importance to logos."

It should be mentioned, however, that the festival did matter to the press, which gathered information on all events each day, making it possible to take it in at a glance, and which provided discussion of the festival's general cultural policies, its share of financing within the city budget, and the capacity of the event to meet social needs.

One of the conclusions of this study is that not only does the city not possess *one* public for culture but that such a public cannot even be brought together by a consolidated program like that of the festival. Despite its encompassing and multidisciplinary character, its appeal to both cultivated and popular audiences, and its location in both enclosed and open-air spaces, the festival turned out to be a kind of laboratory of the multicultural heterogeneity and dispersion of Mexico City. And, like the festival, the city can be said to exist more for the government and the press than for its citizens. Some urban researchers, notably demographers and sociologists, see the city as a whole. In contrast, and with few exceptions, most anthropologists and cultural studies scholars see the city as a disassembled jigsaw puzzle.

This disintegrated conception of the city jibes with ways in which popular urban movements see it. These movements are almost always guided by local and segmented perspectives, linked to the areas of the city in which they live, others to their experience as street vendors, and so on.[12] In each zone, their actions are carried out without contextualizing them in the historical development or more general affairs of the city. Only extraordinary movements, such as the ones that emerged with the earthquake of 1985, or ecological movements and some recently formed political parties, demonstrate an integrated vision of the metropolitan area.[13] These novel cases are characterized by their responses to the deterritorialization and dehistoricization produced by transnational culture and their search for new forms of rootedness. In some cases, they revalorize the neighborhood, in others the historic downtown area, and in a few cases the entirety of the city. For some European authors, such reaffirmations of urban territoriality are ways of holding on to the meaning of the city, insofar as it is an expression of local society, or forms of resistance to incorporation into international markets as one mere component.[14] This hypothesis is useful for understanding some of the current conflicts in the Mexican capital.

Several anthropological studies have revealed that since inhabitants of a megacity such as Mexico City find it difficult to take part in and identify with it as members of its entirety, they identify with the barrio or an even smaller unit. María Ana Portal's work on small historic colonial or pre-Columbian towns, absorbed nowadays into the greater metropolitan area of Mexico City, reveals that the notion of citizenship at work here is limited to a sense of belonging to those towns and to participation in feasts in honor of the patron saint. "In these towns, boys and girls becomes *citizens* upon getting married, at which time they are invited to participate in the festivities, having been informed of their responsibilities. The saint keeps watch; everything has to be done right. If not, he punishes them," commented one resident of San Andrés Totoltepec, a town in which modern jobs such as laborer and chauffeur have acquired greater importance than peasant occupations. Nevertheless, the residents continue to identify with the collectivity and to affirm a sense of belonging by means of rituals whose symbolic meaning is rooted in agricultural contexts.[15]

Even in the most modern of the city's neighborhoods, characterized by social disorganization and the crisis of partisan political representation, individualist reactions and corporatist entrenchment are the rule. When the rules for the right of access to the city lose their effectiveness, or when the access to jobs and services is subject to political arbitrariness and corruption, many residents seek protection in sectorial groupings and subordinate themselves to the paternalism of local bosses or religious leaders. Guillermo de la Peña and René de la Torre's study on urban identities in Guadalajara reveals three modes of organization that may also be found in other cities: *(a)* a "family corporatism" whereby members of an extended family participate in common activities of production and consumption as a defense against competition and uncertainty at the larger social level; *(b)* a "neighborhood corporatism" whereby neighborhood groups, under a strong and often religious leadership, organize the search for housing and jobs, the use of their free time, and the creation of mutual help networks that compensate for the lack of services and protection; *(c)* a "civic association" that pursues similar goals, giving priority, however, to democratic participation over corporatist or authoritarian domination. Right up to the present, according to Peña and Torre, "the old modes of assistance, such as families, churches, and paternalistic bosses," provide the hegemonic context in which identities take shape and citizenship is exercised.[16]

Glocalization or the Globalization of the Local

On the one hand, the majority retreats to its immediate surroundings and seeks to forget the larger urban context. On the other hand, some people begin to think of the city as a whole precisely when its disintegration reaches alarming proportions. It is not only the politicians and government officials who, faced with the need to administer it globally, seek its gestalt. Common problems such as pollution, traffic, and the interactions of the national and international market oblige certain groups to transcend the local in order to understand what takes place in the megalopolis. In addition to the historical city, with its monuments and neighborhoods that bear witness to the historical density of the centuries that have passed, and the industrial city, which emerged in the 1940s, there is the *globalized city,* connected to worldwide economic, finance, and communications networks.

Until recently, urbanization theories characterized cities as being very different from the countryside and as the sites where the agricultural skills of the labor force gave way to secondary or tertiary skills. This process became evident in Mexico when urban expansion followed industrial growth.

Nowadays, however, urban research has given greater importance to informational and financial processes over industrialization as the most dynamic economic agents. This change is leading to a reconceptualization of the functions of large cities. Insofar as today's economic profile is not characterized by the passage from agriculture to industry and then to services, but by the constant interaction of these three sectors by means of information processes (whether in technology, management, or marketing), large cities are the nodes where these movements take place. In an intensely transnationalized economy, the major metropolitan areas are the nodes connecting the economies of different societies to each other. It is no accident that it was Japanese entrepreneurs who coined the neologism *glocalize* to refer to the new "world-entrepreneur" whose culture articulates information, beliefs, and rituals deriving from the local, the national, and the international.[17]

This process is evident not only in the major urban agglomerations, which also happen to be concentrations of high economic power, such as New York, London, and Tokyo. Saskia Sassen has argued that the new strategic role of these cities derives from the "combination of spatial dispersion and global interaction," as well as their capacity to concentrate financial accumulation and innovations in consumption.[18] And Manuel Castells's analysis of the new phase of economic growth in Spain, which started in 1985 as a consequence of integration into the European market, shows that one source of dynamism in such cities as Madrid and Barcelona is their role as articulators of management, innovation, and marketing. The complexity of such international articulation requires increasingly sophisticated mechanisms of entrepreneurial and communications management. Urban communications and information-processing services take on a leading role in the generation of investment and jobs.[19] Both authors point out that the coexistence of a new elite, which administers these services, with migrants and the unemployed generates radically different conditions for the exercise of citizenship.

It is worth asking what sociocultural consequences this reorganization has already had in Mexico City. There is an obvious boom in construction of buildings for financial and information services, and the development of tourism; both initiatives have changed the urban landscape in a number of areas (for example, along the Paseo de la Reforma, in Polanco, and in the southern part of the city). The Festival of Mexico City and the Festival of the Historic Downtown Area, events whose goals include increasing the city's allure for tourists and turning it into an international metropolis, belong to a set of large development projects by means of which Mexico City's current administration is redefining the city's image. Changes undertaken in Alameda Park, Santa Fe, and Xochimilco, as well as projected development proposals and international investment, are resituating local culture within the networks of globalization.[20] Along the same lines, the program of the Fideicomiso de Estímulo al Cine Mexicano [Fund for the Development of Mexican Cinema] promotes the use of Mexico City as a site for filming foreign movies.[21]

Urban accommodation to globalization is not limited to large-scale government and corporate development projects. This redefinition of urban phenomena is discernible even in everyday contexts: executives and mid-level managers talk on cellular phones while driving from home to the office, where they pick up faxes transmitted the night before, answer them, put the information through their computer systems and modems, then go home at night to watch the news in English on channels received by cable or satellite.

Such actions suggest that the city is being reordered through electronic and telematic linkages. It is the same big city that grew along with its industry, as we are reminded every day by spectacular levels of pollution, but it is also a city that has been connected both within itself and with other countries not just by traditional means of air and land transportation, mail and telephone, but by cable, fax, satellite, and other electronic technologies.

Such transformations lead us to a theoretical redefinition of cities. In the fragmented space of this capital city lacking a center, we must work toward combining *sociodemographic* and *spatial* with *sociocommunicational* definitions of the city.

A City without a Map

"Each city receives its shape from the desert counterposed to it," says Marco Polo in Italo Calvino's *Invisible Cities*. When the city invades the desert, the forest, the mountain, everything that surrounds and embraces it, it breaks into pieces, losing its sense of space and challenge to these borders.

How, then, is one to describe the sprawling city from an anthropological perspective? Should we reactivate theories (now considered illusory) of the autonomy of the barrios, of the multitudes' scattered retreat into their homes, of the attempt to preserve exclusive small-scale territories for communities of youths or neighbors? Or should we also try to understand the new forms of identity organized in nonmaterial networks, in the processes of transmission of knowledge, in the diffuse linkages of commerce and the ties of transnational trade?

These options should not be considered mutually exclusive. Anthropologists can study the small histories of the city, and the big ones too. They no longer have a monopoly on the intimate and everyday aspects of urban life. Sociologists and communications specialists also conduct urban field studies. Perhaps as this century comes to a close we can best distinguish ourselves by the old anthropological concern with otherness and others. But the other is no longer territorially distant and alien;

the other is composed of the multicultural realities that constitute the city and its inhabitants. Anthropologists carry the other inside themselves as they participate in various local cultures and as they become decentered in transnational cultures. But, as we witnessed in the tensions and fragmentation of the Festival of Mexico City, it is more arduous to reconcile these multicultural realities within collective processes than in relation to the individual. The current coexistence of indigenous traditions and communications industries, of the local and the global, does not eradicate the struggle and discrimination these antinomies encompass. On the contrary, in trying to achieve cohesion within a single program that encompassed the educated and the popular, the Mexican and the foreign, festival organizers encountered dissension: hisses from rock fans when the romantic music of Marco Antonio Muñiz was announced or the denial of legitimacy for rock music by lovers of ballet or traditional indigenous folklore. Comparable conflicts arise between those who defend local cultures and those who seek to transnationalize or commercialize the city.

The current problems of urban anthropology are not limited to understanding how people reconcile the vertiginous and bewildering rhythms of globalized urban speed with the slow rhythms of their home territories. Our task is to explain how the apparently greater communication and rationality of globalization provokes new forms of racism and exclusion. The ever more frequent fundamentalist outbursts taking place today in big cities such as Los Angeles or Mexico City, Berlin or Lima, make one think that anthropologists must not take too much satisfaction in being apologists of difference. The point is to imagine how the use of international information and the simultaneous need for belonging and local roots can coexist without discriminatory hierarchies in a democratic, intelligent, and egalitarian multicultural society.

Detectives or Psychoanalysts?

This relocation of the anthropologist's task requires a mastery of the many practices that transform the city: of the "real," dispersed practices recorded in surveys or field studies, and of the discourses of the urban imagination that reunify or segregate. To ask about the meaning of the city is to explore the structure and the destructuring of demographic, socioeconomic, and cultural forms that have a certain objective "reality." But it also calls for investigating how subjects represent those acts through which they inhabit these structures and subjective experiences. The meaning of the city is constituted by what the city gives or does not give, by what the subjects can do with their lives within an overdetermined habitat, and by what they imagine about themselves and others in order to "suture" the flaws, the absences, and the disappointments generated by urban structures and interactions in response to their needs and desires.

In an age of globalization, in which the city is constituted not only by what takes place within its territory, but also by the way in which it is traversed by migrants and tourists, messages and goods from other countries, we construct what is ours with greater intensity against the backdrop of what we imagine about others. Not only do we project our fantasy onto the desert in our weekend trips in search of the natural environment surrounding the city, we also find that fantasy in the proliferation of different kinds of discourse created by the multiple groups that inhabit the city or pass through it. Hence our interest in working with texts that describe and imagine the city: informants' stories, journalistic and literary chronicles, photos, radio and television talk, and music that narrates our urban experiences.

Why should anthropologists be concerned with such heterogeneous materials? The idea is to contrast different kinds of discourses, to consider the social facts about which these discourses speak and the experience of the subjects who utter them. We need to bring this research strategy to epistemological debates, laying claim to the need for a *postempirical* and *posthermeneutic* anthropology. What does this mean? Above all, to cease assuming that what is observable in facts acquired through surveys and fieldwork is the truth. Nor do we think that the conflict between empiricists and hermeneuts can be resolved by a confrontation between "facts" and "discourses." The truth does not emerge, as in detective work, by submitting the discourses to a demonstration of the facts. The anthropologist is more the psychoanalyst than the detective, inquiring into the possible correlation of a discourse with facts in order to determine the degree to which it is fantasy or delirium. Simultaneously, the anthropologist inquires after what the facts mean for the subjects who experience them, knowing that the signification (rather than "the truth") of the facts does not inhere in them but lies in the process by which subjects construct and undergo the facts, transform them, and experience the resistance provided by the real. Anthropologists situate themselves in this intersection between facts and discourse. Both have a certain consistency that gives them their relative objectivity and makes scientific analysis possible, but at the same time both are organized by an imaginary regime whose meaning is not exhausted by objective appearances.

This perspective allows us to change the answer to the postmodern question: Who speaks in anthropological studies? This no longer implies choosing between the anthropologists or the informants. What speaks, more than a social agent, is a difference, a fissure, a search for the Other and of that which is Other. Or, rather, the many forms of understanding otherness that coexist in a large multicultural city. This difference and this fissure are usually "sutured" within each society by means of relations of power and rituals of social cohesion. In large cities, we observed, the acts of government and the discourse of the media bring together in imaginary wholeness the dispersed fragments of the urban fabric. We also find that *the* city is able to exist, for a few moments, in the solidarity of the people who suffer disasters like the 1985 earthquake or who take part in a plebiscite, in certain feasts, or in a shared concern about the environment. The perspective of the anthropologist, or of any social scientist, at once local and global, can recognize in those acts projects for social recomposition as well as simulacra of the moment of suturing. In the language of an anthropology influenced by psychoanalysis, we might say that any labor of understanding ends up restoring, by means of criticism, evidence of lack and conflict.

What are the possibilities ensuing from the encounter between anthropology and psychoanalysis today? As in the relation between sociology and anthropology, it is not so much a matter of dialogue between two ways of knowing that deal with different objects. It is, rather, a conversation on what takes place in the act of wanting to know, a conversation on distance and difference, on lack and the resources we mobilize to cover over that lack. In this dialogue, anthropology (and sociology) can learn not to sociologize, to dispense with descriptions of social closure, whether it is of the kind represented by rites or what we find in the simplest acts of survival. In turn, psychoanalysis can learn from the anthropologist about social conditions, collective organization, and stories and rites through which people gather in cities in order to live together with what we lack. We seek to get a better understanding not only of what we as men and women *know* we are, but also of how we attempt to deal with what we never manage to become.

The crisis of the city is homologous to the crisis of anthropology. Perhaps that is why the disintegration of the city exasperates and changes the character of anthropological problems. The debate on whether it is possible or advisable to do anthropology in the city or, of the city, assumed the existence of a territorially delimited urban area whose reality could be grasped. The problem hinged on whether or not anthropological methodology could encompass such a large-scale object. Now we think that what takes place in the city is the sedimentation of a multidetermined set of internal and external global processes that no one discipline can study by itself. Under these circumstances, the best that we anthropologists can do is to rely on our skills in the study of alterity and not worry too much about the scale of the object of study. Instead, we should devote our energies to discerning what happens to what we thought was *the same* as it is *altered* in its encounters with the other. We are interested in the globalized city as a multicultural scenario.

This approach leaves many issues unresolved. But there is one issue that it would be scandalous to omit, given that we are discussing our deterioriated Mexico City. It can be formulated thus: Is there a specific way in which Latin American cities undergo change? Europeans speak of the "rebirth of the city," as a consequence of their highly developed infrastructure and excellent services that are linked to international innovations. Latin American cities, however, are increasingly catastrophic.[22] Intolerable pollution during most of the year, floods and landslides, increases in extreme poverty, a general deterioration of the quality of life, and systematic and uncontrollable violence are characteristics with which Santiago, Mexico City, Bogotá, Caracas, Buenos Aires, Lima, and São Paulo "prepare" for the twenty-first century.

All this calls for cautious engagement with those postmodern urban theories and grassroots movements of recent decades that celebrate dissemination and multipolarity as the bases for a freer life. The advance of grassroots organization and decentered plurality following a period of urban planning that saw the regulation of urban growth and the satisfaction of certain basic needs (as in almost all the cities of Europe and the United States) is different from the explosion of survival tactics that can only count on scarcity, erratic expansion, and the plunder of soil, water, and air. In those countries that entered the twentieth century with low birthrates and with planned cities and democratic governments, the digressions, detours, and loss of power by centralized orders can be praiseworthy paths for a decentralizing logic. But in places like Mexico City, dissemination—generated by the population explosion, the invasion of land by poor people and speculators, without any democratic forms of representation or urban administration—requires both more decentralization and more planning, more civil society, and more state intervention.

I have spoken of the need to complement anthropology with sociology, communications studies, and psychoanalysis in order to get to the bottom of what happens in large cities. I would like to conclude by confessing my dissatisfaction with what some of us experience when we speak only with the voices of the social sciences and why this spurs me to work during the coming years with discourses that imagine the city.

Can ethnographic style describe with expressive effectivity the intersection of cultures and the experience of internal alterity in such complex cities? How can we record the vertiginous and heartrending movement of the city if we remain fixed in the synchronous, depersonalized units with which statistics freezes the social flow? Literary, artistic, and mass media discourses not only document a compensatory imagination, but also serve to record the city's dramas, what is lost in the city and what is transformed. These discourses can help us find a style of explanation and interpretation appropriate to the scale and style of what is taking place. José Emilio Pacheco ended his novel *Las batallas en el desierto* [*Battles in the Desert*, 1982] by talking about the buildings that were demolished during his childhood in the Mexico City neighborhood Colonia Roma: "That city is finished. That country is no more. No memory remains of the Mexico of those years. And no one cares: who could be nostalgic about that horror?"[23]

Shouldn't the discourse of the social sciences contain these daring declarations, especially when we talk about catastrophes? Since I began to study Mexico City, I have asked myself, as have so many other researchers overwhelmed by the data: "Why don't we leave?" I can find no better expression of the threatening and deeply affectionate nature of this city than these lines by Efraín Huerta:

Ciudad negra o colérica o mansa o cruel
o fastidiosa nada más: sencillamente tibia.

Black city, angry city, or city that is tame or cruel
or perhaps just irritating: simply indifferent.[24]

Chapter 3

Urban Cultural Policies in Latin America

What principles should guide cultural action in today's large urban centers? Almost everything written on cultural policies envisions them within a framework of identity, whether national or that of the inhabitants of a particular territory. Similarly, the scant literature on urban cultural policies assumes that they should refer to the ensemble of traditions, practices, and modes of interaction that distinguish the residents of a given city.

But just as the notion of national cultures has been put into doubt, we must also question what it means to belong to a city, especially a megacity. Are there still in Mexico City, São Paulo, or Buenos Aires common features that enable us to identify their inhabitants as *chilangos, paulistas,* and *porteños?*[1] Research on social and symbolic behavior in these three Latin American cities, carried out in the past five years, has led us to reconsider how to formulate cultural policies. My proposals are based in part on the peculiar conditions in metropolitan conglomerations exceeding ten million inhabitants. However, I think that the conclusions derived from the study of these megalopolises make attractive working hypotheses for research on and cultural policies for medium-size cities, at least those in the two-million population range or larger.

This is particularly germane in cities characterized by the influx of migrants and tourists, industrial development, and the transnationalization of communications and finance. These flows deterritorialize local culture, as has been the case in Santiago de Chile, Rio de Janeiro, Lima, Caracas, Bogotá, Monterrey, Guadalajara, and other similar cities.

In what follows, we examine the challenges to cultural policies posed by two changes: (1) the dissolution of monadic identities; and (2) the decreasing importance and displacement of traditional-local cultures (of both elites and popular groups) brought about by the advance of electronic media and communications.

The Dissolution of Monadic Identities

Until recently, cultural policies were thought of as a means to conserve and administer historical heritages that had been accumulated within clearly delimited territories. These in turn were defined by a nation, an ethnic group, a region, or a city. The state assessed what should or should not be supported, guided by the criterion that practices should be faithful to the territory and the given ensemble of traditions that distinguish each people. Moreover, each modern nation-state arranged diverse and dispersed ethnic and regional traditions in harmonious display in its national museums and in textbooks that are still identical today across the many zones of a country.

On the basis of this unifying strategy, the cultural differences identified with the various cities of a given country were taken to be particular variants of a common "national being." It is true that the difference between *porteños* and provincials, between *paulistas* and *cariocas*,[2] between *chilangos* and the inhabitants of the cities of the interior provided attractive materials for folklore and regional humor. No one doubted, however, that these confrontations between brothers were held in check by the profound unity of Argentines, Brazilians, or Mexicans.[3]

In the second half of the twentieth century, the simulacrum of monadic identities loses verisimilitude and disintegrates, quite ostentatiously, in large cities. What does it mean to be a *chilango* in a city like Mexico City, where more than half of the inhabitants were born in other areas of the country? In the preceding chapter, I noted that there are 263,000 Indians in this capital city. Additionally, there are several million city dwellers who come from predominantly indigenous regions (Oaxaca, Guerrero, Michoacán, etc.). These people leave their ethnic mark on the capital city when they build homes, eat, seek health care, or weave their networks of solidarity.

In São Paulo, the most modern and industrialized city of Brazil, there are more than one and a half million northeasterners and even more migrants from Minas Gerais, Rio Grande do Sul, and other states. Several anthropological and sociological studies have taken note of the enormous heterogeneity of the *paulista* population, including that segment which is usually lumped together as "urban popular sectors." Large cities create patterns of uniformity, refashion local habits, and subordinate them to "modern" styles of work, dress, and entertainment. To live in a large city means that the majority of migrants, wherever they come from, aspire to have their own home on a paved street, with electricity and running water, near schools and health clinics. Nevertheless, the homogenization of consumption and sociability, fostered by common patterns according to which these services are organized, does not do away with particularities. "The social construction of leisure time," Antônio Arantes explains, "is not the result of one overdetermining factor (economic or educational), but of the play of multiple variables that condition each other reciprocally." In addition to social position, gender and age are also quite important.[4] Following Eunice Ribeiro Durham's lead, it is also possible to speak of the different ways in which society is seen from the periphery.[5] But even then, it should be noted that the populations in diverse peripheral zones develop peculiar ways of gathering, speaking, and satisfying their necessities. The popular sectors, especially those who do not have a car or a telephone, tend to identify the boundaries of the city with those of their own neighborhood. There they elaborate their networks of interaction, which display differing modalities within the same urban space. Neighborhood dwellers move into the wider space of the city, but only in a limited manner, as they travel the larger arteries on their way to work, to make transactions, or to seek a special service.

Research on consumption in large cities carried out by the Working Group of the Latin American Social Science Council (CLACSO) in Buenos Aires, Santiago de Chile, São Paulo, and Mexico City revealed a destructuring effect in urban experience.[6] This is especially the case in the latter two cities, where the metropolitan area grew at a much faster rate than public cultural facilities. Researchers have observed an atomization of symbolic practices and an ever-declining attendance at movie houses, theaters, concerts, and other collective venues of cultural

consumption. This dispersion can also be detected in cultural and political popular movements, characterized by their local and compart-
mentalized points of view. In our studies of São Paulo, Buenos Aires,
and Mexico City, we observed that the mayor, the governor, or the re-
gent, who are charged with administrating the entire city, are distant
figures and only become recognizable when they are associated with
some aspect of the neighborhood or of the immediate surroundings.[7]
Whether in their political demands or in the organization of artistic
events or other forms of entertainment, neighborhood movements may
have to strategize around the disturbances generated by street peddlers,
celebrating the feast of the local patron saint, or getting public transport to come to the locality. It is unlikely, however, that they will take
the global problems of the city into consideration. The cultural policies of popular movements are local, they relate to what is of immediate interest and have little to do with large-scale issues such as ecology
or the programs of large institutions. Even when these movements enter into alliances, their vision of the city is a sum of fragments and it is
difficult to coordinate or rank their demands within programs of wider
scope.

Perhaps the two best examples of why one cannot speak of a homogeneous identity in large cities are youth gangs and discrimination
against migrants. The gangs compensate for atomization and fragmentation in large cities by offering group belonging. Faced with diminished expectations of attending school or getting a job in lean labor
markets, gangs offer thousands of youths other forms of socialization
and other means of access to commodity consumption. But gangs also
take intercultural conflicts to their most exasperating extremes, such as
the acrimonious encounter of natives and migrants or the clashes between migrants of diverse origins, their turf battles and struggles for
sociopolitical control. The irritation conveyed by their very names says
it all: Sátiros [satyrs], Ratas Punk [punk rats], Niños Idos [runaway kids],
Bastardos [bastards], Funerales [funerals]. These are some of the gangs
active in Mexico City.[8] Youth gangs, like the informal economy and
other fractal phenomena, are indicative of the inadequacy of macro social and cultural policies in providing effective and wide-ranging solutions.
The suspicion of large sectors of the population toward these macro
policies and the irreducible and often irreconcilable multiplicity of languages and lifestyles, of strategies of survival and communication, are
evidence of the decomposition of megacities.

Another promising, yet unexplored means of documenting the discrimination that inhabitants of different parts of a given city thrust upon each other, but especially against migrants, is to study the ways in which humor reworks racism and class prejudice. In Buenos Aires, the massive arrival of provincial migrants since the 1940s was characterized as a "zoological avalanche." The newly arrived are called *cabecitas negras* [black heads], sometimes "public telephones," the joke being that they are "black, square, and don't work."

The mass migration of the poor from the northeast and the infusion of Arab capital into São Paulo in the 1980s provided grist for jokes such as the following: An Arab contractor looks for good northeastern bricklayers in construction sites throughout São Paulo. He tells them they will have to reemigrate to Iraq, but they will be paid in dollars. Those who agree board a plane that makes an emergency landing in the Sahara. They deplane, and when they see the vast stretch of sand, they ask: "Where's the cement?"

In Mexico City, humor based on class prejudice has increased with every catastrophe, as if satire provided an escape from the terror of an earthquake or an explosion, or, simultaneously, from the fear provoked by the "invasion" of migrants and popular sectors. In November 1984, soon after a gas storage plant in San Juanico, on the periphery of the capital, exploded and killed five hundred people and destroyed 1,500 homes, dozens of macabre jokes were heard throughout Mexico City. "What did you think of the explosion in San Juanico?" "What a shame! But if it were to occur in Las Lomas, it would be a tragedy."[9] "In San Juanico they don't make grilled tacos; instead they serve grilled *nacos*."[10]

We know that this kind of humor does not circulate only among middle and upper sectors in large cities. It is also part of radio and TV programs, that is, of communications cultural policies. As Carlos Monsiváis has observed, sarcasm directed at subaltern people does not emanate only from elites. The mass media disseminate it quite successfully and mass audiences celebrate it.[11] Many comedians, from Cantinflas to Héctor Suárez, who ridicule popular stereotypes find great resonance in discriminatory mass-media policies as well as in the self-denigrating tendencies of the ridiculed. The subaltern's complicity in the reproduction of inequality suggests that we should reconsider the possibilities of democratizing cultural policies and our idealizations of civil society.

One of the few Latin American texts that has dealt with this issue is Antônio Flávio Pierucci's study of racism toward northeasterners in

São Paulo. This researcher sought to understand the mechanisms of political culture that explained Fernando Henrique Cardoso's defeat when
he sought the mayoralty of São Paulo in 1985.

Pierucci conducted his research in the areas of the city where the
most votes were cast for Jânio Quadros, who was elected, and Paulo
Maluf, the candidate of the right. He found that a major factor among
the lower middle class was dislike of northeastern migrants, whom they
blamed for the decline of the city. The most visible problems in São
Paulo, attributable to industrialization and modernizing expansion, promoted by *paulista* elites, were overshadowed by the conviction that the
city's past, imagined in all its splendor, had been ruined by the "lowly"
migrants. Pierucci concluded that the "conservative common sense" and
the right-wing vote of a large proportion of popular sectors was due to
the idealization of differences. They perceived racial and ethnic differences as fixed and concrete, while rejecting egalitarian thinking as abstract. Hence his wariness regarding populist idealizations of the rights
to difference and the celebration of irreducible differences in certain
postmodern trends.[12]

Fragmentation of Traditional Culture, New Electronic Linkages

The cohesion of national and urban cultures was generated and sustained, in part, because high and popular cultures provided specific
iconographies to express local identities. The tango, Jorge Luis Borges's
writing, and Antonio Berni's painting represented the symbolic universe
that made Buenos Aires distinctive (although its origins and influences
obviously extended to other territories). Mexico City was characterized
by the films of Pedro Infante, the architecture of its historic center, and
the music of Chava Flores (although the repercussions of and capacity
for sociocultural representation of all of these cultural forms encompassed people from other regions).

What happens to the connections between certain cities and certain symbols when national musics are hybridized with those of other
countries or when films are the result of international coproductions?
In order to reach wider audiences and make a profit, film and television
favor spectacular plots that are easily understood by all cultures. National references and local styles dissolve in those films, and paintings
and television series increasingly resemble each other in São Paulo and
Tokyo, New York and Mexico City, Paris and Buenos Aires.

Local folkloric repertoires, whether they spring from high art or popular culture, do not disappear. But their impact is diminished in a market made hegemonic by transnational electronic cultures, particularly because the social life of cities no longer takes place exclusively in historic or traditional centers but is largely displaced to commercial centers on the beltways. People promenade less in the parks specific to each city and ever more in the shopping malls that mirror each other from one corner of the world to the other.

In a study of Bogotá and São Paulo, Armando Silva explored the sites where the inhabitants tend to congregate. He found that adults, especially those over fifty, tended to gravitate to the most traditional places (churches, plazas, cafés, and, in Bogotá, bakeries). As his subjects decreased in age, he found that they preferred shopping centers and metro stations.[13] This trend, which is observable in other cities with dense historic and noteworthy areas, such as Buenos Aires and Mexico City, suggests that younger generations are drawn to what Marc Augé has called "nonplaces." The proliferation of these "installations necessary for the rapid circulation of people and commodities,"[14] which affects the use of space and the citizenry's habits, reveals a displacement in urban agglomerations, a decrease (but not the disappearance) of the distinctive in favor of the deterritorialized and the dehistoricized. Beatriz Sarlo is correct in characterizing shopping malls as "spaces without qualities: an interplanetary jet set of Cacharel, Stephanel, Fiorucci, Kenzo, Guess, and McDonalds." "The relationship of the mall to the city that surrounds it is one of *indifference*." The mall "offers the model of a miniature city, sovereignly independent of tradition and environment." "It has been constructed too rapidly, without attention to the variations, ups and downs, corrections, destructions, or the influence of more ambitious projects." "And when there is history, there is no passionate conflict between the resistance of the past and the drives of the present."[15] But can't these neutral sites, like the malls, turn into *places* by means of the ways in which new generations mark them and make them significant though use, incorporating them into their own history?

Our research on cultural consumption in Mexico City bears out this decrease in the use of emblematic places, in keeping with a different, complementary process. We found that attendance at public spectacles and gatherings increasingly shifted to home reception of radio, television, and video. Survey results, which we summarized in the preceding chapter, showed that the institutionalized sector (i.e., film, theater, music and dance concerts) fell short of 10 percent of all cultural consumption. Regular attendance at traditional, popular spectacles and feasts also failed to reach a higher market share. That this situation holds in a country like Mexico, with strong ethnic and popular traditions and with greater state sponsorship than elsewhere, suggests that in other countries there is even less receptivity for local cultural fare.

On the other hand, we found that almost all homes in Mexico City have television and radio. The amount of time that these appliances occupy in people's use of free time reveals that there has been a reorganization of cultural habits, increasingly oriented to home reception of audiovisual product, which conveys international symbolic codes. The majority of people receive their information and entertainment more from a dislocated, international system of cultural production than from culture linked to particular territories and local products specific to them.

The disintegration of the city as a result of demographic expansion and urban sprawl diminishes the organizational significance of the historic center and shared public spaces that once encouraged common experiences in the Mexican capital. Territorial expansion and the massification of the city that reduced interaction among neighborhoods are processes that date from the 1950s to the present, precisely the same period in which radio, television, and video spread throughout the city. These are the new invisible, electronic links that have reorganized relations among inhabitants in a more abstract and depersonalized manner, while connecting us all to a transnational symbolic order.

Do cultural or communications resources still have the power to bring people together in live gatherings, without mediation, in cities that are wired for cable? A good part of communication takes place via newspapers or television. These very media, however, show that the inhabitants also gather in political demonstrations, in fairs and feasts, and even in the chaos of the subway at rush hour, in waiting lines, and among crowds of shoppers. Can cultural policies bring together these multiple groups who at the end of this century are dispersed throughout our megacities? Or does this interest in designing policies that might encompass the diversity of megacities betray outdated nostalgia for those times in which we still believed in totalities?

Policies for Citizenship

1. Consideration of these data brings us to our first conclusion, that the cultural needs of large cities require multisectorial policies tailored to

particular zones and economic, educational, and generational strata—in sum, to the complex heterogeneity of what is referred to simplistically as "the public." Perhaps the cities we mention here have never been homogeneous. Perhaps the point of departure for urban policies should not be to think of heterogeneity as a problem, but rather as the point of departure of a democratic plurality.

2. The most democratic and popular cultural policies are not necessarily those that offer spectacles and messages that reach the majority, but rather those that take into account the variety of needs and demands of the population. Neither elites nor popular sectors constitute a homogeneous mass, as revealed by the fragmentation of their practices. The very same city that massified them connected them at the same time with a great variety of (national or foreign) symbolic offerings, thus encouraging the pluralization of tastes. Therefore, they require differentiated cultural action. Cultural policies that dogmatically uphold one legitimate identity in each city or nation will not be more democratic. Only those that encourage the coexistence of multiple forms of being *porteño* in Buenos Aires, *paulista* in São Paulo, and *chilango* in Mexico City will achieve that end.

3. Policies that promote local traditions enable the maintenance of adherents, thus contributing to the preservation of the historical features that give the inhabitants of a city their distinctive identity. Without a doubt, urban imaginaries continue to be constituted by memories sedimented in each city, by particular emblematic neighborhoods, idealized trajectories and scenarios, by rituals through which inhabitants take possession of the urban terrain, or by singular narratives that glorify it. It is the complicitous synergy of all of these phenomena that activates ecological movements and local feasts even in the megalopolis. To cultivate this fervor may be a resource for inspiring citizen responsibility. Few are the urban movements that do not base their organization and political mobilization on that fervor. We are, however, also familiar with reactionary cultural policies that foster xenophobia, as a nostalgic refuge for what some see as resistance to modernization and globalization. In any case, the predominance of mass-media consumption and the population's need to receive international information indicate that the promotion of traditional cultures acquires meaning and efficacy by linking those cultures with the new conditions of internationalization.

4. The culture industries today are the principal means of enabling reciprocal knowledge and cohesion among the segmented organizations and groups of large cities. In order to re-create a shared imaginary for urban experiences, territorially identified neighborhoods and groups should come together in solidarity for the purpose of information and cultural development prompted by the mass media, so long as these provide forums for public interests. Citizenship is no longer constituted solely in relation to local social movements, but also through the communicative processes of the mass media.

Chapter 4

Narrating the Multicultural

I would like to propose a discussion of the current state of multiculturalism and its function in urban studies of culture. My work is situated primarily in the social sciences; however, insofar as I take interest
in the city not only as an object of knowledge but as a site in which to
imagine and narrate, I attend to certain issues that belong to the domain of literature. Multicultural intersections and the industrialization
of the symbolic have induced literary theory to expand its analytical
repertoire to include signifying processes that textualize and narrate the
social differently than in canonical literary works. Rather than dwell
on what the literary field might look like after its object is shattered, I
prefer to air a concern raised by the studies alluded to: What do we do
when we narrate the multicultural and what is the significance of this
narration in contemporary societies?

Constructivism versus Fundamentalism

My first concern is that narratives of multicultural society are currently
divided between academic theories and sociopolitical movements. The
social sciences and humanities conceive of identities as historically con-

stituted, imagined, and reinvented in ongoing processes of hybridization and transnationalization, which dissolve their ancient territorial
roots.[1] In contrast, many social and political movements unequivocally
emphasize the original territorial foundations of ethnic groups and nations, dogmatically avowing the telluric and biological traits associated
with that origin, as if they were unaffected by historical vicissitudes and
current changes. Interethnic and international conflicts betray obstinate
tendencies to treat each identity as if it were a hard, compact kernel of
resistance. For this reason, they demand absolute loyalty from each member and demonize their critics and dissidents. In many countries, purity is invoked as a defense against modern trends that relativize the
specificity of each ethnic group and nation with the objective of creating democratic forms of coexistence, complementarity, and multicultural governability.

   In truth, the opposition between the constructivist discourse of cultural studies and the fundamentalist doctrines of ethnic or national
movements is a recent one. Over the past two centuries, literature, philosophy, and anthropology, on the one hand, and fundamentalism, on
the other, reveal powerful complicities. Folkloric romanticism and political nationalism were allied in the effort to bring about, on the basis
of tradition, ordered ethnic and sociocultural groupings in fewer than
two hundred juridico-territorial containers called nations. It was determined that the inhabitants of a given space were to belong to one homogeneous culture and therefore have one single distinctive and coherent identity. A culture of one's own was to be created in connection
with a territory and organized conceptually and practically in relation
to collections of objects, texts, and rituals that would enable the affirmation and reproduction of the signs of distinction for each group.

   It was determined that to have an *identity* was the same as belonging to a nation, to a spatially delimited *entity*, where everything shared
by the inhabitants—language, objects, customs—would differentiate
them neatly from others. Those identitarian referents, although historically variable, were embalmed in folklore as markers of the "traditional"
phase of national development, and enshrined as essences of national culture. Even today they are exhibited in museums, transmitted in schools
and through the mass media, affirmed dogmatically in religious and political discourses, and defended by military authoritarianism as it begins to lose power.

   This model was so persuasive that it brought into existence nationally circumscribed zones of culture, knowledge, sports, and other fields.

Art and literary histories, for example, were written as histories of national arts and literatures. Even the avant-gardes, which attempted to
transgress sociocultural conventions, were identified with certain countries, as if national profiles defined their projects for renewal of culture.
That is why we have Italian Futurism, Russian Constructivism, and the
French *nouveau roman.*

Many literary studies have shown the fictive and arbitrary character of the multicultural "solutions" assayed within the purview of those
nationalisms. Let me give two examples. Josefina Ludmer demonstrated
that in salvaging from illegality the voice of the gaucho and establishing an ensemble of oral markers for culture and politics, *criollismo* also
excluded Indians, blacks, and immigrants from this national definition.[2]
Antonio Cornejo Polar argued that each definition of the legitimate cor-
pus of Peruvian literature excluded important components of the historical process. It was first defined as a Hispanic literature (Riva Agüero
y Prado), then as *mestizo* literature (Luis Alberto Sánchez and others),
with the purpose of harmonizing the contradictory tendencies of modern Peru into a homogeneous system "sufficiently differentiated so that
it would merit the qualifier 'national.'"[3]

A great part of artistic and literary production continues to be created as an expression of national traditions and circulates only within
each given country. The plastic arts and literature continue to be sources
of the nationalist imaginary, providing scenarios for the consecration
and communication of regional signs of identity. But an ever-larger por-
tion of the production, diffusion, and reception of art is carried out
nowadays in a deterriorialized manner. Many writers publicized as "great
national artists" by cultural diplomats and marketers, for example, the
writers of the "Boom," display in their works a cosmopolitan sense that
enables them to resonate internationally.

I wonder if the shift from national monadic identities to global multiculturalism is not accompanied by the survival of fundamentalism today in the guise of Latinamericanism. As we noted, ethnic and national
political movements continue to exist, seeking to justify themselves with
supposedly distinctive national and symbolic heritages. But the process
that has achieved the most verisimilitude is the fundamentalism of *Macondismo.* It freezes the "Latin American" in a premodern sanctuary
and sublimates this continent as the place where social violence casts
its spell through the affects. This literary mode includes texts from very
different countries, from those of the Cuban Carpentier to those of the
Colombian García Márquez, the Peruvian Vargas Llosa, the Chilean

Isabel Allende, and the Mexican Laura Esquivel. It aligns them into one paradigm of reception, which is also one particular way of pitching Latin America's heterogeneity in the marketplace of cultural globalization.[4]

The exaltation of irrationalism as the supposed essence of the Latin American gains its "consistency" from the mediation of the market and the hype of many critics and contributes to the opposition that the fundamentalist fixation of identity poses to social constructionist interpretations of multicultural societies. Market and critics normalize this identity so that it becomes difficult to recognize it as imagined, polyphonic, and hybrid. Hence the importance of cultural studies analyses of how the culture industries and urban mass life are organized to preserve local cultures and at the same time foster the most open and transnational phases in their history. This observation can also be phrased as a question: How is it possible for the ideologies that represent and dignify these two movements—fundamentalism and cosmopolitanism— to coexist?

Currently, the social sciences consider identity not as an eternal essence but as an imaginary construction. Globalization diminishes the importance of the foundational events and territories that supported the illusion of ahistorical and self-absorbed identities. Today, identitarian references are shaped not by the arts, literature, and folklore—which for centuries gave nations their distinctive features—but by textual and iconographic repertoires furnished by electronic communications media and by the globalization of urban life. What is the meaning, within this process, of the imaginary constructions that contradict it?

The Flaneur and the Narrative of Consumption

It may be easier to conduct research on social processes if we adopt a social constructionist perspective on multiculturalism. The prevalence of fundamentalist interpretation in accounts of these processes leads us to ask whether or not every narrative implies some form of uncritical celebration. Let's examine, in this regard, what occurs in the megacity of the Mexican capital.

How do cultural studies encompass the dispersed meanings of a large city? The problem is largely a narrative one. This is what Wim Wenders insinuates when he says that maps make him uneasy, especially if they represent a country or city in which he has never been. He considers each name and seeks to find out what each indicates. "Looking at a map is tolerable only if I try to find a path, draw an itinerary that allows me to travel through the country or city at hand."[5] Urbanism, Wenders observes, poses similar problems to those that are intrinsic to constructing narratives. Both entail describing routes and coordinates in a universe where, without these heuristics, one would reach thousands of different places without arriving anywhere.

This anxiety-producing uncertainty in the face of a disordered multiplicity is encountered in many Latin American cities that have grown vertiginously and without any planning. Let's review the figures presented in chapter 2: Mexico City had a population of one and a half million in 1940; by 1960 it had grown to five million, and by 1990 it reached fifteen million inhabitants. The city sprawled beyond its perimeters over an enormous territory almost without any coordinates to organize it.

It is obvious that the city today cannot be narrated, described, or explained as it might have been at the beginning of the century. The sense of living together in the capital was structured in relation to shared historical markers, within a space that all inhabitants felt could be circumscribed in their daily meanderings. The identifying heritage of Mexico City could be portrayed as a realist representation of a territory and a history. To be sure, all heritages and every historical or literary narrative is a metaphor of a social alliance. Every construction of national heritages and legitimation narratives in a given era is the result of selective, combinatory, and performative processes shaped by the struggles of social groups in their bids for hegemony. These processes change relative to the objectives of the actors in struggle for the hegemony and renewal of their pacts. In every period, the resulting policies have, of course, been weighted unequally to the benefit of "noble" neighborhoods vis-à-vis poor ones, and toward "distinguished" cultural goods vis-à-vis "vulgar" ones. But since the revolution, these differences were partially subordinated to an experience of national unity, of Mexicanness, which the capital city represented more or less coherently.

Newspaper chronicles from the end of the nineteenth and the beginning of the twentieth centuries conditioned the meaning of urban life by instilling a sense of modern commercial development that complemented pride in the city's monuments. Mexico City was articulated in the web of its urban design, its monuments, and its historical celebrations. To this transcendental, patriotic ritualism was added another, secular mode of representing the city: the promenade and the chronicle that recorded it. The writer and statesman Justo Sierra wondered how the expression *flâneur*, which the French used to designate the taste for strolling through the city, might be translated in Mexico City. Julio Ramos has observed that *flânerie* is a mode of entertainment associated with modern commercialization and its spectacular display in consumption.

What is it that one looks at as one strolls through the modern city? Manuel Rivera writes: "The streets of Platero have establishments that can satisfy the most demanding whims of taste and fashion: great showcases filled with merchandise behind the display windows; a multitude of elegant ladies promenade on those streets."[6]

To be a flaneur, adds Ramos, is not only a way of experiencing the city. "It is, rather, a way of representing it, looking at it, and telling what one saw. The private, urban subject of *flânerie* approaches the city with the gaze of someone who sees an object on exhibition. The show window, therefore, becomes an emblematic object for the chronicler."[7]

The promenade is a process of symbolic consumption that integrates the fragments of the modern metropolis that emerged in an already splintered condition. By stringing together the segments of the chronicle into a narrative, an urban order is achieved by means of what Ramos calls the "rhetoric of the promenade." The chronicles published in newspapers are the proper communicative medium of this incipient modernity, where the partial meanings of urban experiences are intertwined.

This function still holds even today. From Salvador Novo to Carlos Monsiváis, José Joaquín Blanco, and Herman Bellinghausen, the journalistic chronicle is a way of organizing the discontinuities of urban life. The chroniclers of today, especially those who write after 1968, add to the playful narrative the presence of political demonstrations by students and new social movements. Through these the chronicler seeks to understand how the city is being transformed. It is significant, for example, that Monsiváis should have published collections of more or less frivolous chronicles, such as *Escenas de pudor y liviandad,* and other more critical pieces on urban movements such as *Entrada libre. Crónicas de la sociedad que se organiza.* In their attempt to witness and articulate urban experiences, the chroniclers of today devote a good part of their work to the culture industries and the new modes of consumption.

Is it possible to grasp the multiple narratives that "organize" the economically and communicationally industrialized city? One would have to figure out not only how to bring together the novels, journalistic chronicles, political speeches, radio and televisual representations of the city, but also the more complex task of connecting the multiple internal and external narratives that traverse the city. Like so many other large cities, Mexico City contains indigenous languages from all over the country, whose speakers are migrants to the capital: Mixtecos from

Oaxaca, Purépechas from Michoacán, Nahuas from Guerrero, and another twenty ethnic groups. One also finds English, French, German, and Spanish with Chilean, Argentine, and Central American accents, as well as information and advertising, *telenovelas* and cop shows that are transmitted in transnational circuits. The Mexican capital is thus reordered multiculturally in the articulation of international mechanisms of negotiation, innovation, and commercialization. The narratives of the megacity are also created through telephone, fax, televisual and finance communications that link it with other countries.

The City as a Video Clip

There coexist in Mexico City all the different places of Latin America and many from throughout the world. As if peering into Borges's "Aleph" or looking at a video clip, we ask ourselves how we might enumerate even one sequence of this infinite ensemble. To live in this "gigantic instant," which is every instant in a city such as this, is bewildering not so much because of the "million delightful and atrocious events" that take place in it, but rather because "everyone occupies the same spot, without being superimposed or transparent."

It occurred to me to apply this Borgesian story to Mexico City after reading Edward W. Soja's *Postmodern Geographies,* where it is used to refer to Los Angeles. Like Soja, I do not see any other way to refer to the "pool of cultures" that constitute the Mexican capital than to assemble a "succession of fragmentary glimpses, a free association of reflective and interpretive field notes," observations that are "contingently incomplete and ambiguous." Soja takes this approach because he knows that "any totalizing description of the LA-leph is impossible."[8]

In the final instance, says Soja, megacities such as Los Angeles—with its juxtaposition of historical temporalities, of what comes from east and west, north and south—lead us to ask whether the meaning we sought in a unified temporal logic should not be explored in the simultaneous relations that take place in a single space. We can see this in certain foundational texts of Latin American urban literature, such as Borges's, and before him Macedonio Fernández's. It is even more evident in Ricardo Piglia's Macedonio-like Museum, *La ciudad ausente* [The absent city]. There Piglia exasperates his readers with superimposed histories and digressions, which, like symptoms of impossibility, defy unifying the infinity of stories into one single narrative. He attempts to "use lost words to narrate everyone's history."

Large cities torn by erratic growth and multicultural conflicts are the sites where we can best observe the decline of metanarratives, of utopias that projected an ascendent and cohesive human development throughout time. Even in those cities laden with signs of the past, like the Mexican capital, the weight of the present and the perplexity of an anticipated uncontrollable future erode temporal experiences and privilege simultaneous connections in space. In the preceding chapters it was suggested that this may be one of the reasons why emancipatory movements based on the great historical narratives (the proletariat, nations) lose their effectiveness. On the other hand, urban social movements and ephemeral, fragmentary actions earn a higher rating.

Borges's story "The Aleph" anticipates all this in an exemplary way. Like the narrator who is rendered speechless before the Aleph, that point in space that contains all others, we find ourselves incapable of encompassing the Mexico City of today in one description. If we look at it from the inside, from the purview of everyday practices, we see only fragments, instants, locations fixed in place by a myopic perception of the totality. From afar, it all seems a confused mass difficult to discern according to theory-driven models of urban organization. There is no organizing focus because Mexico City "is everywhere and yet, completely, nowhere," as the author of *Ficciones* wrote.

To narrate is to know that it is no longer possible to have the experience of order that the flaneur expected to find in his strolls through the city at the beginning of the century. Nowadays the city is like a video clip, an effervescent montage of discontinuous images. We can no longer travel downtown twenty kilometers on the bus and expect a story by Carlos Fuentes or the *Kaliman* to transform the crowded and bumpy ride into a peaceful reading experience. Some of us still insist on smuggling in the newspaper or a *fotonovela,* but soon the constant braking of the bus or the crowds on the subway force us to give up.

That's why three million drivers prefer to get in their cars and risk bottlenecks, perhaps hoping to find in them a momentary refuge. No sooner do I enter the beltway than the traffic seems to harmonize with the strings of the Telemann concerto I am listening to. The Dodges and Chevrolets changing lanes to pass me are the intrusive trumpets and saxophones, the Mercedes that overtakes us all moves like an oboe, smoothly, almost imperceptively. Just when the second movement begins, always an adagio or an andante when I listen to Baroque music, the traffic slows down as we near the ramps where those who come from the Viaduct join us. It is a movement of many changes, from third to second, from strings to piano, and back to strings, while the cars limp to a halt and the sleepy traffic makes it impossible for us, for all of us together, to reach the final allegro.

The cars stop. I change the station. I search for that other, contemporary Baroque, the vertiginous rock that does not pretend to go anywhere. It is better attuned to the fast tracks that get bottlenecked, to the furious horns of cars trapped by a demonstration, or to the disorder of pedestrians crossing haphazardly when blackouts disable the traffic lights. "It's difficult to walk / in a strange place / where you can see hunger / as in a great circus in action." . . . "The great circus in this city / stop, continue, stop," sings the group Maldita Vecindad [Cursed neighborhood].

Walking through the city is like a video clip in which diverse musics and stories are mixed, but in the intimacy of the car, with a backup of external noise. One alternates passing by seventeenth-century churches with nineteenth-century buildings and constructions from every decade of the twentieth, interrupted by gigantic billboards layered with models' phony bodies, new cars, and newly imported computers. Everything is dense and fragmentary. As in the videos, the city has been created by plundering images from everywhere, in any order whatsoever. Good readers of urban life must adapt themselves to the rhythm and bliss out on the ephemeral visions.

I end up asking myself if we will be able to narrate the city again. Can there be stories in our cities, dominated as they are by disconnection, atomization, and insignificance? It is no longer possible to imagine a story from the purview of a historical or modern center that would permit us to draw the only possible map of a compact city that has ceased to exist. At this late stage we can only glimpse fragmentary reinventions of neighborhoods or zones, timely triumphs over anonymity, and disorder made possible by signs of belonging and multiple spaces of participation. Perhaps the only totalizing narratives of Mexico City that achieved some verisimilitude in recent years have been the chronicles of Carlos Monsiváis and Elena Poniatowska; they describe the solidarity of the survivors of the 1985 earthquake participating in their political and ecological performances. Confronted with the city's chaos, they sought to restore some measure of national unity. Something similar has occurred with radio and television, which function as urban narrators. It is as if these media can only surmount the simultaneity and dispersion of the video clip, the daily obsolescence of sound bites, when the pain and the disorder of extraordinary events prompt them to "recuperate" the historical density and meaning of living together in a city or a nation.

Monsiváis takes this difficulty in narrating the chaotic megacity to an exasperating extreme when he tells us that "now we can only rely on a legend in the making: the miracle of endurance and survival. How can we fail to admire the coexistence of millions of people who in the midst of disasters act to distribute water, build housing, organize transportation, innovate work schedules, and provide public security?"[9]

Simultaneously modern and postmodern, we oscillate between two positions, which coexist in the paradoxical text by Wim Wenders quoted earlier: "I fully reject stories because they only generate lies for me, and the biggest lie is that they create a connection where there is no connection whatsoever. On the other hand, we need these lies, so much so that it is totally senseless to organize a series of images without lies, without the lie of a story."

I read Wenders as if he were speaking of the myths that have been used to order the multicultural history of Mexico with the purpose of re-creating meaning and solidarity in the midst of a changing urban life. "Insofar as humans create linkages and connections, stories make life more tolerable and help dispel terror."

Part II

Postnational Suburbias

Chapter 5

Identities as a Multimedia Spectacle

I dentity is a narrated construct. It involves the establishment of a set of founding events, which almost always refer to the appropriation of a territory by a people or the independence gained in the struggle against foreigners. The narrative proceeds by adding up the feats through which the inhabitants defend their territory, order their conflicts, and establish the legitimate ways of life there in order to distinguish themselves from others. Textbooks and museums, civic rituals and political speeches were for a long time the mechanisms by which each nation's Identity (with a capital I) was formed and its narrative rhetoric consecrated.

Radio and film contributed in the first half of this century to the organization of identity narratives and the meaning of citizenship in national societies. In addition to epic tales of heroes and great collective events, they introduced the chronicle of everyday life: common habits and tastes, ways of speaking and dressing, that differentiated one people from another. Radio helped previously distant and unconnected groups from diverse regions of a country to recognize each other as part of a totality.[1] The news programs that linked disparate zones, like the films, portrayed intercultural conflicts and showed the migrating masses how to live in the city, and proposed new possible syntheses of a national identity in transformation.

Whereas in the 1940s and 1950s, Mexican and Argentine cinema projected their identity narratives through mass visual culture, in the 1960s, allied with the emerging television industry, they changed course and structured the imaginary of developmentalist modernization. The mass media were agents of technological innovations, they sensitized us to the use of electronic appliances in everyday life, and they liberalized customs within a more cosmopolitan framework; but they also unified the patterns of consumption in line with a national vision. Because the media were owned predominantly by national capital and adhered to a developmentalist ideology, which sought modernization through import substitution and the upgrading of industry in each country, even the most internationalized agents at this point in time—such as TV and advertising—beckoned us to buy national products and encouraged the dissemination of local knowledge.

All of this waned throughout the 1980s. The opening of each country's economy to global markets and processes of regional integration diminished the role of national cultures. The transnationalization of technologies and the commercialization of cultural commodities attenuated traditional forms of identity. Now it is within globalized networks of symbolic production and circulation that trends in art, publishing, advertising, and fashion are set.

An Anthropology of Transcultural Citations

Where does identity reside? By what media is it produced and renewed at this end of the century? To answer this question, we shall contrast the way in which classical anthropology defined identity with how it is constituted today.

If anthropology—the social science that has studied the formation of identities more than any other—encounters difficulties today in dealing with transnationalization and globalization, it is because of the habit of considering the members of a society as belonging to one homogeneous culture and, for that reason, having one distinctive and coherent identity. That singular and unified vision, confirmed by classic ethnographies and many national museums established by anthropologists, is not adequate for understanding intercultural situations.

Theories of "cultural contact" have always posited contrasts between groups only on the basis of what differentiates them. The problem with this approach is that most intercultural situations today are constituted not only in relation to *differences* among cultures that have developed separately, but also by the *unequal* ways in which groups appropriate, combine, and transform elements from several societies. Subject to fewer restrictions and greater speedup, the circulation of people, capital, and messages brings us into daily contact with many cultures; consequently, our identity can no longer be defined by an exclusive belonging to a national community. The range of legitimate objects of study should therefore not be limited to differences, but should extend to hybridization.

According to this alternative view, nations become multidetermined scenarios where diverse cultural systems intersect and interpenetrate. If social science is to say anything significant about identity-formation processes in an age of globalization, it will have to attend to the heterogeneity and coexistence of various symbolic codes in a group and even an individual subject, as well as discern intercultural borrowings and transactions. Identity today, even among broad sectors of the popular classes, is polyglot, multiethnic, migrant, made from elements that cut across various cultures.

We thus confront a double challenge. We must endeavor to understand, simultaneously, postnational formations and the remodeling of subsisting national cultures. A great part of current artistic production still expresses national iconographic traditions, circulating only within the confines of a given country. As such, the visual arts, literature, radio, and film remain sources of nationalist imaginaries, providing scenarios in which the signs of regional identity are consecrated and communicated. Yet an ever-expanding sector of the creation, dissemination, and reception of art operates today according to deterritorialized procedures. As with the writers of the "Boom" mentioned in the preceding chapter, the great national painters—say, Tamayo or Botero—have gained an international resonance by opening up local iconographies to the international avant-gardes. Even those who choose to speak for the narrowest imagined communities—Rio de Janeiro or the Bronx, Zapotec myths or the Chicano borderlands—achieve their meaningfulness precisely because their work operates as a "transcultural citation" within art markets and exhibitions in [hemispheric— *Trans.*] American metropolitan centers.[2]

It is not unusual to see the particularities of each country condensed into the framework of transnational conceptual networks at international exhibitions. "Paris–Berlin," "Paris–New York," two shows at the Centre Georges Pompidou, revisited contemporary art history not by parceling it into national patrimonies but according to trends that cut across borders. The art market, however, is inflexible in subordinating the local meanings of artworks, converting them into secondary, folk-loric references within a homogenized international discourse. The lead-ing galleries, with their headquarters in New York, London, Milan, and Tokyo, circulate these works in a deterritorialized fashion and encour-age the artists to accommodate to "global" publics. Fairs and biennials also contribute to this multicultural enterprise, as evidenced in the 1993 Venice Biennale, where most of the fifty-six countries represented did not have their own pavilions. Almost all Latin American contributions (from Bolivia, Chile, Colombia, Costa Rica, Cuba, Ecuador, El Salvador, Mexico, Panama, Paraguay, and Peru) were included in the Italian sec-tion. This was not apparently of great concern in an exhibition titled "The Cardinal Points of Art" and dedicated to demonstrating that art today is constituted by "cultural nomadism."[3]

The Regional and the Global

As in other eras, when identities were displayed in national museums, a new phase in economic transnationalization and in the very character of communications technologies (from television to satellites and fiber optic networks) has, since mid-century, contributed to the increasing protagonism of those world cultures exhibited as multimedia spectacles. Consider that today no "national" cinema can recoup investment in a film from ticket sales within its own borders. It has to target multiple sales venues: satellite and cable TV, networks of video and laser-disk rental outlets. All of these systems, structured transnationally, facilitate the "defolklorization" of the messages they put into circulation.

Cinema's survival problems have been dealt with by acquiescing to the tendency to transnationalize, eliminating in the process most na-tional and regional features. This involves the promotion of a "world cinema" that seeks to use the most sophisticated visual technology and marketing strategies in order to gain a foothold in a market of global proportions. Coppola, Spielberg, and Lucas, for example, construct spec-tacular narratives—*Jurassic Park, Frankenstein, Batman*—from myths intelligible to most spectators, independent of culture, educational level, national history, level of economic development, or political system. World cinema, according to Charles-Albert Michelet, "is closer to Claude Lévi-Strauss than to John Ford."[4] The point is to fabricate such a daz-zling spectacle that it will persuade viewers once or twice a year that it is worth the trouble to leave the living room sofa for the lesser comfort of a dark theater.

Regional cultures, nevertheless, persist. Even the global cinema of Hollywood leaves some room for Latin American, European, and Asian motion pictures that, precisely because they capture certain local issues, have the power to interest multiple publics. Brazilian cinema of the 1970s and the first half of the 1980s, for example, widened its mass-market appeal inside and outside of Brazil by combining testimonies about identity with an imaginative and parodic treatment of the internationalization of the country. *Macunaíma, Doña Flor and Her Two Husbands,* and *Xica da Silva* are representative of this tendency. We could also mention the example of political rereadings of detective stories in the Argentine context, as in Adolfo Aristiráin's films; or historical narratives told from the perspective of everyday intimacy as in the Mexican pictures *Red Dawn* and *Like Water for Chocolate.* The latter, which in a few months surpassed Mexican box-office records (1.5 million), is at best a well-filmed *telenovela.* Its success is not, however, unconnected to the themes dealt with by other, less conventional Mexican films—*La Tarea, La mujer de Benjamín, El bulto*—that ironically, irreverently, and without complacent nostalgia rework stock crises in family identity and national political projects.

Such films reveal that identity and history—including local or national identities—can still be custom-fit into cultural industries that require a high profit margin. The deterritorialization of art does not tell the whole story; simultaneous to it, there are strong reterritorializing tendencies, represented by the local demands of social movements, on the one hand, and mass-media processes, on the other. Differences and forms of local rootedness are produced and reproduced by regional radio and television, niche markets for folkloric musics and crafts, "demassified" and "mesticized" consumerism.[5]

Research on the ideology of global managers suggests that corporate globalization, which tends to homogenize in order to reap profits, should pay greater attention to local and regional differences. What do anthropologists discover when they read the *Harvard Business Review* and the *Journal of Consumer Marketing*? In his most recent book, Renato Ortiz, for example, finds that the intellectuals of corporate globalization foster universalization by exploiting the coincidences in thought and taste in all societies. Computers, credit cards, Benetton clothing, Barbie dolls have all contributed to this form of globalization. However, once these forms of homogenization come to be understood as the antithesis of the local, a new view envisages universalization and regional particularization to be complementary:

Coca-Cola was only able to make profits in the Spanish market when it shortened its bottles to the size of other soft drinks in the country; a German publicity campaign using U.S. basketball stars had little effect because they were unknown to European sports fans; Brazilian jeans are cut more tightly in order to emphasize women's body shape; Japanese manufacturers know that Europeans tend to buy high-end compact stereo components that can be kept hidden in a cabinet, while U.S. consumers prefer jumbo speakers.

Once it is evident that a recognition of multicultural differences does not disappear even in the most pragmatic of corporate strategies, the contrast between homogeneous and heterogeneous, Ortiz argues, loses importance. It then becomes necessary to understand how world segments—youth, senior citizens, the oversized, the disaffected—share converging habits and tastes. "The world is a differentiated market constituted by strata defined by their affinities. Rather than produce and advertise commodities for 'all' consumers, they are promoted globally among specific groups." Consequently, Ortiz advocates abandoning the notion of homogenization and speaking, instead, of "cultural leveling" as a way of "capturing the process of convergence in cultural behavior, while preserving the differences in the various strata."[6]

Nations and ethnic formations continue to exist. For the majorities, however, they are less and less important as determinants of social cohesion. We need not fear that these forms of identity will be eradicated by globalization; rather, ethnic, regional, and national identities are being reconstructed in relation to globalized processes of intercultural segmentation and hybridization. If we conceive of nations as relativized settings, crisscrossed by other symbolic matrices, then the question that arises is what kinds of literature, film, and television are capable of narrating the heterogeneity and coexistence of several codes within a group and even in one individual subject.

In the Media: Identity as a Coproduction

Current reflections on identity and citizenship have couched themselves within several cultural contexts characteristic of nineteenth- and early-twentieth-century nationalisms; they can no longer be confined, however, to folklore or political oratory. These reflections have to take into account the diversity of artistic repertoires and communications media that contribute to the reelaboration of identities. Moreover, the study of identities cannot be the task of a single discipline (anthropology or political sociology), but the concerted effort of transdisciplinary work, with contributions from specialists in communications, semiology, and urbanism.

Multimedia and multicontextuality: these are two key notions for the redefinition of cinema, other communications systems, and culture in general. Just as the survival of cinema depends on its relocation to a multimedia audiovisial space (along with television and video), so too national and local identities will endure to the degree that we resituate them within multicontextual communications processes. Dynamized in this way, identity will not be seen simply as a ritualized narrative, the monotonous repetition proclaimed by certain fundamentalisms. As a narrative that we renew continually, that we reconstruct with the collaboration of others, identity should also be understood as a coproduction.

Nonetheless, this coproduction is accomplished under unequal conditions among the various participating actors and powers. On the one hand, national economies and cultures have eased their border controls in response to the pressures of cultural globalization and regional economic integration. On the other hand, the asymmetrical circumstances in which international agreements are crafted can be aggravated by trade liberalization. A theory of identities and citizenship has to take into account the diverse forms of their recomposition as they move through unequal circuits of production, communication, and cultural appropriation.

Globalization processes have a lesser effect within the space of *historical-territorial culture,* that is, the set of regional and ethnic knowledges, habits, and experiences reproduced more or less according to a set profile throughout the centuries. Inasmuch as profits on investment are small and symbolic inertia quite protracted in the areas of historical heritage, artistic and folkloric production, and certain forms of peasant culture, the impact of economic liberalization is likely to be limited.

In a second circuit, that of the *mass media* that disseminate (via radio, television, video) entertainment and information to majorities, we can speak of certain peripheral countries such as Brazil and Mexico that have the human, technological, and economic resources to continue producing nationally, with a measure of autonomy, and even expand to international markets. The majority of Latin American countries, however, are quite dependent, not so much on global capital in general but on U.S. production.

The dissolution of national and regional identities is even greater in the third circuit, composed of computers, satellites, fiber-optic networks, and other *information technologies* linked to decision making as well as expanding and highly profitable forms of entertainment (video, video games, etc.). The effects on the reconstitution of identities of this kind of technological and economic globalization, particularly in the workplace and in consumption, are just beginning to be studied. Current discourses on competitive productivity, the rituals of integration among workers and corporate management, the subordination of entertainment iconography in keeping with delocalized codes are some of the processes in which the refashioning of local identities according to global matrices is quite evident. Many traditional habits and beliefs survive in these spaces, providing input for the differential styles that manifest themselves in different countries, even where production and consumption are high-tech. But it should be obvious that as we come under the logic of world competitiveness, as we watch television and inform ourselves electronically, use computer systems for many everyday activities, identities based on local traditions are reformulated according to "cultural engineering."[7]

One of the greatest challenges for rethinking identity and citizenship today is finding a way to study how relations of continuity, discontinuity, and hybridization are produced among local and global, traditional and ultramodern systems of cultural development. We have to examine not only coproduction, but also conflicts that revolve around the coexistence of ethnicities and nationalities in the workplace and in sites of consumption. Although *hegemony* and *resistance* continue to be useful analytical categories, the complexity and nuances of these interactions also compel us to study identities as processes of *negotiation,* inasmuch as they are *hybrid, flexible,* and *multicultural.*

When we take into consideration the social conflicts and the multicultural changes that accompany globalization, it becomes evident that the media spectacles we see cannot account for what takes place in industry. It is necessary, then, to clarify a statement made at the beginning: identity is a construct, but the artistic, folkloric, and media narratives that shape it are realized and transformed within sociohistorical conditions that cannot be reduced to their mise-en-scène. Identity is theater *and* politics, performance *and* action.

Chapter 6

Latin America and Europe as Suburbs of Hollywood

December 1993, in Brussels: for the first time, controversies over cultural policies took center stage in international economic debates. This meeting of the General Agreement on Tariffs and Trade (GATT), at which 117 countries approved the most far-reaching trade liberalization in history, nearly broke down because of disagreements in three areas: agriculture, textiles, and the audiovisual industry. The conflicts in the first two areas were resolved through mutual concessions negotiated between the United States and European governments. An analysis of the discrepancies that led to the exclusion of film and television from the agreement is of the greatest importance for understanding the predicaments confronted by national cultural policies in this age of globalization and the possibilities for waging a more effective politics of citizenship from the purview of culture.

The Conflict of Economic and Cultural Strategies

The United States demanded unrestricted circulation of audiovisual products; the Europeans sought to protect their media industries, especially cinema. The discrepancy derives from two ways of conceiving of culture. The U.S. position is that entertainment should be treated as a business—not only because it is, but also because it is the second-largest, after aerospace, of all sources of export income. In 1992, U.S. producers sent more than $4.6 billion in entertainment programs and films to Europe.[1] In this same period, European exports totaled $250 million.[2]

This asymmetry is evidenced further in European movie-theater and television programming. U.S. distributors controlled 80 percent of the French and 91 percent of the Spanish film markets in 1993. The resulting loss of screen time for the national cinemas of these countries generated great unrest among local artists and producers. The greatest expressions of irritation occurred when *Jurassic Park* premiered simultaneously in 180 Spanish and 400 French theaters.

Latin America is not to be outdone in this competition among the largest importing nations of U.S. entertainment. The figures have grown in the past few years because we receive not only film and television programs, but also films, games, and other forms of entertainment on video. Mexico, for example, barely in sixteenth place in 1990 among importers of U.S. films, had the distinction of reaching tenth place worldwide in 1993, with investments totaling $36.9 million.[3]

In debates prompted by GATT negotiations, European motion-picture worker associations defended their jobs, but they also put forth the argument that film is not exclusively a commodity. It is also a powerful instrument for the expression and self-affirmation of one's language and culture, and their dissemination beyond one's borders. They made reference to the contradiction whereby the United States demands the free circulation of its communications in foreign countries, while article 301 of its own commercial law permits restrictions on cultural products from abroad. U.S. radio and television stations broadcast nationally produced programming almost exclusively and, furthermore, disqualify imports through advertisements such as "Why buy music you don't understand?" Various experts have asked what if any advantage there might be for Europe to open its telecommunications markets without restriction to the two countries—the United States and Japan—that have closed their own markets to European products.[4]

Until a few years ago, each national film industry was allotted, for the sake of survival, a quota of screen time (50 percent in several Latin American countries). This was one means of limiting U.S. expansionism. We know that movie-theater attendance is falling worldwide for very complex reasons. In France, where 411 million tickets were sold in 1957, sales reached only 121.1 million in 1990.[5] Latin American movie theaters closed their doors en masse in the 1980s when attendance fell off by an average of 50 percent. In Mexico, 410 million in sales in 1984 had shrunk to 170 million in 1991.[6] In reality, the decrease in moviegoers does not signal the disappearance of film; instead, television and video have taken up the slack, propagating home viewing.[7] If U.S. enterprises have taken the lead in capitalizing on these changes in technology and cultural habits, it is because they can adapt more rapidly than the film industries of other countries. In fact, they encourage these innovations enthusiastically, thus gaining nearly worldwide control of television and video distribution as well as surviving movie-theater chains.

What can producers, filmmakers, and distributors who are not from the United States do? They do not constitute a bloc that reacts in the same way in all countries or all industry sectors. In the recent GATT debates, the English and the Germans washed their hands of "whatever might happen to the image industries: they had already given up many years earlier the possibility of creating their own culture in that sector."[8] France, Spain, and Italy tried to maintain national and European film quotas as a means to better production and to establish new sources of subsidy for their own film industry. This practice was criticized by the United States as a form of "unfair competition."

Even in Europe's Latin countries, who defend the "cultural exemption" to free trade, there are some who see film and television as nothing more than merchandise. As such, it is up to the spectators to decide what should or should not be exhibited. "They deserve what's coming to them," said a radio commentator, arguing that 90 percent of Spanish cinema is terrible. "But why take it out on film?" Eduardo Haro Tecglen responded in a newspaper article: "What percentage isn't equally bad in literature, theater, painting, carpentry, plumbing, the priesthood, or people's qualities overall?" One encouraging by-product of the debate is that it sharpened the self-criticism of Spanish cinema and society, particularly regarding the criteria of evaluation to be implemented in a democracy. Taking the size of the audience as an indicator of quality, Haro Tecglen argued, is like using election results to evaluate a government. "This is what is happening. It could be said that American film is slightly less bad: 80 percent. Perhaps because they can attract the best filmmakers in the world, they have greater economic potential. Be that as it may, it is here to stay."[9] In sum, the crisis of the film industry can no longer be understood as a problem internal to each country, nor in isolation from the transnational reorganization of symbolic markets. It is situated at the intersection of tensions between free trade, cultural quality, and particular ways of life.

The European debate offers useful insights for the analysis of these issues in the Latin American context. In Europe, too, neoliberal reforms of the state have led to the privatization of radio stations, TV channels, and a sizable segment of informational and telematic circuits. In some countries, the cultural action of the public sector was reduced to protecting the historical heritage (museums, archaeological sites, etc.) and promoting traditional arts (visual arts, music, theater, literature). The premise here is that, given declining attendance, these forms of culture would not survive without artificial respiration from the government. Communication and information media linked to the new technologies, which require greater investment but have the power to reach vast audiences, have been sold off to private enterprise, most often U.S. and Japanese corporations.

It is becoming evident that national identities are no longer defined exclusively by cinema, television, and video, but by the whole ensemble of "communication highways." Satellite transmission and fiber-optic cable have transformed scientific communication (electronic mail, telemedicine), office information systems, financial services for banks, intercorporation transactions, and, obviously, the distribution of cultural products. From the United States, Turner Communications masterminds the distribution of films, cartoons, and news in many Latin American countries and is now even operating in several European countries, such as France. Before long, U.S. films will arrive in movie theaters via satellite in hundreds of cities in all continents, without the complexities of customs' checks, as in the case of packaged pictures and videos. Television and home computer access to video games, electronic shopping, national and international news is also becoming more common. The Europeans are asking who will control these networks: information and entertainment audiovisual production is predominantly in the hands of U.S. companies, and 70 percent of worldwide sales of electronic devices for the mass market is controlled by Japanese firms. Europe is almost as ill prepared as Latin America to compete in the mass-mediated reorganization of culture. Furthermore, because of limited production and technological innovation in this area (the exception is Phillips), only small countries—Belgium, Switzerland, Ireland, Holland, and the Scandinavian countries—have been cabled. This technology is almost nonexistent in France, Spain, Portugal, and Greece, where the preferred means of delivery is the airwaves.[10]

Europe's weakness in the recent GATT negotiations prompted pointed responses from leading filmmakers (Pedro Almodóvar, Wim Wenders, Bernardo Bertolucci), actors' unions, television and film directors' associations, executives, and politicians. Their interests were at stake in the options given to audiovisual communication and they urgently sought a reformulation of the concepts used in drafting cultural policies, inasmuch as such policies have to factor in how new interactions between local cultures and global processes affect the public good. Several directors and writers involved in this debate have created works of great sensitivity to regional traditions. Their films and novels are incontrovertibly Spanish or German, or even more locally based in the urban cultures of Madrid, Berlin, or Rome. Nevertheless, they understand that the possibility to go on filming or distributing pictures, videos, and books relevant to local cultures depends on the degree of control that they secure within the most advanced networks of transnational communications.

And what about Latin America? The situation in Europe may help to bolster the demands of Argentine, Brazilian, and Venezuelan filmmakers who, among others, have won international prizes in recent years, but who find little support in their home societies, racked as they are by financial and legal crises. In some countries, government institutions that provided subsidies have folded, as did Brazil's Embrafilme. Film production is bound to fall (from 40 to 70 per year to 3 or 4, as in the early 1990s in the above-mentioned countries) if those who draft cultural policies continue to ignore the importance of mass communications. It is difficult for the state to make strategic interventions if the majority of cultural ministries and councils persist in believing that culture and identity are shaped predominantly by fine arts, with a pinch of indigenous and peasant cultures, traditional crafts and musics.

If it is true that part of our identities is still rooted in those traditional symbolic formations, it should also not be forgotten that 70 percent of the population are city dwellers and that an increasing number of these live in an almost exclusive connection with the culture industries. Lacking national cultural policies, these industries are condemned to importing and distributing that world folklore whose most characteristic examples are U.S. television series and Spielberg's and Lucas's movies. Meanwhile, the public in each country becomes accustomed to a media "normalcy" embodied by the most spectacular narratives contrived from myths that are intelligible to spectators from any country. Will our cultural policies continue to trod dirt roads or will they gain access to a paved culture, to international information and communications superhighways?

From Cinema to Multimedia Space

In the GATT negotiations, Europe proved to be more flexible in the areas of agriculture and industry than in audiovisual space. "France can forgo producing potatoes and still be France, but if we stop speaking French, lose our cinema, our theater, and our own narrative, we will become just another slum suburb of Chicago," said a French television executive.[11]

Five days before signing the GATT accord, the Spanish government passed a law establishing minimum screen-time quotas for European cinema. In cities with more than 125,000 inhabitants, at least one film from a European Community nation will be screened for every two from other continents. Other measures require television channels to pay higher rental fees for airing films. There is even talk of video distributors and rental outlets having to contribute part of their profits toward the financing of film production. It is increasingly evident that the survival of cinema does not depend on movie-theater screenings alone, but on its new role within the ensemble of factors in the audiovisual field. Nowadays, film is a multimedia product that can only be financed by contributions from the various venues in which it circulates.

When all is said and done, however, the survival of cinema, important as it is, pales in comparison to the total deregulation of the entire area of communications, the goal of U.S. trade policy. Fiber-optic networks and the digitization and compression of images will bring a "downpour of five hundred channels on Europe" before the end of the century. Juan Cueto, until recently director of Spanish TV's Canal +, has said that cinema is a McGuffin (scenes in Hitchcock films that add nothing to the plot but serve to thicken it). "Cinema is a locomotive, Hitchcock's McGuffin, and what is important is what it drags behind it."

Forecasts predict a similar fate for Latin America in the near future. Movie theaters have closed in Buenos Aires, São Paulo, Caracas, Bogotá, and Mexico City, while upwards of 50 percent of homes in these cities count videocassette recorders and cable television among their possessions. Video rental clubs, the major outlet for cinema, offer from 70 percent to 90 percent U.S. films, depending on the country. Productions representative of European cultures, with which we Latin Americans have the closest ties, together with works from other countries in the region, do not exceed 10 percent of all the disposable fare on television and video.

U.S. hegemony is even greater when it comes to the control of information and telematics. There is not one country in Latin America, except for Brazil, with state policies for investment in high-end research, production of equipment, and personnel training, all necessary to compete in the development of cultural innovations associated with cutting-edge technologies. Subordination to U.S. technological and communications production is becoming even more accentuated in Mexico since the signing of NAFTA, an eventuality to be repeated in those Latin American countries that will follow suit in joining the accord. The reason for this is that the economic opening negotiated in NAFTA actually limits investment from countries outside the region in the national economies of this hemisphere. At the very least, the United States and Canada can request preferential treatment whenever a Latin American country signs an accord with a country outside the region.

Nationalism All Over Again?

The United States has benefited in many ways from industrial development in Germany and Japan. It also has an overwhelming control of almost all postindustrial software production, that is, of electronic information and communications programs. After the collapse of the Soviet bloc, the "American Way" has jurassically expanded the dissemination of its spectacles throughout the universe. Europe's energetic negotiations in the recent GATT rounds and the measures taken by some countries to protect their audiovisual production are a few of the alternatives that make it possible to envisage a symbolic world in which not everything is in the hands of Hollywood and CNN. At least, according to Régis Debray, it helps to question whether what is good for Columbia and Warner Brothers—which we already know is good for the United States—is also good for humanity.[12]

Some intellectuals become alarmed by what they consider to be a resurgence of nationalism, an "anti-North Americanism, based on ideological myths" and statist interventions that are conducive to authoritarianism. For Mario Vargas Llosa, "when it functions freely, the market allows, for example, for films produced in the 'periphery' to reach millions of movie theaters throughout the world, as in the case of *Like Water for Chocolate* or *El Mariachi*."[13] These exceptions are exactly that, rare cases, as one can easily confirm by surveying the meager space given to Latin American and European films (and also Asian and African films) in movie listings, television offerings, and video club holdings in any North American city, and in every country in which programming is controlled by U.S. distributors. In the United States, only 1 percent of all movie tickets sold are for films in languages other than English.[14] The numbers do not support what Vargas Llosa says: "the disappearance of borders, the integration of the peoples of the world in a system of exchange that benefits all, and especially those countries that urgently need to overcome underdevelopment and poverty." "Those ideals of our youth" that socialism could not attain have been made possible by "capitalism and the market."[15] A novelist's fiction?

To conclude, we might say that the current European debate reformulates transnational mass communications policies, in at least three ways:

1. *It calls for a reformulation of the relations between the national, the continental, and the global.* There is no dearth of racist and chauvinist outbursts as Latin Americans and Europeans confront the transnational restructuring of markets by proposing a return to a telluric nationalism, as if "national roots" were the only source of true art. This "horticulture of creation," as André Lange has called it, has always been a meager aesthetic and sociologically unverifiable: "What are Mozart's roots? Salzburg, which sent him off with a swift kick in the ass, or all of Europe, which provided him with forms, themes, librettos?" "Should André Wajda, the Polish filmmaker, have refrained from giving us a provocative Danton?"[16] It is not difficult to give a similar repertoire of Latin American examples, from the hybrid multicultural "roots" of tango or revue theater to internationally recognized writers, musicians, and painters (for example, Octavio Paz, Ástor Piazzolla, and César Paternosto, to mention only those surnames beginning with P). They are renowned for the quality of their innovations, for their way of speaking on "their own" without taking refuge in the local. The question is how to make it possible, in the current phase of the industrialization and transnationalization of communications, for Mexican, Argentine, or Colombian artists not only to communicate with one or ten thousand compatriots but to gain entry into the circuits of a *Latin American cultural space,* from which vantage point they might dialogue with the voices and images that come to us from the entire planet.

A crucial issue that will determine whether or not this Latin American space represents our multicultural societies is the degree to which it channels action in a decentralized manner, recognizing the diversity of regional styles and aesthetics. The current tendency is to concentrate television and other audiovisual media in two or three oligopolies: the 6,000 radio and 550 television stations in Latin America "represent, in reality, 6,550 times the same fare; they compete vigorously to get a piece of the advertising pie, but to get this they all have to have the same kind of programming."[17]

2. *The articulation of public services and private interests.* Precisely because their influence is so great, and because they require huge investments and a high level of efficiency, the new audiovisual technologies should not depend predominantly on the bureaucratic apparatuses of the state. But because they constitute the cultural space where inequalities and asymmetries among societies are most accentuated, they cannot be left unmonitored and exclusively to the dictates of competition in international markets. Once the euphoria of the fall of the Berlin Wall subsided, and the complications this brought to Europe were discerned, thinkers such as Alain Touraine explained that the market might be good for demolishing the "centralized, clientliest or totalitarian state," but not for providing a principle for the construction or management of social life." New questions arise: "How can the state be made to intervene without falling into the trap of defending inward-looking national traditions?" How is it possible to combine support "for creation and the survival of enterprises capable of competing in the market" with "policies for patronage and indirect support for cultural institutions, schools, museums, universities, and associations"?[18]

Other authors, from Jürgen Habermas to Dominique Wolton, insist on the need to give greater depth to the "construction of a European public space" that provides for the combined administration of the public and the private—expanding in proportion to the multiplication of translated books, and film and TV coproductions (e.g., the Franco-German channel Arte)—and the opening of daily columns in national newspapers to foreign writers. One challenge yet to be met is the broadening of intercommunications in high culture so that they also include a public space for popular sectors. This broadening is especially needed in media such as television that are more disposed to celebrate their national sports or to disseminate "quaint" views of other societies than to provide historical references and significant intercultural confrontations.

I see in these European polemics an attempt to ensure that the neoliberal paradigm does not become a self-fulfilling prophecy. They also exemplify the search for a path that does not confuse the inevitability of the globalization of economy and culture with U.S. hegemony. We too, on this side of the Atlantic, can benefit from this distinction. We too must recalibrate the balance of public and private on a scale larger than that of the nation by creating a Latin American culture of democratic citizenship and a Latin American space for communications. This requires that states, international organizations such as UNESCO, OAS, and others, nonmonopolistic business enterprises, and NGOs foment transnational coproductions and distribution programs. Furthermore, the continental range of these initiatives must be buttressed by national laws that establish minimum screen time in movie theaters and on television, not only for the cinema of each country, as in the past, but for a continental Latin American production, more in keeping with the European model, which has a realistic vision.

3. *The need to reposition each culture industry—film, television, video—within a multimedia policy* that also includes advertising and other commercial by-products of mass symbolic practices. Currently, the European and U.S. film industries are sustained through a combination of exhibition in movie theaters and other venues such as national and foreign television, cable and satellite broadcasts, and video. In Italy, France, and Spain the crisis generated by low movie-house attendance for local film production is mitigated by television broadcasts, which comprise up to 90 percent of financing. In the United States, two hours and forty minutes of advertising are enough to finance one hour of a series. In France, it takes ten hours of advertising to raise that amount. In Mexico, on the other hand, private television can show a film as many times as it wants over a year and a half for only twenty thousand dollars, even though the first minute of advertising during the transmission of the film earns the channel two hundred thousand dollars. We know it is not easy to balance public and artistic interests with the tendency to seek easy profits among audiovisual entrepreneurs. For example, an Argentine initiative to tax videos and films transmitted on television in order to subsidize and therefore help reinvigorate the film industry was denounced by the channels and video club owners. In order to change this situation, it is indispensable for Latin American states to take on the public interest and regulate entrepreneurial activity.

December 1994. At the end of the year, presidential and parliamentary elections were held in several Latin American countries with the largest audiovisual industries: Venezuela, Colombia, Mexico, and Brazil. Argentina held a constitutional assembly in 1994 and scheduled its presidential election for 1995. There is no reason to assume that the gov-

ernments that privatized radio stations and television channels in recent years, and that—with the exception of Mexico—tore down the
infrastructure that supported cinema, are going to recognize the disas-
trous consequences of neoliberal deregulation and absolute commercialization of audiovisual space for national cultural production. Most
of the opposition parties also seem unconcerned that we will produce
fewer films and books, fewer cultural television programs, or that our
video clubs have become the branch stores of Hollywood. Will the integration projects and free-trade agreements being negotiated throughout America help reactivate the culture industries? We can only imagine that this will be possible if they reanimate regulation policies and
publicly financed promotion of Latin American culture. These questions will only enter electoral agendas and international negotiations if
there is mobilization by artists, independent producers, and some form
of organization on the part of cultural consumers, say, moviegoers and
television viewers. That such organization does not exist in Latin America is one of the most alarming symptoms of our lack of protection as
spectators. Is it still possible for us to produce, create, and choose as
citizens? Or will we become complacent with the modicum of liberty
that channel surfing affords us?

Chapter 7

From the Public to the Private

The "Americanization" of Spectators

The future of multiculturality depends not only on policies of national and international integration. The habits and tastes of consumers condition their capacity to become citizens. Their exercise of citizenship is shaped in relation to artistic and communicational referents, and to their preferred entertainment and forms of information. Let's examine how cultural practices and preferences are being restructured in relation to the transformations taking place in the film, television, and video industries.

The crises of the film industry have almost always been related to technological changes. The appearance of the talkies, cinemascope, and competition from television were some of the innovations that cast doubt on the cinematographic industry and language. In the past decade, the questions about the continued existence of cinema are really about diminishing audiences.

Thousands of movie houses have shut down in all Latin American countries, as in other continents. Movie theaters have become video game parlors, evangelical churches, or parking lots in Montevideo, São Paulo, Bogotá, and Mexico City. In a country such as Argentina, with a strong cinematographic tradition, seven provinces no longer have movie houses.[1]

Nevertheless, more films are seen now than in any prior period. But they are watched at home, on television, or on video. Of 16 million Mexican homes, more than 13 million have a television set and more than 5 million own a video player. There are 9,589 video clubs distributed throughout the country, including popular areas and small peasant villages.

The dissemination of video and the growth of its profits are the greatest in the United States. Income from the rental and sale of videos went from $3.6 million in 1985 to $10.3 million in 1991. It is not usual for a cultural industry to triple its earnings in six years. These figures increased in the same period in which audiences vacated movie houses. In 1989, these constituted 80 percent of film revenues; currently they provide barely 25 percent.

In what ways is it different to view film when it passes from the movie house to home projection? This chapter, which synthesizes several research findings in four Mexican cities,[2] highlights four transformations:

1. A new relation between the real and the imaginary.

2. A different positioning of the phenomenon of film between the public (urban cultural consumption) and the private (reception of entertainment at home).

3. A reorientation of cinema in relation to national and transnational culture.

4. The emergence of multimedia spectators, who relate to film in various ways—in movie houses, or via television, video, and entertainment magazines—and who consider it part of a broad and diversified system of audiovisual programs.

Intimacy in a Crowd

The film viewer is an invention of the twentieth century. We can trace its origins in Robertson's camera obscura, in nineteenth-century experiments with photography and X rays, and, of course, in Lumière's, Félix Mesquich's, and others' first projections, when people still did not know how to look at those "animated scenes," and the public, on seeing the locomotive approaching on the screen, frantically rushed out.[3]

Only with the construction of permanent movie theaters, from 1905 on, did there begin to emerge habits of perception and attendance, a new distinction between the real and the imaginary, another sense of verisimilitude, of solitude and collective ritual. People learned to be film viewers, to go to dark auditoriums periodically, to choose to sit at the proper distance from the screen, to enjoy movies by themselves or in the company of others, to pass from the intimacy of the projection to the exchange of impressions and gregarious celebration of the stars. Films thus came to be selected by the names of the actors or the directors, to be situated in film history or among the ads in culture and entertainment sections.

What remains of all this when movies are viewed on television, in one's illuminated living room, interrupted by ads, the telephone, or other members of the family? What becomes of cinema when we no longer go to the movie house but to the video club, or when we watch whatever appears on television?

Video is appealing above all because it costs more or less the same to rent as to buy a movie ticket. Moreover, each video is watched by several people, and viewing it at home eliminates extra expenses (carfare, food), the dangers of the city, the lines, and other inconveniences. Older moviegoers, accustomed to the theaters, may lament the loss of the spectacle and the poor quality of the television screen, but video viewers welcome the possibility of operating the projection themselves, stopping it, going back over scenes, and above all not having to put up with commercial breaks.[4] It is logical for broad sectors of the viewing public to prefer home entertainment instead of having to travel throughout the city. But for film—a traditional stimulus for going out and using the city, where urban themes are generated—to become a reason for staying in the privacy of the home means that a radical change has taken place in the relations between cinema and public life.

Film widened its communicative action thanks to television and video. But this expansion transformed the productive process and the ways of viewing films. Instead of going to the theater to seek, in Carlos Monsiváis's words, "intimacy in a crowd," a devoted community gathered in the dark silence in front of the screen, television and video encourage the restricted sociability of the couple or the family and a diminished attention to the film. They permit distractions and even enable other activities while one follows the story line. Also changed are the ways of getting information on what to watch, on how to develop tastes and locate them within the history of film and the history of the nation.

From the National to the Transnational

The success of what is known as Mexican cinema's "golden age"—approximately 1940 to 1954—was due to the creativity of several filmmakers (Emilio Fernández, Luis Buñuel, Ismael Rodríguez) and the presence of actors capable of becoming idols (Pedro Infante, Jorge Negrete, María Félix, and Dolores del Río, among others). Also important was the convergence of entrepreneurs and state support, and a distribution system that reached almost all of Latin America. These factors combined with the capacity of the cinematic narratives and characters to represent Mexican national culture and contribute to the sentimental education of the masses who migrated to the cities in those years.

The mass media contributed to the formation of cultural citizenship. Through radio and cinema, Carlos Monsiváis says, Mexicans learned to recognize themselves within an integrated whole, above ethnic and regional divisions. Ways of acting and speaking, tastes and codes of customs, disconnected or in conflict in the past, were brought together in the language with which films represented the emergence of the masses, legitimizing their styles of feeling and thinking.[5] The continental expansion of Mexican cinema, like that of Argentine cinema, during World War II and subsequent years was aided by Hollywood's abandonment of the Latin American market as it concentrated on producing propaganda films for U.S. troops stationed in Europe. "We had a privileged position," observes Ignacio Durán Loera, "because we had greater access to raw materials—acetate and celluloid—which in Argentina were very difficult to obtain in time of war."[6]

This favorable international situation was key for the success of Mexican cinema. But its contribution to the modernization and massification of national culture was also a key factor in the development of this art industry. Cinema was not merely a prosperous commercial activity; it became that because it also played a major, imaginative role in the renewal and growth of society.

Mexican cinema's role in shaping a mass audiovisual culture and a symbolic language to express social process lost its effectiveness because of a combination of factors. The most important were the reduction of state support; the closing off of the Cuban market with the revolution and the contraction of South American markets due to economic difficulties; the rapid expansion of television as a new agent of entertainment and conditioner of the social imaginary; competition from U.S. cinema, which, revamped thematically and formally and strengthened by large investments and greater effectivity in distribution, gained control of international markets.[7]

To these processes one should also add the changes in the relation between film and national culture when its principal means of diffusion are television and video. On the one hand, these new means enable a more balanced distribution throughout the national territory of what is shown in Mexico City. In contrast with the situation in museums, libraries, and theaters, most of which are concentrated in the capital, the dissemination of TV channels and video clubs throughout the country, with homogeneous programming designed by monopolies, makes it possible for viewers in large and small cities to have access to almost the same cinematographic repertoire. This "egalitarian democratization" is heightened by the designers of television programming and video club catalogs who cater to tastes based on the premise that everybody in the country resembles one another.

But such a "national unification" achieved by the mass distribution of cinema is, in a way, paradoxical. In contrast to education and cultural policies that throughout this century sought to construct a common Mexican identity on the basis of national symbols, of actors, objects, and customs issued from the nation, almost 80 percent of the films available on video are of U.S. origin. European cultures with which Mexico has long had relations, particularly the Spanish, as well as Latin American cultures, with which we share a common language, history, and political projects, are represented in less than 10 percent of available film on television and video. Mexican film available in video clubs also fails to reach 10 percent of the total and the inventory virtually excludes films that document contemporary conflicts. When we consider all this together with the preponderance of North American film, it is logical, as Déborah Holtz observes, that video viewers should relate to cinema with the assumption that "reality resides elsewhere."[8]

The predominance of one foreign film industry can be even more disconcerting on taking into account that corporations linked to U.S. capital, Multivisión and Blockbuster, control minority stakes in television and video markets. The hegemonic role of Televisa in these media suggests that the unilateral audiovisual repertoire is solely of its own making and conforms to its cultural objectives. Televisa's interests in Spanish, Latin American, and U.S. Hispanic markets are evident in only a few entertainment programs (*Siempre en domingo*), news magazines (Eco), and short-lived series of Mexican films or spectacles (Cadena de las Américas). We can assume that most viewers' preferences for U.S. pictures and the overriding popularity of North American stars (Kevin Costner, Arnold Schwarzenegger, Tom Cruise, Sylvester Stallone, Mel Gibson), confirmed by a survey we conducted in Mexico, are determined in part by the bias of the repertoire and the near absence of other national cinemas.

What do video viewers think of Mexican cinema? They see it through the comparative framework established by U.S. film. This is borne out not only by the predominance of U.S. movies and actors mentioned in surveys, but also by development of aesthetic taste, the value placed on spectacle and types of stars, and of course on the skewed proportion of programming. U.S. film is thought of as the norm precisely because U.S. product has a 60–85 percent market share in all venues: movie houses, television, and video. Blockbuster video outlets make a glaring classificatory slip that bears this out. The majority of their racks are classified by "genre" (action, suspense, comedy, children, etc.), represented almost exclusively by U.S. films, with a few Mexican exceptions. In a corner, we find a few dozen European, Latin American, and perhaps a couple of Asian films, all united under the category "foreign film." U.S. film does not appear in this section. Is it therefore not a national cinema? Is it then film pure and simple?

There is a significant difference between male and female viewers of national and U.S. cinemas. Majorities of both genders prefer U.S. film, but because men are most attracted to action films (thrillers, adventure, and espionage films), their answers on surveys show a higher preference for North American movies. Women, on the other hand, show a preference for "sentimental" and "family" dramas, which leans them more toward Mexican cinema. In any case, for both men and women the relation between the national and the North American is negotiated symbolically through action and social violence, while Mexican cinema— where these modes are less prevalent—provides scenarios for the portrayal of sentimental and family conflicts.

That Mexican film occupies such a low standing in movie theaters and video clubs does not mean, at least so far as our data indicate, that there is an equally low interest in and value placed on it by film, TV, and video viewers throughout the country. A considerable percentage of those interviewed, when asked what they did not find in video clubs, mentioned Mexican films. Although it is clear that the majority prefer U.S. films, it is not the case that all sectors judge Mexican film in the same way, nor show preference for the same films. The 25 to 40 age group showed greater interest in some new national films such as *La tarea* and *Like Water for Chocolate*. Others that can be included in this category, *Danzón, Rojo amanecer,* and *La mujer de Benjamín,* on the other hand, sparked the interest of those in the 45 to 60 age group, because of the greater correspondence between the events presented and the age of the protagonists (e.g., those who lived through the student demonstrations of 1968). The percentage of new films mentioned in our question regarding the most recently rented video, also indicates that national cinema is not neglected by the majority. Nor is this interest limited to the golden age of Mexican cinema. What is evident from the declared preferences is that there is not only *one* national film public. Diverse eras, genres, styles, with different proportions of entertainment and artistic pursuit, find faithful or recently interested publics. The question that arises here is whether current cinematographic policies, in which the aesthetic dimension of films is subordinated to ratings, can take into consideration this multicultural diversity of publics.

Film, Television, and Radio: Multimedia Spectators

Up to twenty years ago, films could recoup their cost through national and international movie-theater chains. As we noted in the preceding chapter, now they have to venture into many other venues to attempt to make good on their investment: national television and that of other countries, cable, parabolic antenna, and video broadcasts. In Mexico and other countries, these latter circuits are usually under the control of transnational corporations. As cinema becomes more dependent on new technologies, it is increasingly difficult to produce film and video in Latin American countries, where investment in these areas has fallen off in recent years, as a result of reductions in public spending and the lack of interest in providing incentives for innovation in cutting-edge technologies.

Video has become, in less than a decade, the most diffused venue for viewing films. Those who go to movie theaters once a week or every two weeks rent two or three films on video per week. Add to them those who have lost the custom of going to movie theaters, or who shrink from traversing the city to a theater showing the film they want to see, and the masses who never had the custom to go to movie theaters and nevertheless see from two to four films per week on video or television.

The study we carried out in Mexico City provides a profile of these new spectators. Sixty percent of video club clients are less than thirty years old. Only those who grew up watching video have a "natural" relation to the television screen and are less bothered by it than those who go to movie theaters. Video, however, is popular not only among the young. More video viewers have children than those who go to the movies, which implies that they stay at home because of family obligations. Many of those who watch videos at home also go to the movies,

but for them the family promenade or friendly gathering is as important as the choice of film. People go out not only to enjoy the film but
also for the rituals before and after the showing.

The moviegoer, that invention of the beginning of the century, has
been changing in the past decade. Surveys that ask about moviegoers'
and video viewers' knowledge of film history show that the majority of
both groups do not know the names of the directors. Almost all moviegoers leave the theater before the credits. In video clubs, arrangement of
films by genre, with little or no information about the directors, contrasts with the saliency of actors' names and "intense" (dramatic, sex-
ual, violent) scenes represented on the box covers. This suggests that these
businesses have no interest in locating the films in cinema history or in
relation to their "authors." Whereas access to the movie house is usually
guided by consulting newspaper listings and one's own viewing history,
which often involves having to go to other parts of the city, video viewers go to rental clubs near their home without making prior decisions.

One of the most notable differences between cinephiles and videophiles is that the relation of the latter with film takes place in a present
without memory. Video clubs in Mexico City consider films older than
eighteen months to be of no interest, and for them to remain on exhibition that long they must turn a good profit. Video renters' dissatisfaction almost never refers to the lack of films from other periods or from
countries other than the United States, but rather to the lack of suffi-
cient copies of films that have recently premiered. What is important is
not the film itself, nor the director, but the most recent film available,
especially if it is an "action-adventure," the most requested genre in
video clubs.

> Immediacy and the value of the instantaneous are reflected in what young
> videophiles seek. The number of images that succeed each other by frac-
> tions of a second are the beginning of a challenge to time that does not
> correspond to time. It is the illusion of a transgression emanating from
> the rhythm that this fictitious reality imposes. The pleasure of expecta-
> tion thus modifies the way of seeing. This survey confirms that the new
> image consumers are addicted to rhythm more than they are to plots.
> (Déborah Holtz)

The proliferation of video clubs throughout the city and the uniformity of available repertoires make it possible for consumption to be
a neighborhood activity. Everyone has all the available titles near their
home. In the Federal District there is one movie theater for every 62,868

inhabitants, and some districts have fewer than five theaters. There is, on the other hand, one video club for every 4,500 inhabitants (Déborah Holtz).

If the passage from movie houses to video clubs means fewer trips throughout the city, the selection of films to view on television, as is well known, is even more passive. Pay-per-view is available only for the smallest minorities, and almost all TV viewers have their options limited by the four or six films that the channels air during the evening. People do not see what they prefer, but they prefer what they are offered.[9]

Diversification of Tastes and Citizenship

Let me review two of the conclusions pertinent to the analysis of cultural policy that ensue from our research on viewers' aesthetics: on the one hand, the preponderance of spectacular action over other dramatic and narrative modalities; on the other, the possibility that national cinemas can subsist in the midst of the transnational and multimedia reorganization of audiovisual production and markets.

1. It is thought-provoking that cinematographic and televisual repertoires, as well as audience tastes, should give precedence to an aesthetics of action in an age that has seen the demise of the heroic phase of political movements. Politics has often put a premium on action: the antitheoretical pragmatism or "militance" of political parties, the exaltation of everyday heroism and of "what-can-be-demonstrated-in-concrete-practice" in social movements, and, of course, the extreme subordination of politics in guerrilla hyperactivism. The failure of many armed groups, the decline of militant cadre in political parties, the displacement of political *action* by *acting* in the media, and the institutionalization of social movements all led to a shift from radical heroism to negotiation and other mediated forms of resolving power struggles.

Of all these changes, the transference of political staging to the electronic media is the process that best preserves in a depoliticized mode what there is of action in politics. After all, we are speaking of theatrical action. Let's not forget that politics, from solemn parliamentary speeches to everyday rituals in which hierarchies are acknowledged, has always had a theatrical side. But televisual spectacularization accentuates it, and thus modifies political action.

Fernando Collor, Carlos Menem, and Alberto Fujimori are some of the leaders who in recent years have cultivated this change. Their publicity campaigns, both preelectorally and while in power, cast them in the role of sports figures and thus constructed their public images. Menem has sought to display his omnipotence by playing soccer and tennis, piloting airplanes, driving race cars, and going out with exuberant models all in the same day. Renato Janine Ribeiro has said that Collor's image crafters transmitted "an impression of efficiency, energy and youth, suggesting to public opinion that through his physical energy and will the president could conquer the problems of Brazil, from inflation to underdevelopment.[10] It is not political action itself (an even less reasoned argument) that is offered to resolved social problems, but rather, brute force. The mass-media political hero bases himself more on brute force than on his intelligence or ability. Of all the examples of this semantic shift in what can be understood as political action—or its convergence with media action—there is none better than George Bush's welcoming of Brazil's president at the White House with the sobriquet "Indiana Collor." Ribeiro recalls Bush's curious interpretation of the *Indiana Jones* films:

> Spielberg's character is, above all, an archaeologist, an intellectual. The filmmaker's strategy to make him likable, even if he is in the service of knowledge (a cause that generally makes characters hateful to mass audiences), was to have him carry out his quest with the utmost energy, giving him a kind of second existence. Neither Bush nor Collor, however, showed any interest in research, or in Indiana's knowledge-producing dimension. Moreover, the "heroic" phase of Collor's presidency was marked by a strong and explicit aversion to the academic, scientific, and cultural sphere. In sum: *Indiana Jones* is, in Bush's universe of references, a hero of force rather than knowledge."[11]

The denouement of the transubstantiation of political action into communicational action is not always so felicitous as in the impeachment of Collor in Brazil. Ribeiro concludes his analysis by arguing that the destruction of the public sphere provoked by these heroic presidents can boomerang on them when citizens and media ally to restore the dignity of the public. However, Latin America's recent history suggests that there are numerous situations in which societies accept the transubstantiation and prefer a political scene in which political heroes resemble those of film and television.

The majority consensus held on to by the governments of Menem and Fujimori seems to be based on the complacency with their omnipotent exhibitionism and their capacity to confirm it through financial stability. If we take into consideration the signs of productive stagnation, the increase in unemployment and poverty, one cannot but think that the overwhelming vote for these figures is not due to their power to transform their countries and generate well-being, but to that more modest power that consists of overcoming the panic produced in periods of hyperinflation and instability. Correlatively, the recent electoral failures of opposition parties are interpreted in Argentina, Peru, Mexico, and other countries as an expression of fear of what might be lost if there are changes, if the economy is destabilized, if inflation returns, and it is not possible to continue enjoying certain commodities. The fact that these interpretations are linked to worries about consumption shows the degree to which it is operative in shaping citizen opinions. Consequently, it is not so surprising that the media should play an important role in generating consensus or that the frivolous actions that politicians use to demonstrate their power should take on a positive meaning.

The consensus achieved among majorities by politicians who act against their interests has been explained by reference to the evasive effects of the media, whose model is the preponderance of alienating entertainment over consciousness-raising information in North American culture industries. I prefer another hypothesis: the correspondence (rather than mechanical determination) of, on the one hand, narrative structures, the rise of spectacular action, and the fascination with a memoryless present in film and television, and, on the other, an anecdotal rather than argumentative vision in political discourse, as well as a media-constructed political heroism that enables leaders to show their power not through their intervention in the structural changes of history but in the mininarration of feats of virtuosity linked to corporal ability and consumption. In this same vein, we can correlate the declining attendance at places of public cultural consumption (movie houses, theaters) and the retreat to the home for electronic entertainment with declining public forms for the exercise of citizenship.

2. I should like to explore whether it is possible for national cinemas, as integral parts of the cultures of each country, to survive under the current conditions in audiovisual markets. To answer this question implies knowing what possibilities there are for Latin American cinemas to reformulate their projects so as to insert themselves in the new relations among financing sources, producers, directors, distributors, promoters, and, of course, the diverse types of audiences, some of whom go to movie theaters, but most of whom devote their evenings and weekends to video rentals and their television screens.

Nevertheless, we can report that audience surveys do not condemn movie theaters to the ash can of history. Although surveys show that the youngest, the unmarried, and those over fifty prefer to see films there, movie theaters continue to be attractive for all ages and social strata. The desire to see films in movie houses surpasses 50 percent of viewers in the four Mexican cities studied, but the percentage of those who actually attend theaters does not rise higher than 36 percent. Practice would be closer to desire, the surveyed explain, if movie-house projections were of better quality, if they were more diversified, if the theaters were cleaned and renovated periodically, and if complementary services (parking, drinks, etc.) made attendance more pleasant.

The mass success of some Mexican pictures, such as *Sólo con tu pareja,* that deal with topics of interest to youth, or of films that relate national history to everyday intimacy, as, for example, *Like Water for Chocolate, Rojo amanecer,* and other similar films, indicates that Mexican pictures that transcend the stereotypes of commercial success can find an audience. Our research confirmed that quality films can attract a relatively broad, albeit selective, public predisposed to relate to demanding films and capable of establishing a more complex relation with them than mere entertainment. A good example are the Muestras Internacionales de Cine [International Film Festivals] in Mexico City, which have an excellent public resonance.

Nevertheless, the most salient feature in the restructuring of markets is the segmentation of publics. On the one hand, we have an elite with knowledge of film history who attends the Cineteca, annual festivals, cine clubs, and views television film showings with few commercial breaks (channels 11 and 22); on the other, an enormous audience that is not even aware that there are options other than Televisa and video clubs.

It may be possible to construct intermediate circuits. This is beginning to take place in large and medum-size cities where small "art cinemas" with daily multiple programming have been established. In some cases, commercial television, and not only the "cultural channels," carries out this function. Surveys at movie theaters and video clubs on what people want to see on television and video show that mass audiences are more diversified and complex than is assumed by those who divide them into the educated and the entertained.

The system of video clubs seems condemned to being the most monotonous circuit in terms of repertoire. This is due to its speedy economic success as a purveyor almost exclusively of U.S.-made entertainment. In Mexico, as in other countries, this aesthetic unilateralism is more the result of the pragmatic criteria of business than a careful attention to the interests and preferences of viewers. In a way, the "neglect" of the internal differences in the mass of videophiles corresponds to a depersonalized form of consumption: videophiles are less inclined to ritual than moviegoers, and have not made prior choices about what to see. The vast majority of video viewers declared in our surveys that they go to the clubs without knowing what they will rent.

Nevertheless, a minority of viewers are beginning to inform themselves in newspaper sections on what's new in video and in other media that provide brief reviews. Moreover, there are enough examples of Latin American countries with better equipped video clubs, as regards quality and international representation (Argentina, Brazil, Colombia). They also make good profits, which suggests that including Jim Jarmusch, Derek Jarman, and the best of Latin American cinema will not sink similarly stocked businesses in Mexico. Some examples of the new Mexican cinema lead us to such optimistic predictions. *Danzón,* which sold twenty-five thousand cassettes, is not the only example. On this view, neither television nor video are substitutes for movie houses; there is, rather, an interdependence between the three media that can contribute to the revitalization of cinematographic production, which is what happened in European coutnries.

It is reasonable to think that the integration of the audiovisual field is based not only on the complementarity of cinema, television, and video as regards production and distribution. When we observe changes in audience habits, we have grounds for surmising that viewers might propose solutions for the combination of cinema with repertoires available in movie houses and on television and video. Movies today are a multimedia process, followed by multimedia spectators.

Perhaps this integrated vision of the various distribution circuits for film and the greater attention to the cultural diversities of publics will liberate us from the spectacular uniformity with which the crisis of the audience is currently being addressed. World cinema does not seem to be the only way to intensify the connections of film and publics, nor to give a shot in the arm to sagging national cinemas. Even Spielberg's films and those of other astute market multiculturalists can backfire from too much of a good thing: the obsession to chock their films with attractive ingredients from eveywhere. No need to even mention what happens in the hands of less expert filmmakers who kill a story's verisimilitude to satisfy the demands of international coproducers, who must have or get rid of this or that actor. When it seemed that Raúl de la Torre's *Funes, un gran amor* was going to receive U.S. financing, the owner of the whorehouse was cast as a North American. When the money came, it was Italian, so Gian María Volonté was chosen to play that role.

> Such a circumstance brings into existence a new category of characters: the foreigners. In many recent Argentine films, curious characters wend their way through the plot without the slightest idea of what they are doing there; sometimes they even admit it. The most obvious example is Volonté's *Funes...*, who meanders through the film muttering unintelligible utterances and who finally flees terrified, at the same time as the whorehouse disappears, this whorehouse of the fictive narrative, of the absurd story of the film and the grotesque project that he was bamboozled into.[12]

The large demand for films that deal with historical themes or contemporary social problems is evidence that light entertainment is not the only reason why people continue to see films. For large numbers, which are even higher among the youngest viewers or the most educated, the problematic treatment of current issues, close to everyday life, as well as intercultural matters and artistic innovations, is the motivation for watching movies. The diversification of tastes might have something to do with the cultural formation of a democratic citizenship.

The question is to what extent this variety of interests will be considered in policies for the production and distribution of films, even when they are not the most profitable. Without a more active role on the part of public power in the definition of the rules of use and circulation of film, seeking, for example, greater financing in the television and video sectors, it is unlikely that a quality cinema can be promoted, one that will also serve to fill movie houses and help increase profits. Will we have film for publics or for corporate executives? Are these mutually exclusive options?

Chapter 8

Multicultural Policies and Integration via the Market

In 1994 the Latin American presidential summit held two meetings in two emblematic cities to try to reanimate a project that had languished for some time: regional integration. The first, held in June in Cartagena de Indias, included a representative of the Spanish government; the second, held in December in Miami, included Clinton but not Fidel Castro.

The first attempt to include this continent in the world economy took place five hundred years ago. Homogeneous labor-control methods in different regions facilitated the unification of local styles of production and consumption. The Christianization of the Indians, their introduction to literacy in Spanish and Portuguese, the design of colonial and subsequently modern urban space, the uniformization of political and educational systems engendered enabled one of the most effective homogenizing processes on the planet. With the exception, perhaps, of the Arab countries, there is no other area of the world where such a large number of independent states share the same language, history, and dominant religion, or have occupied for more than five centuries a more or less shared position in their relation to metropolitan countries.

Nevertheless, this historic integration contributed little to consistent economic development or to competitive participation in global exchange. In the cultural sphere, despite the multiplication of integrating organizations since the 1950s—Organization of American States (OAS), Economic Commission for Latin America and the Caribbean (CEPAL), Latin American Free Trade Association (ALALC), and so on—Latin American countries have not even been able to establish lasting forms of collaboration and reciprocal knowledge. It is still almost impossible to find Central American books in Montevideo, Bogotá, or Mexico. We can learn through U.S. news agencies that Argentine, Brazilian, and Mexican films have won prizes in international festivals. But such news sources do not distribute them throughout the continent. Our publications, films, and musical works have just as much difficulty entering North America and Europe as do our steel, our grain, and our crafts.

Two decades ago, developmentalism—like other evolutionary modernizing tendencies—attributed Latin American disintegration and backwardness to "cultural obstacles," that is, to those traditions that differentiated the region. There was confidence that with industrialization our societies would be able to modernize homogeneously and establish fluid linkages among themselves. This did happen, in part. It is now easier to communicate via television networks than through books, or via fax than through the mail.

Nevertheless, there persist marked ethnic, regional, and national differences among Latin American countries. And we no longer believe that modernization will do away with them. On the contrary, the social sciences tend to accept Latin America's heterogeneity and the coexistence of diverse historical temporalities that are articulated to a degree but not dissolved in a uniform style of globalization. Multitemporal and multicultural heterogeneity is not an obstacle that needs removal but a necessary piece of information for any development and integration program.

However, the free-trade agreements that promote greater economic integration (such as NAFTA among Mexico, the United States, and Canada; MERCOSUR and other accords among Latin American countries) have little interest in the possibilities and obstacles presented by greater social disintegration and the low level of cultural integration in the continent. The cultural policies of each country and their exchanges with others are still programmed as if economic globalization and technological innovations had not already begun to reconfigure identities, beliefs, conceptualizations of what is one's own, and one's connections to others.

Indigenous Peoples and Globalization

In order to understand the current challenges of the multicultural character of Latin American development projects, we should distinguish between two of its modalities: on the one hand, its multiple ethnicities; on the other, the multicultural outcome of modern forms of segmentation and the organization of culture in industrialized societies.

Indigenous rebellions and mobilizations bring home the importance of Latin America's multiethnic relations. Their complexity, however, is quite evident in everyday life circumstances. Many branches of our economies cannot develop without the participation of the 30 million indigenous people who live in Latin America. These groups possess differentiated territories, their own languages (whose speakers are increasing in certain regions), and work and consumption habits that distinguish them. Two and a half million Aymaras, 700,000 Mapuches, more than half a million Mixtecos, 2 million Mayas, 2 million Nahuas and 2 million Quichés, and approximately 10 million Quechuas have remained a fundamental part of Chile, Bolivia, Peru, Ecuador, Guatemala, and Mexico throughout their five centuries–long resistance.

There is no dearth of research on what these multiethnic relations represent in processes of modernization and integration. As modernization becomes problematic and it is obvious that metropolitan models of development are not applicable mechanically in Latin America, that version of history that considered modern technologies incompatible with non-Western traditions is no longer compelling. It is thus feasible to focus on the sometimes positive role of cultural diversity in economic growth and in popular strategies of resistance. On this view, ethnic and religious solidarity is seen as contributing to social cohesion and production techniques and traditional consumption habits are understood to be the basis of alternative forms of development.[1]

In some societies, consensus is achieved through multicultural policies that recognize diverse modes of economic organization and political representation. Some examples are ethnodevelopment programs in various Latin American countries, legislation to guarantee the autonomy of indigenous peoples on Nicaragua's Atlantic Coast, and juridical reforms of ethnic issues that are currently being negotiated in Mexico. These are examples of a partial shift from paternalistic *indigenismo* to modes of greater self-determination.[2] But these attempts at reformulation are not instituted without resistance from racist elites, who still see indigenous cultures as antiquated remnants or mere survivals that are of interest only to folklorists and tourists. On the other hand, many indigenous groups refuse to be integrated, even in pluralist societies, because they consider ethnicities to be "potential nations," completely autonomous political unities.[3]

Neoliberal economic policies have intensified these conflicts. In the past decade, they accentuated poverty and marginalization among Indians and mestizos, and they continue to aggravate migration, displacement, and struggles over land and political power. Intercultural conflicts and racism are on the increase in many national border areas and in all large cities on the continent. Never before has it been so necessary to develop education, communications, and labor-regulation policies in the interest of greater interethnic democratic coexistence. In countries such as Peru and Colombia, peasant and urban economic conditions have deteriorated, spurring guerrilla movements, alliances between peasant struggles and narcotraffickers, and other explosive expressions of social disintegration. The segregationist fundamentalism of ethnic or paraethnic movements such as Sendero Luminoso only makes it more difficult to implement integration projects. In the United States, the restructuring of labor conditions and increasing racism have led to intensified repression of Latin American migrants, contradicting the integrative tendencies of free-trade agreements.

Despite the social upheavals that continue to vex intercultural relations, an analysis of the issues raised by these relations cannot be understood only in terms of the antagonism between dominant and subaltern groups. There are also promising changes in some government policies and new modes of relating traditions to modernization among indigenous groups.

Presently there are movements that balance their energetic claims for cultural and political autonomy with demands for full integration in modern development. They appropriate modern forms of knowledge as well as technological and cultural resources. They combine traditional healing procedures with allopathic medicine, ancient techniques of artisanal and peasant production with international credit and the use of computers. They seek autonomous democratic changes in their regions and egalitarian integration in modern nations. Guatemalan, Mexican, and Brazilian peasants send fax reports on the violation of human rights to international organizations. Indians from many different countries use video and E-mail to lobby for the defense of alternative ways of life.

At least in these cases, the problems of socioeconomic integration do not seem to ensue from the incompatibility between tradition and modernization. The failure of globalizing policies stems from a lack of flexibility in modernization programs, cultural incomprehension in their application, and, of course, the persistence of discriminatory habits in institutions and among hegemonic groups.[4] State reform in the guise of deregulation of services and subordination of public responsibilities to private interests does very little to expand the social agency of these multiple styles of life and the various forms of participation of marginalized sectors.

The Failure to Coordinate Cultural Policies and Consumption

The problems raised by multicultural phenomena at the end of this century cannot be reduced to multiethnic conflicts, nor to the coexistence of diverse regions within each nation. The forms of thought and life connected to local or national territories are only one part of cultural development. For the first time in history, the majority of commodities and messages received in each nation have not been produced in their own territory, do not result from the particular relations of production, and do not convey meanings connected exclusively with given regions. They operate, in our view, according to a transnational, deterritorialized system of production and diffusion.

Since the 1950s, the principal means of access to cultural commodities, aside from schooling, are the electronic communications media. The number of homes with radio and television in Latin America is equal to, and in some areas even greater than, that of homes in which family members have completed primary school. Although textbooks have provided a modest integration of Latin America, they are usually limited to a national-historical perspective and often distort the history of neighboring countries. These shortcomings are not overcome by the historically weak information and "up-to-the-minute world reports" on television and radio. Our enormous consumption of the mass media, greater than that of the metropolitan countries, as pointed out earlier, is not nourished by endogenous media production with better information and greater potential to bring Latin American countries together. Like cinema, television—and radio to a lesser degree—give priority to information and entertainment that originates in the United States. The representation of the diversity of national cultures is low in all of our nations, and there is even less airtime given to the cultures of other Latin American countries.

As we near the end of the century, we must turn to the actions and decisions of those responsible for cultural policies if we are to deal effectively with the problems raised by the culture industries (the primary agents) and globalization (the main tendency) for our multicultural societies. We also need to ask who can be integrated into these processes and what are the conditions for the democratization of transnational integration.

The following summarizes the approaches taken by those organizations most involved in dealing with (or neglecting) these problems:

1. State cultural policies are still focused on the preservation of monuments and folkloric heritages, and in the promotion of the fine arts (visual arts, theater, classical music), whose audiences are diminishing. Public action regarding electronic industries has been reduced to the privatization of radio and television stations as well as other circuits of mass diffusion, precisely those in which there have been attempts to sustain—almost always with little success—artistic and information programs that represent cultural diversity.

2. In contrast, large transnational private corporations (mostly U.S.-based, but also Latin American–based conglomerates such as Televisa and Rede Globo) have dedicated themselves for decades to the most profitable and most influential communications media. They have thus penetrated into family life and become the principal organizers of mass entertainment and information. Some Latin American corporations have produced recreational programs with broad transnational coverage, thus favoring a greater presence of national or "Hispano-American" themes and styles. Recent audience surveys show that they have high receptivity among the popular classes. More educated people prefer U.S. TV series, films, and music.[5] But the main question today, in my view, is not how many foreign or national messages circulate (although this may still be important), but rather the disdain or apathy of all programs (whether *Dallas, Cristina,* or *Siempre en domingo*) toward minority or regional cultures that have not been sanctioned by world folklore. Also deplorable is the censorship of debates about society itself and the lack of a diversity of information indispensable for the construction of citizenship and integration with other countries in the region.

3. The cultural actions of international organizations and those promoted by the meetings of ministers of culture reproduce on a Latin American scale the view of states, which gives priority to high culture,

on the one hand, and monuments and folkloric heritage, on the other. They give preference to a conservationist vision of identity and to an integrationist view based on traditional cultural goods and institutions. For example, of the sixty-seven projects recognized by UNESCO as activities of the "World Decade for Cultural Development" in Latin America in 1990–91, twenty-eight were dedicated to conservation of cultural heritage; seventeen to participation in cultural life and development; ten to the cultural dimension of development; eight to advancement of creativity and activity in the arts; three to the relation between culture, science, and technology; and only one to the mass media.[6]

Some Latin American governments have recently signed accords to facilitate the exchange of books, works of art, and antiquities through customs houses. Mutual cooperation programs have also been created. Worthy of mention are book collections such as the Biblioteca Ayacucho and the Biblioteca Popular de Latinoamérica y el Caribe; the journal supplement series Perio-libros, which includes works by prominent writers and artists; the decision to create a Latin American Fund for the Arts and another for Cultural Development; Latin American endowed chairs and Latin American and Caribbean Culture Houses in each country. All of these are definite advances in the mutual knowledge of the continent's nations. But these measures are limited to the field of written culture and "classical" plastic arts and music.

Meanwhile, the Working Group on Cultural Policies of the Latin American Social Science Council (CLACSO) has carried out research on cultural consumption in large Latin American cities that offers data similar to ours in Mexico City. For example, audiences for high culture do not exceed 10 percent of the population.[7] It is no doubt necessary to expand support for literature and the nonindustrialized arts, but at the end of the twentieth century it does not seem convincing to say that we are promoting cultural development and integration if we lack public policies for the mass media through which 90 percent of the inhabitants of this continent inform and entertain themselves.

4. Cultural resources involving everything from traditional artisanal knowledges to radio and video programs also circulate in nongovernmental organizations and associations of independent artists and media workers. Festivals, exhibitions and workshops, networks of alternative audiovisual programs, magazines, and books in which cultural development is documented—all of these are sponsored with scarce local funding and a great amount of free work, sometimes with subsidies from universities and international foundations. According to a directory put

out by the Institute for Latin America, there are more than five thousand independent groups of education, culture, and communications producers in our region. We value their contributions toward the formation and organization of popular sectors in defense of their rights, and toward the documentation of their life conditions and cultural production. But their actions are strictly of local scope and cannot be taken as a substitute for the actions of states. These independent groups almost never include the mass media and consequently have little influence over the majority's cultural habits and ways of thinking.

That states, corporations, and independent organizations work in isolation hinders the development of multicultural societies in Latin America; instead, it produces greater segmentation and inequality in consumption, impoverishment of endogenous production, and discouragement of international integration. In recent years, the reduction of public investment and weak action on the part of private enterprise have produced the following paradox: greater trade among Latin American countries and with metropolitan ones is promoted at the same time that we produce ever fewer books, films, and records. Integration is encouraged at the same time that we have fewer things to export and lower salaries reduce what majorities can consume.

The drawbacks are even more dramatic with regard to Latin America's access to cutting-edge technologies and communications highways: satellites, computers, faxes, and the other media that provide information necessary to make decisions and innovate. The subordination of Latin American countries will get even worse with the elimination of free-trade agreements, trade barriers to foreign products, and the few surviving subsidies for local technological development. We will be left more vulnerable to transnational capital and cultural trends devised outside the region as there is an increase in cultural and scientific dependence on cutting-edge communications technologies, which require high financial investments and generate more rapid innovations. The multiculturalism generated by these trends does not represent diverse historical traditions but rather stratification resulting from the unequal access to advanced communications by countries and sectors internal to each society.

How do the modes of access to transnational communications systems produce new forms of sociocultural stratification? The incorporation into global culture of the great majorities, especially in peripheral countries, is limited exclusively to the first phase of audiovisual industries: free entertainment and information on radio and television. Small sectors of the middle and popular classes have updated and upgraded their information as citizens through access to the second stage of the media, which includes cable television, environmental and health education, as well as political information on video, and so on. Only small fractions of the corporate, political, and academic elite are connected to the most dynamic forms of communication, to that third stage that includes fax, E-mail, satellite dishes, as well as the informational and playful interactivity of aficionado videomakers and horizontally organized international networks. In some cases, a handful of popular groups gain access to these latter circuits through the dissemination of community newspapers, radio stations, and video production.

The extension of the last two models of communication is a key condition for the development of democratic forms of citizenship today. People need access to international information and must have the capacity to intervene in meaningful ways in global and regional integration processes. The multinational complexity of problems such as environmental contamination, drug traffic, and technological innovations requires information that transcends local spaces still circumscribed by nations, and coordinated action in a supranational public sphere.[8]

What is being done in Latin America to develop the forms of citizenship that require the most advanced and interactive forms of cultural diffusion and consumption? If we believe that endogenous production and the representation of regional interests in these fields require not only the organization of civil society but also state initiatives, then we need to keep track of the amounts invested to this end.

Latin America has more than 8.3 percent of the world's population but only 4.3 percent of engineers and scientists active in research and development, and it only invests 1.3 percent of all the resources in this field.[9] These figures raise questions about the participation of a continent such as Latin America in international markets and about its capacity for self-management in the future.

Cultural Integration in an Era of Free Trade

The multicultural integration of Latin America and the Caribbean requires constitutional and political reforms that guarantee the rights of diverse groups in the context of globalization, that promote understanding and respect for differences in education and in traditional forms of interaction. But it is also the responsibility of public institutions to develop programs to facilitate reciprocal information and knowledge in culture industries that provide mass communications—radio, TV, film, video, and interactive electronic systems—to different peoples and subgroups within each society.

We need policies to promote the formation of a Latin American audiovisual space. In an era in which film, video, records, and other industrial forms of communication are unable to recoup their high costs if distributed exclusively in a given country, the integration of Latin America becomes an indispensable resource for the expansion of markets, thus facilitating our own production. I would like to mention three proposals that adumbrate what these policies might look like:

1. The creation of common Latin American markets for books, film, television, and video, accompanied by concrete measures to promote production and favor the free circulation of cultural commodities. (The steps taken in this direction, more declarative than practical, demonstrate the need for more fine-tuned diagnostics of the consumption habits in Latin American countries as well as their most determined public policies.)

2. The establishment of quotas for minimum screen time, radio airtime, and other Latin American cultural commodities in each country of the region. (Notice that we do not recommend returning to the narrow policy that established a 50 percent quota for national music and cinema; this new suggestion is inspired by a 1993 Spanish law that took into account regional conditions of production and circulation and decreed that movie houses in cities with more than 125,000 inhabitants should show 30 percent European films.) The promotion of a Latin American market for cultural commodities will not be effective unless it is accompanied by measures that protect that production through its circulation and consumption.

3. The creation of a Latin American Fund for Audiovisual Production and Diffusion. Its role would be to finance in part film, television, and video production, to provide smooth coordination of state, corporate, and civil institutions, to imagine new channels of distribution (video rental outlets, high-quality cultural programs, mass audiences for national and regional television networks, a Latin American cable signal).[10]

Free-trade agreements should not foment an indiscriminate opening of markets, but take into consideration the unequal development of national systems as well as the protection of the rights of production, communication, and consumption by ethnic and minority groups. It is necessary to regulate the participation of foreign capital, including that of larger Latin American economies or of transnational corporations based in the region, in order to prevent monopolies from strangling the cultural industries of the smaller countries. But more important than restrictions, it is necessary to seek collaboration agreements that balance the relations between "truly exporting countries (Brazil, Mexico), emerging exporters (Argentina, Chile, Venezuela), and those that only import (the rest)."[11]

A democratic multicultural development will be realized in each nation only if there are favorable conditions for the expansion of regional, ethnic, and minority radio and television stations; or at least of programming designated for the expression of different cultures, subject to collective public interest rather than commercial profitability.

The promotion of these policies requires a reformulation of the role of the state and of civil society as representatives of the public interest. It has been said that it is necessary to put an end to overly protectionist populist states in order to reduce the risks of centralization, clientelism, and bureaucratic corruption. But after a decade of privatization we have not seen private corporations make telephones or airlines function any better, or even elevate the quality of radio and television programs. Rather than mire ourselves in the quagmire of the state versus the market, we have to create policies to coordinate the diverse actors who participate in cultural production and intermediation.

The goal is not to reinstall the proprietary state, but to rethink the role of the state as an arbiter or guardian against subordinating collective needs for information, recreation, and innovation to the profit motive. To guard against the risks of state intervention and the frivolous homogenizaton of diverse cultures by the market, it is necessary to get beyond the binary option between the two and to create spaces where the multiple initiatives of civil society can emerge: social movements, artists' groups, independent radio and television stations, unions, ethnic groups, and associations of consumers, radio listeners, and television viewers. Only the multiplication of actors can favor a democratic cultural development and the representation of multiple identities. The new role of states and international organizations (UNESCO, OAS, SELA [Latin American Economic System], ALADI [Latin American Association for Integration], etc.) will be to reconstruct public space, understood as a multicultural collective space where diverse agents (states, corporations, and independent groups) will be able to negotiate agreements for the development of public interests. Such changes in communications and cultural policies are necessary for the exercise of diverse forms of responsible citizenship, as conditioned by transformations in sociocultural settings, current forms of consumption, and transnational integration.

Part III

Negotiation, Integration, and Getting Unplugged

Chapter 9

Negotiation of Identity in Popular Classes?

Any serious attempt at rethinking citizenship should endeavor to understand how the process of negotiation relates to the other concepts invoked in the title of this chapter. Indeed, recent studies seeking to redefine the concepts of identity, class, and the popular have taken the analysis of negotiation processes as a key heuristic. But I place the question mark at the end of the title to ask whether or not negotiation is possible in the current context of the restructuring of political and communicational spheres.

Without playing down the history of each of these terms or what specific sets of issues they evoke, I would like to deal conjointly with the crises of identity, social classes, and the popular. What makes this joint analysis possible is the convergence of crises in each domain: ontologico-fundamentalist conceptions of identity, historico-dialectical conceptions of class, and melodramatic conceptions of the popular. Historically, the trajectory of this triple crisis might be characterized as the passage from the epic affirmation of popular identities, which is an integral feature of national societies, to the acknowledgment of transnational conflicts and negotiations in the constitution of popular and other identities.

As this century winds down, however, we are also experiencing a reorganization of symbolic and political markets resulting in the dissolution of the spaces of negotiation. We have already noted in previous chapters that the subordination of political action to mass-mediated spectacle undermines the importance of parties, unions, strikes, and public mass demonstrations, that is, those very instances in which negotiation takes place.

I should explain that in speaking of "negotiation of identity," I will be concerned only with cultural aspects and will only occasionally refer to the political dimensions of negotiation. Likewise, I focus only on questions of daily life, or of the interaction of cultural policies and popular viewers and listeners, rather than on negotiation as a matter of institutions, labor unions, or well-organized movements.[1]

Fundamentalists and Eclectics

Today a reflection on these matters should begin with a critique of *ontologico-fundamentalist conceptions of identities,* which we have carried out in part in the preceding pages. We examined the waning of romanticism and nationalism as ideological bases for conceptualizing identity. We can no longer consider the members of society as belonging to one homogeneous culture, with a corresponding single distinct and coherent identity. The transnationalization of the economy and symbols has eroded the verisimilitude of this mode of legitimizing identities. If we follow Arjun Appadurai's classification, there are at least five contemporary processes that challenge this territorial and nationalist characterization of discreet identities: (1) *ethnoscapes:* demographic movements of immigrants, tourists, refugees, exiles, and temporary workers; (2) *technoscapes:* the flows produced by technologies and multinational corporations; (3) *finanscapes:* currency exchanges in international markets; (4) *mediascapes:* repertoires of images and information created for planetary distribution by culture industries; and (5) *ideoscapes:* representative ideological models of what might be called Western modernity, that is, conceptions of democracy, liberty, welfare, and human rights that transcend the definitions of particular identities.[2] To these ideological matrices, I would add other forms of traditional non-Western thought (for example, Eastern, Latin American) that are diffused throughout other continents.

Confronted by these contemporary transformations that have relativized the foundations of national identities, some have turned to popular cultures as the last preserve of traditions. As ahistorical essences, they are appealed to as the last resistance to globalization. The recrudescence of nationalisms, regionalisms, and ethnicisms at the end of the twentieth century acts to reduce the *historical work* of the incessant construction and readaptation of identities to a simple exaltation of local traditions. The warlike fundamentalism of many movements—ranging from those in the ex-Yugoslavia and the ex-USSR to certain groups in Latin America—annuls any space of transaction. For such groups, identity is not something that can be negotiated; it is simply affirmed and defended.

These movements express, in part, identitarian demands that have been suppressed or incompletely incorporated in the constitution of modern nations. In some cases, their dogmatism and violence are proportional to the oppression suffered by broad social sectors and to the stupidity demonstrated by the neoliberal mode of globalization in ignoring ethnic and regional particularities. Why, then, do we claim that these fundamentalist reactions are in crisis and have no future? Limiting ourselves to Latin America, it can be said that such ways of "resolving" identity questions are untenable in countries with a very hetereogeneous sociocultural composition that have been undergoing centuries-long processes of modern internationalization. It is quite unlikely and impracticable that the multiple ways of being Argentine, Brazilian, or Peruvian can be reduced to a fixed package of archaic features, to a monochrome and ahistoric heritage.

Policies that acknowledge the important contribution of negotiation are based on the constitutive role of transactions in the development of cultures. I have already referred to anthropological studies of Latin American indigenous groups' strategies of work, commerce, and consumption. The energetic defense of their ethnic heritage and their political autonomy is not at odds with their intercultural transactions and their critical integration into modernity. Indigenous peoples often seek the most advanced techniques of production and consumption of industrial commodities, and demand access to education and to mass communications. Although there may be ethnic movements that resist Westernization, broad sectors nevertheless appropriate knowledge as well as modern technological and cultural resources.

Adopting modernity does not mean that they necessarily substitute their traditions. Indigenous groups are often eclectic because they have discovered that the pure preservation of traditions is not always the most appropriate path to reproduce and better their situation. As I showed in a previous book dealing with the transformation in craft production,[3] the negotiated reformulations of their iconography and traditional practices are tactics that enable them to expand trade and earn money that will permit them to better their daily life. Multicultural consumption, through which they seek to satisfy their needs by taking advantage of their traditional resources and those of different modern societies, reveals great flexibility in how popular sectors reconstitute themselves.

We should not, however, idealize the imaginative adaptations of traditional groups. As Eduardo Menéndez's research shows, the transactions of popular sectors in combining traditional and scientific medical practices supposes "that they accept and 'solve' their problems within the limits established by the dominant classes." Within these limits, subaltern groups try to achieve effectivity through self-exploitation and the subordinated appropriation of "external" production.[4] In contrast to the analyses of Friedrich Barth and R. C. Harman,[5] who understand transactions as relations of reciprocity, the choice of intermediary means of negotiation, adopted as their own by popular groups, demonstrates that it is also difficult to shake loose of the conditions of oppression. In the midst of economic recession, these groups demand higher salaries at the same time that they limit their consumption. Their reaction to political hegemony, which they are unable to modify, is to transact personal arrangements to obtain individual benefits. The meaning of these acts can only be considered as an impoverishment if they are interpreted within the domination–subordination paradigm. A broader and more detailed consideration of the daily interactions of subaltern majorities reveals that Latin American countries are hybrid societies where different forms of disputing and negotiating the meaning of modernity are in constant contention.

From Epic to Melodrama: The Postrevolution

The reconversion of traditional symbolic heritages in contemporary economic and symbolic markets erodes the coherence and future receptivity of the fundamentalist epic. However, the binary opposition between what is and is not popular continues to organize a great part of political and academic thought, not only in the traditional currents of the right but also in those of the left, not only in folklore studies but also in sociological research on modern processes. This is borne out in what remains of Marxism, as well as other theories that deal with social conflict. Their historicism had greater explanatory power than the natural-ization of the popular by fundamentalists. The notions of class and class struggle served to show that identity is modified in keeping with historical changes in the productive forces and struggles among the relations of production. Consequently, the popular was no longer defined by a series of internal features or a repertoire of preindustrial contents, predating the massification of culture, as is the case in national-populist doctrines and in the majority of folklore studies. The Gramscian current, which best represents this historicism, characterized the popular not according to its essence but by its *position* in relation to the hegemonic classes.

It is not the purpose of this chapter to analyze the waning receptivity of the Gramscian framework as a perhaps too mechanical effect of the collapse of so-called socialist political systems and projects. I am more interested in exploring what this model facilitates and makes difficult from a heuristic perspective, particularly in the style of research that it foments. These difficulties emerge precisely from the scarce or empty role attributed to negotiation in many of these studies.

Neo-Gramscian anthropologists—especially in Italy, where the most valuable contributions to the study of the popular have been realized—generally avoid the risk of the Manichaean. They pay attention to the "network of reciprocal exchanges, borrowings, and conditionings" among hegemonic and popular cultures.[6] However, the numerous Latin American studies that adopted this orientation in the 1970s and 1980s reduced the complex relations between hegemony and subalternity to a simple bipolar confrontation. The most political and voluntaristic Gramscian currents emphasized the autonomy and resistance of the popular classes with little substantiation. Many research projects turned into a partial catalog of the actions through which popular sectors gave continuity to their traditions of opposition to hegemonic ideology and politics. Certain tendencies of anthropological ethnicism and local "grassroots" thought still share this schematic view.

The defeat of popular movements in recent years brings to the center of debate a question ignored by those who base their research and political practice on this hypothesis of popular autonomy, which is associated with revolutionary or insurrectional voluntarism. The question is: Why do the subaltern classes collaborate so frequently with those who oppress them? For example, they vote in elections, and make pacts with their oppressors in matters of daily life and in political confrontations.

Answering this question requires a more complex conception of power and culture. We suggest that the reduction of interactions among classes to permanent conflicts, and of politics to war, overlooked the complicities and reciprocal uses that knit the web of relations between hegemonic and subaltern groups. The construction of this new perspective in sociology, anthropology, and communications has been achieved by a triple reconceptualization: of power, the action of subalterns, and the structure of intercultural relations.

Thanks to Michel Foucault's contributions,[7] and empirical studies on social movements, power is no longer seen only as top-down domination over the dominated but as decentered, multidetermined political relations, whose conflicts and asymmetries are tempered through compromises among unequally positioned actors. Not even in monopolistic concentrations of power, intensified by neoliberal policies, is there an omnipotent manipulation of sociocultural relations. A range of studies, from anthropological research on government institutions that work with popular cultures to investigations into the strategies of communications corporations, have demonstrated that power is won and renewed through centers that are disseminated, initiatives that are multipolar, actions and messages that are adapted to the variety of addressees and cultural references that in every case provide an order that shapes identities.

For example, in our own research on the Fondo Nacional de Fomento a las Artesanías [National Fund for the Promotion of Crafts] in Mexico and on the private businessmen who trade in these products, we found that the relative consensus achieved by them was a result of the fact that not only do they not exploit artisans economically but they even offer them services: loans, assistance with bank credits, technical and stylistic training to increase their marketability, and help with the rules of commerce, which artisans do not fully understand.

The "solidarity" expressed through these interactions does not diminish the degree of oppression suffered by the majority of the thirty million indigenous Latin Americans, and among them the eleven to fourteen million artisans. However, when economic domination is combined with an exchange of services, it is understandable that their first course of action is not confrontation. Rather, their actions reveal them to be a complex combination of workers, subordinates, clients, and beneficiaries who try to take advantage of the rivalry among institutions and private agencies.[8] Symbolic interactionists might say that negotiation is a key component in the functioning of institutions and sociocultural fields. Identities are constituted not only in the bipolar conflict between classes but also in contexts of institutional action—in a factory, a hospital, a school—that operate insofar as all of their participants, whether hegemonic or subaltern, consider themselves part of a "negoti-ated order."[9] Conflicts among different and unequal actors are processed within the (revisable or negotiated) order established by institutions and more or less institutionalized everyday structures of interaction.

How are subaltern urban groups positioned in relation to conflicts and negotiation? In answer to this question, I will mention briefly two evaluation studies of cultural policies in two very different countries, Mexico and Argentina, that nevertheless share one characteristic: asym-metric and intense intercultural relations.

The first study was conducted in Tijuana, on the border between Mexico and the United States. We evaluated the activities of the Pro-grama Cultural de las Fronteras [border cultural program].[10] This pro-gram was created by the Mexican government in 1982 to "affirm Mexi-can identity" on the northern border against the threat posed by increasing U.S. influence. The activities of this program were guided by appeal to a Mesoamerican identity more in congruence with the central section of the country and with traditional features deriving from the evolu-tion of indigenous and colonial cultures, which were stronger in the center and south than in the arid lands of northern Mexico. The largely bilingual inhabitants of Tijuana and other border cities, whose interac-tion with North Americans has led to exuberant hybridization, claim that they are no less Mexican than their compatriots from other regions. Indeed, they argue that the sixty million crossings per year between Ti-juana and San Diego keep them constantly aware of difference and in-equality. Consequently, they claim that they have a less idealized image of the United States than the residents of the capital who are similarly influenced by television and imported consumer commodities. They add that those who encounter U.S. culture from a distance, through the consumption of images and objects detached from social interac-tion, are subject to a more abstract and passive "gringo" influence. In contrast, those who negotiate economic and cultural matters on a daily basis necessarily distinguish between what is one's own and what is for-eign, between what they admire and what they reject from the United States. In this regard, it is instructive to consider how migrant Indians organize on both sides of the border according to their ethnic group and the region from which they come (Oaxaca, Michoacán, Guerrero). At the same time that they express their original identity in specific spaces and rituals, they also reformulate their cultural patrimony, acquiring knowledges and customs that enable them to reposition themselves in new labor, sociocultural, and political relations. They undoubtedly continue to be Mexican (of which U.S. racism continually reminds them), but their identity is polyglot and cosmopolitan, endowed with a flexible capacity to process new information and understand habits that are different from those of their original symbolic matrices.

The other study, which complements these observations, examined how the Programa Cultural en Barrios [neighborhood cultural program] in the municipality of Buenos Aires fared in dealing with the needs and demands of Bolivian immigrants who enrolled in the program in Villa Soldati, one of the poorest zones of the Argentine capital.[11] Initiated in 1983 after the military dictatorship, this program was conceived as part of Raúl Alfonsín's governing policy. Aimed at democratizing access to culture and promoting new modes of political participation, it endeavored to eradicate what survived of authoritarianism in the social fabric. On the one hand, the program sought to deliver cultural goods that were almost always restricted to elites (conferences, concerts, and art workshops), the hypothesis being that democratization of opportunities would by itself bring about the appropriation of those goods. On the other hand, some cultural promoters who celebrated the ethnic origin of the inhabitants encouraged activities rooted in the local culture. Some of these, such as the celebration of the Virgin of Copacabana, were successful; others, which also seemed to be related to what the Bolivian migrants considered "their own," found little receptivity. One of the reasons for the difference in uptake was that the inhabitants of the barrio were organizing their culture in order to adapt it to the demands of living and working in Buenos Aires. For example, it was observed that among the new generations the affirmation of their own culture did not automatically entail the continuity of language and other traditional features of the group. For example, consider the answers of one young Bolivian who studied at the university but continued to live in the barrio:

> "Have you ever considered learning Quechua?"
>
> "No, because one tends to do what is practical in everyday life. I would only need to learn Quechua if I wanted to become an anthropologist, return to Bolivia, to a little town in Bolivia, or maybe if I wanted to speak with a newly arrived Bolivian woman to explain to her... I don't know... something. Then, for example, I would need to learn... But, I don't know, you leave behind those things that are not going to help you..."
>
> "Does your mother speak it?"

"Not all of the time . . . we never made an effort to learn."

"And what does she think of your not learning Quechua?"

"Well, she too doesn't think it's so necessary. She sees us thrust into this society and . . . simply believes that we have to live here, in this society with whatever exists here, with what prevails in this culture."

It is not common for shantytown dwellers to express themselves in so complex a manner. I deliberately chose the son of Quechua speakers who was enrolled in the university. The oscillation between his original circumstances and his acquired intellectual position gives us an idea of the speed of transitions, especially in the urban areas of Latin America, and the broad range of negotiations through which these actors move. This example also reveals that the loss of language is not necessarily accompanied by the loss of ethnic cohesion. Cohesion is provided by the *residential community* in an urban barrio in Buenos Aires, experienced by Bolivians as if it were their own territory. Their experience is analogous to that of Mixteco or Purépecha migrants from Mexico who take up residence in the poor barrios of California in the United States.

This research showed that the continuity of the group is also achieved through the conservation of family and festive traditions, the strongest of which are *compadrazgo* [godparenthood] and other "non-modern" bonds of power, often in contradiction with the democratization of social and cultural relations. How can a program that is democratic and respectful of a group's structures be established if the structures in question are paternalistic, authoritarian, and based on bonds of blood rather than affinity? Moreover, what if the state that promotes democratization is also racked by these same nondemocratic characteristics?

The migrants who adapted to life in Argentina and to the large city demanded in turn that cultural promoters accommodate their cultural codes, formulated in part through processes of apprenticeship in negotiation with the state. They had learned that the different sections of the bureaucracy with which they dealt generated different images: a "clientelist and corrupt" state, a "bureaucratic and inefficient" state, a "public and no-charge" state, a "welfare" state, or an "authoritarian" state. Consequently, they guided themselves according to the following rule: "Our strategy depends on what bureaucrat we deal with." These fragmentary and sometimes contradictory representations of the state are articulated in the structures of bossism and clientelism, in the hierarchical and asymmetric hierarchies proper to the political culture of each popular group.

It is not easy to discern what counts as popular within this play of relations. If we define the popular as the traditional and local culture of a given group, it seems to characterize only private family life or feasts. Meanwhile, modern hegemonic culture is acquired by these groups in order to move within the public world. Yet this culture is not only nor primarily part of enlightened modernity, which is usually expressed in objective and democratic rules for political representation. It is also a complex amalgam of modern and traditional relations of power. Hence the paradox: those who sought to bring democracy to the locality soon learned that they had to make pacts with neighborhood bosses in order to gain access to the dwellers and to insert themselves into local sociocultural structures.

The difficulties that "culturally well-meaning" promoters have in gaining a space within the paternalism of the state and vis-à-vis the mixture of resistance and authoritarianism of subaltern groups reveal that the "popular" cannot be defined neatly according to the criteria of socioeconomic class analysis. The culturally hybrid features resulting from cross-class interaction force us to recognize that alongside struggle there is also negotiation. And negotiation does not appear as a process external to the constitution of the actors, to which they might resort on occasion for political convenience. It is a mode of existence, something intrinsic to the groups that take part in the social drama. Negotiation is located within collective subjectivity, in the most unconscious culture of politics and daily life. Its hybrid character, which in Latin America derives from a long history of mixtures and syncretisms, is accentuated in contemporary societies through complex interactions between the traditional and the modern, the popular and the elite, the subaltern and the hegemonic.

What do we understand by *popular* once we accept this perspective? It is not a scientific concept, with a series of distinctive features that can be univocally defined. It does not, therefore, warrant an epic vision of its history or its practices, according to which what is "popular" is neatly and firmly opposed to whatever is not. *Popular* designates the position of certain actors in the drama of struggle and transaction. That is why some of us have suggested shifting from an epic characterization of the popular to a theatrical or melodramatic one.

I would like to recommend reformulating the original question— Why do popular sectors collaborate with those who oppress them?—as well as the following one: Why does the melodrama, from tango and Mexican film to the police beat and the *telenovela,* have greater receptivity among popular sectors than any other genre? Jesús Martín Barbero's research on the *telenovela* identifies the "recognition drama" as the pivotal element of these narratives: the son recognized by his father or mother, the wife by her husband, lover, or neighbors. Instead of references to the social contract and large sociopolitical structures, the melodrama gives greater importance to other primordial forms of sociability, such as kinship, neighborhood, territorial, and friendship solidarities. Martín Barbero asks, "To what extent does the success of melodrama in these countries relate to the failure of social and political institutions that have developed without any concern for that other sociality, and that are incapable of assuming its cultural density?"[12]

From Melodrama to Video Games: Postpolitics

A major feature of the 1980s and 1990s has been the disappearance of spaces for political negotiation. In this regard, *communications* analysis will provide insights analogous to those of *anthropological* microsocial analysis by discovering the role of transactions and pacts in social conflicts. *Communications* research helps us understand how the reorganization of social interaction by video politics strangles possibilities for negotiation.

Political struggles have become "abstract" owing to the incapacity of bureaucratic leaders to deal with the sociocultural density of everyday life. This abstraction is exacerbated as direct action gives way to electronic mediation. The first decades of Latin American populism, from the 1930s to the 1950s, also saw the expansion of the first mass media (press and radio). Popular participation, simultaneously promoted and mediated by these communications agents, was combined with labor and political organization. Public spaces such as parliaments, and grassroots action such as street meetings and demonstrations, strikes, and *physical* confrontations between the actors of civil society and government powers, put "teeth" into the "concrete" forms of negotiation.

Nowadays, social conflict and the management of its transactions have been displaced to hermetic places, channeled by forces that the citizenry has no way of confronting. Where and by whom are decisions made about electoral campaigns that cost millions of dollars? What forms of monitoring are there for the image-engineering of candidates whose appeal is not based on their political platforms but on the opportunistic machinations of political *marketers?* Even the stylization of the product (the candidate's plastic surgery and change of dress, for which image consultants receive fat fees) is publicized by the press and television as part of the preelection political spectacle. This dissolution of the public sphere as a space for popular participation is aggravated by technobureaucratic decision making in neoliberal governments. The conflicts are negotiated by politicians (increasingly technicians rather than politicians in the traditional sense) and businessmen; labor unions and social movements find out about it in the newspapers and television newscasts. What is left for the citizens?

In this play of simulacra, the leaders who competed for the presidency of their respective countries in the last round of Latin American elections all share one feature: they do not want to be taken for politicians. Alberto Fujimori, who does not know karate, was photographed during the campaign in a white gi, in the act of cracking a brick with a karate chop. He looked like an angry angel, remarked Beatriz Sarlo, a prophet, a karate fighter who exploited his Japanese physiognomy. He was anything but a Peruvian politician. Carlos Menem and Fernando Collor de Mello were filmed engaging in sports, dancing, or chatting about frivolous topics with everyday people. Here the contact with popular culture is sought through the construction of mass-media icons, not through the exchange of information or the analysis of the problems of popular sectors. There are no "intellectual" discourses, nor direct confrontations or impromptu engagements with social conflicts. In this postpolitical phase, in which everything takes place without struggle, there also seems to be no place for negotiation. Everything is photographed, filmed, televised, and all the images are consumed.[13]

This tendency to substitute spectacle for conflicts became evident most eloquently when the Gulf War was presented as a video game. We did not see bodies in direct fighting—only the "representation *en abîme*" of a monitor screen displaying another monitor screen. Nor was there any debate, for which reason there was also no negotiation. Instead, we witnessed two unchanging rivals pitched in battle against each other with no explanation. In this video game, in which signs are replaced by simulacra, "any question of truth [disappears] (regardless of whether truth is defined as an effect of discourse or otherwise); all questions turn on efficiency, skill, velocity, and distance."[14]

When the difference between reality and the symbolic, and the question of the legitimacy of representations, are abolished—when everything is a simulacrum—there is no place for a reasoned confrontation of positions, nor for change, not even for negotiation. The struggle for identity disappears because there is no discourse that positions itself in relation to a reality of one's own. There is only an unordered succession of images, as in the video game, without external references to the visual pseudonarration.

Despite its all-encompassing intentions, video politics does not become the only form of culture. The mass receptivity of melodramas transmitted by television and other media, as well as the persistence of critical reflection and oppositional social movements, keep open the quest for recognition among people and questions about struggle among groups.

I would therefore like to hazard a conclusion that might prompt new investigations. Conflicts today are not limited to classes or groups. They are also found in two cultural trends: reasoned negotiation and critique or the simulacrum of consensus induced through a devotion to simulacra. There is no choice between two absolutes here, for simulacra, as we know, are part of the signifying relations of every culture. However, how we negotiate a compromise between both tendencies is decisive for whether democratic participation or authoritarian mediation will predominate in the future society.

Chapter 10

How Civil Society Speaks Today

It is said that when Jack Lang was the French minister of culture, upon being asked what he understood by the term *culture,* he answered: everything for which there is a General Directorate. The majority of cultural policies carried out by Latin American countries still seem mired in this bureaucratic inertia. Or, to express it more graphically, they are ruins from a lost era.

The critiques of government action and the analyses of sociocultural changes presented in this book deal with the inability of policies to respond to what takes place in civil society. Forty years after the electronic communications media appropriated the public-sphere scene and became the principal agents in shaping the collective imaginary, the ministers of culture still look after the fine arts. In the best of cases, they give some support to traditional popular culture, but they almost never have anything to say about modern urban cultures: rock, comics, *fotonovelas,* videos, that is, the media through which mass thought and sensibility move. They ignore the sites of consumption where the aesthetic foundations of citizenship take shape.[1]

State cultural bureaucracies still draw their interests, rhetorical styles, and communicative strategies from the era when literature, painting, and music provided the codes and key concepts for interpreting the world. They lack departments for dealing with video and informatics, and what is left, after privatization, of film and television production is relegated to the margins of the budget. Although politicians have learned in recent decades the importance of managing their mass images electronically, they manage their cultural budgets as if they were nineteenth-century leaders seeking to cast their magnificence in the luster of bronze sculpture.

This is not to say that cultural policy should surrender to the mass allure of ratings. We should not, of course, forget Brahms and Joyce, Alfonso Reyes and Heitor Villalobos, simply because they have few customers. When I point out that states give artificial respiration to concert halls and art and literature reviews, I am questioning only their exclusive support for these cultural forms, which in any case is insufficient: they give them just enough oxygen for them barely to survive. I belong to a group of advocates who still see the need for supporting high and popular traditions of preindustrial art as a means of discovering the memory of what has made us what we are. We ask, with less fascination, ingenuousness, and irresponsibility, if this voyage through technological culture and mass markets is worth the effort.[2]

Contemporary culture lives in tension between an accelerated modernization and the critiques of modernity. The most radical and lucid challenges of the 1990s to the sensibility, thought, and imaginary of the postindustrial era are brandished today by those who experienced the tumultuous breaks, renewals, and disillusionments of this second half of the twentieth century. Let me cite two examples, among the many that could be offered. The first is *Time* and *New York Review of Books* art critic Robert Hughes's collection of articles on the alliances between art, television, and markets. His assessment of the transformation of high and mass culture enables him to explain "the numbing eclecticism" of the art of the 1980s in New York. "Its imaginative drought recalls a sad Russian joke: nowadays when you place a phone order for a filet mignon it is delivered by television." Only a long-range perspective, rooted in the history of art, makes it possible to realize that the two hundred thousand artists that can be considered active in the United States today are no more important for the development of culture "than, say, the Japanese neopaladins that Charles Jencks categorizes as a subgroup left out of the history of architecture." You cannot expect more, says Hughes, from a period in which artists rewarded by the market resort to synthesizing fashions, dispensing with any "ideal of slow maturation," taking advantage of "whatever stylistic devices bring notoriety, without regard for the sterility that results over the long term."[3]

Besides homogenization and short-term commercial interests, Hughes also finds that U.S. art is menaced by judgmentalism, ranging from moral prescriptions to dogmatic conceptions of citizenship. I am interested in how he confronts the two moralisms: on the one hand, the puritanism and racism of those who censored Mapplethorpe's photographs or advocated cutting funding for public-supported radio; on the other hand, a populist multiculturalism that justifies exhibition of "kitschy farragos" or applauds ethnic groups for their "naive hobby crafts."[4] Neither the rejection of difference nor its unrestricted approval encourages art that "challenges, refines, criticizes," and "aims for excellence," which are the ways in which modern artists help citizens resist a submissive viewership. Hughes puts his hopes in artistic explorations that will continue to dispel the leveling, abstract illusions of Western democracy. He warns, however, that these possibilities will not flourish if artists fall prey to the dictates of the market or the well-meaning endeavors of a homogenizing multiculturalism. Aesthetic inquiry is still the means whereby differences of quality and intensity, perspective and experimentation emerge. Through it we realize that the coexistence of ethnicities and cultures, their unequal hybridization, do not constitute a happy, peaceful world family.

Nevertheless, not all art produced today shows this inability to relate to conflictive forms of citizenship. I am thinking, by way of contrast, of the "unplugged" singers of today's jazz-rock. Ever since Eric Clapton cut his *Unplugged* album and found millions of fans who preferred the acoustic versions of his greatest hits, MTV has sponsored, beginning in 1990, a series of de-electrified concerts, with fewer arrangements and simulations. Other musicians who had achieved celebrity using the playback and the clip also decided to re-create small jam sessions affording them a space in which to improvise and take risks. Sinéad O'Connor and Joe Satriani, Gilberto Gil and Stevie Ray Vaughan, and a hundred others in their wake, are cutting unplugged albums and turning down stadium concerts for more intimate concert halls. The market is too vigorous and astute to throw away the opportunity to use this revival of direct experience between musician and audience as a way of lifting sagging sales. Returning to the past as a way of generating new business was a lesson already learned in retro fashion, nostalgia films, and graphic design. But perhaps the most interesting outcome is the willingness of musicians and listeners to reencounter the moment in which music is composed, simply and interpersonally, with no touch-ups.

In the plastic arts, in music, and in any cultural creation, we necessarily swing between the plugged and the unplugged. One cannot do without international information, not only to be technologically and aesthetically up-to-date, but also to nourish symbolic production grounded in multicultural migrations, exchanges, and hybridizations. But there are moments too when we need to return what is our own, to our national or ethnic peculiarity, to personal interaction in our domestic spaces or to our modest individual quests.

Integration and competition with others can be stimulating, but there continue to exist local needs in the midst of globalization. I know that it is not necessarily tenable to lump together the dynamism of artistic creation and the demands for autonomy of social groups, especially oppressed ethnic minorities. But there is a coincidence between the experiments of some jazz and rock musicians who renounce some forms of intermediation—particularly electronic enhancement—and endeavor to capture the flavor of African and Latin American musics, and the mobilization of indigenous peoples and popular classes who question who benefits from transnational commercial integration and for what reasons, when they do not have paved roads, schools, transport, or any of the basic resources that would enable them to stand alongside others as peers.

Integrate or Unplug

I have tried to explain in this book why setting up a choice between these two options is not a good formulation. Unlike the epoch in which those who placed all their hopes in some magic transformation of the state were diametrically opposed to those who staked all change on the proletariat or the popular classes, now it is a matter of trying to remake the state and civil society in relation to each other. In order not to simplify what we mean by one or the other, we need to rethink simultaneously policies and forms of participation. This means that we have to understand ourselves as citizens and consumers.

It is clear that at the heart of this reformulation there is an attempt to reconceptualize the public sphere. Neither subordinated to the state nor dissolved in civil society, it is reconstituted time and again in the tension between both. I am therefore interested in the hermeneutic line of reasoning that incorporates Habermas's and Bakhtin's contributions:

the public sphere is a "field of competing traditions," "a space of het-eroglossia," in which "certain meanings and traditions are reinforced" (the role of the state), "but, in the process, new forces can attribute different meanings or emphases to the same concepts" (the role of civil society), thus avoiding the danger of exclusivity and authoritarianism.[5]

The future of multicultural society and the competitive participation of (material and symbolic) Latin American industries in the world market depends on how we combine these two notions of the public. After a decade that saw a spate of privatizations, too readily conceded by state leaders, it is now evident that private enterprise does not necessarily mean that telephones, airlines, or cultural communications function any better. This failure does not justify reinstalling the state as the guardian of territorial nationalism, or as an efficient administrator, or as the agent of populist forms of assistance. The real challenge is to revitalize the state as the representative of the public interest, as the arbiter or guarantor that will not allow the collective need for information, recreation, and innovation to be subordinated to commercial profitability.

To this end, it is necessary that cultural policies, political parties critical of neoliberalism, and social movements go beyond a Gutenbergian conception of culture and develop strategies for action in the media. We must, of course, also reformulate the reasons why we need "high culture," that is, schools, publishing houses, libraries, and public museums. But above all we need to imagine how to valorize the public interest in radio and television, in cutting-edge technologies, scientific experimentation, and aesthetic innovation that circulate through the mass media and information networks

Is it possible to unplug, or at least decondition, ourselves from hegemonic information networks? This question, which independent organizations rooted in "civil society" tried to answer in the 1960s and 1970s, has been much enriched since the 1980s by information networks. In the hard sciences, the use of modems has enabled the development of fluid international communications, with access to innovations for established and younger researchers. The costs are low and often paid by their institutions. In the social sciences, the process has been slower and perhaps there are not many possibilities of creating a scientific public space, in which qualitative information can be absorbed and transmitted, without reducing the sociocultural particularity of given countries or their contribution to differences of opinion and theoretical debates.

It seems to me that these conditions point up the opportunities and the limits of efforts to establish an alternative *sociopolitical public space.* Indeed, nongovernmental organizations and other international action initiatives benefit from uncensored rapid access to knowledge about conflicts in the ex-Yugoslavia or Chiapas, but there is still much to decide when wading through the hundreds of "pages" of unprioritized information that electronic listserves deposit every day on subscribers' computer screens. How does one assess opinions and rumors, how does one differentiate them from certified information, and how does one situate each fact in its proper historical and sociopolitical contexts when one lacks the direct experience of living in the region from whence they come? There were discrepancies in information about the events in Chiapas in 1994 among those directly involved, the press, and nongovernmental organizations that got their information through electronic means; these discrepancies revealed the ambivalences that these alternative modes of communication generate. On the one hand, they made it possible for a multiplicity of local, national, and international actors to exercise influence on the development of the conflict, above all, to defend human rights. But the expansion of these informative channels has also revealed difficulties for those who, from a multicultural perspective, seek to apply abstract principles concerning democracy and justice in the specific conditions of the region.

International Redefinition of the Public

When we look into processes of transnational integration, we realize that reclaiming the public cannot be carried out only within the purview of each nation. The megacorporations that have restructured the market according to principles of global administration have created a kind of "world civil society" in which they are the protagonists.[6] Enjoying much greater decision-making power than political parties, labor unions, and social movements of national scope, they have remodeled the *public space* that had been shaped by the coordinating action of modern states. These corporations now construct this space on a global scale, subordinating the social order to their own private interests. For this reason, to think of the exercise of citizenship only at the local or national level is the political equivalent of confronting Sony or Nestlé with commercial strategies at the retail level.

Strategies for reconstituting the public as a *multicultural collective* can avail themselves of the competitive spaces in which political organizations and networks of international studies participate, using them in a way analogous to that of transnational corporate practices. However, when we look to the proceedings of the Organization of American States or the meetings of ministers of culture, we see how utopian are our hopes that there might be space within these precincts for constructing a democratic multicultural society and defending an international public interest. But we cannot dispense with this hope if we want multiculturalism and national integration to mean more than the Cadena de las Américas network on Televisa or Benetton's billboards.

When we examine the globalization of urban consumption or the transnational character of the mass media, we realize that the public sphere is not limited to political action or national space. The reach of the public extends beyond state activities and practices directly linked to political actors. It also encompasses the ensemble of national and international actors capable of influencing the organization of collective meaning and the cultural and political foundations of citizens' endeavors.

> The public is virtually all of humanity and, correlatively, "public space" is the medium in which humanity surrenders itself unto itself as a spectacle. The word *spectacle,* to be sure, may provoke a wrong interpretation because public space does not reduce the media to spectacular images and words. It is also composed of discursive elements, commentary, discussion, with the most "rational" objectives of elucidation. What is most important to point out, however, is that "social public space" does not at all honor the national borders of each "civil society."[7]

This extension of the field of national political representations is evident, in the context of European integration, in the importance given economic and political "metadiscourse" of continental scope. This is also taking place in the newly constructed space of free trade in North America, evident in the spillover effects on the consumption habits and the exercise of citizenship in the three national societies implicated.

"European citizenship," "internationalization of citizenship," and even "global citizenship" are expressions that began to have currency in the 1990s.[8] Can the processes of democratization, which have operated with much difficulty within national borders, be extended to transnational systems for the administration of power, commodities, and communications? How can the notions of rights and responsibilities established in the West on secular foundations and on the basis of individual evaluation be made compatible with "communitarian" societies based on religious principles? In spite of the globalization of material goods and information, local or regional traditions and beliefs continue to differentially shape the public and the private as well as the procedures for inclusion and exclusion. At the same time that multicultural relations and integration projects among nations require supranational and post-local forms of administering conflicts, analysis needs to take into consideration the differences that persist: some due to the continuation of particular ways of life, others because global restructuring assigns unequal places to elites and masses. In any case, these less integrated sectors also participate, as we pointed out, in globalization, through human-rights, feminist, and ecological movements. In sum, globalization appears as a necessity that has to be expressed in a global endeavor for citizenship. Yet there are diverse ways of being a global citizen.

All of this poses challenging consequences for so-called civil society. If there is any hope that modernization in Latin America will prevail over the decadence experienced in the past decade, and that states will renew their interest in the public, its principal site of realization will be civil society. The little that has been done recently to carry out this cultural priority, which entails fending off the inevitability of the neoliberal project and questioning the absolutism of the market, has been generated in civil society. But who, at this late stage, can say what exactly we should understand as civil society, especially if we take into consideration the international expansion of the notion?

Several chapters in this book included attempts to deconstruct the confusion of civil society with the market, and of Latin American integration with agreements between governments and corporate executives. But we also pointed to the risk involved in a reactive celebration of civil society, rehearsing the disillusionments experienced by those who placed their hopes in fundamentalism and populist voluntarism.

In consideration of the manic oscillation between modernization and decadence in Latin America, and in consideration of the inability of state bureaucracies to extricate themselves from it, we hear again that, regardless, all this is not very important because "the people are strong" or because there continue to be (ecological, human-rights, women's, and youth) social movements in which we might see realized the promise of social regeneration. These movements are and continue to be valuable sites of resistance but—as Norbert Lechner states so well—they almost never rise above a "corporative reaction against crisis."[9] After thirty years of attempting to construct alternatives to parties and governments, there is no country in which comprehensive projects have been implemented, much less policies to restructure state bureaucracies and declining economies.

If we look at the entirety of civil society, there are even greater causes for alarm. We asked earlier why majorities elect and reelect presidents and parliaments that do not represent their interests. The explanations reviewed are inadequate. There remain questions for future research: How do we interpret the preference of parties, unions, and many social movements for negotiation over confrontation? The preference of sectorial and even individual "solutions" over political democratization and the redistribution of material and symbolic goods? To what degree are the failure and distrust of popular movements the result of their alliances with corrupt forces (narcotraffic, mafias) or the resigned acceptance of primitive exploitation in informal markets? I know of few sociocultural research projects that have begun to give convincing answers to these questions. They are, nevertheless, crucial for understanding the answers most frequently given for the decadence of neoliberal modernization: consensus or collapse.

Citizenship and Consumer Communities

A key issue for redefining civil society, one that has come up constantly in this book, is the crisis of the nation. Lechner speaks of a "desire for community" which he believes acts in reaction to the disbelief provoked by promises that the market will bring about social cohesion. We might ask what community he is referring to. The recent history of Latin America suggests that if there is anything like a desire of community, it is held less by large entities such as the nation or a class than by groups such as religious communities, sports leagues, age cohorts, and mass-media fans. A feature common to these atomized "communities" is that they cluster around symbolic consumption rather than in relation to productive processes. It is difficult to imagine, therefore, how they might contribute to reanimating the economy. Only in cases of extreme need do economic solidarities appear: strikes, popular soup kitchens, disaster aid. Civil societies appear less and less as national communities, understood on the basis of territorial, linguistic, and political unity. They behave, rather, as *interpretive communities of consumers,* that is, ensembles of people who share tastes and interpretive pacts in relation to certain commodities (e.g., gastronomy, sports, music) that provide the basis for shared identities.

It is not possible to generalize the consequences for citizenship of this increasing form of participation through consumption. Apocalyptic criticisms of consumption point to its individualist organization as the reason for disconnecting from citizenship, from our shared circumstances, from collective concern about inequality and solidarity. These criticisms are partially correct, but the expansion of communications and consumption generates associations of consumers and social struggles, even among marginal groups, who are better informed about national and international conditions. Imaginary communities are sometimes "scenes" that make evasion possible, and at other times circuits where the social bonds, sundered by urban sprawl or delegitimized by the loss of authority by parties and churches, are reconstituted. This ambivalence is also found in sports communities or music fans, capable of reviving the fundamentalist and racist stereotypes of nationalism (such as intercultural battles during world soccer championships) or generational violence (the moralizing discrimination aimed at rock fans or the furious rejection of "society" by youth groups after rock concerts). Consumption is good for thinking, but not only in keeping with modern rationality. Not even parties and social movements have succeeded working exclusively in this way. We might conclude, then, that the problems entailed in the transition from the public to the citizen are not very different from those experienced by party or union militants (or clients) when they attempt to act as rational citizens.

Popular epics still exist. The gimmicks of video politics are not enough to reduce them to simulacra or lead them astray among so many sports, music, and telenovelesque spectacles. The seduction of the media cannot anesthesize society to the point that the 40 percent to 50 percent of the population that lives in extreme poverty ceases to elicit a response or their rebellions evaporate into thin air. But it is true that the conditions for civil society to dialogue with itself have been structurally transformed. So long as the actions of the masses are not commensurate with the reach and effectiveness of the media, dissent will continue to be atomized, and group behavior erratic, connected more by consumption than by communitarian desires. Social research is only beginning to deal with these new relations between civil and political society, so different from those conceptualized by the modern liberal paradigm. Meanwhile, I find an apt description of this drama of dispersed social communication in some literary texts. Diamela Eltit begins her study of a marginal person's speech in Santiago de Chile thus: "Tatters of newsprint, fragments of extermination, syllables of death, pauses that lie, commerical slogans, the names of the dead. A profound crisis in language, an infection of memory, a disarticulation of all ideologies. What a shame, I thought. But that shame is Chile, I said to myself."[10]

An interpretation of contemporary society without voluntaristic illusions is not much of an encouragement for taking the side of the excluded and the exploited. Only by love of the desperate do we manage to conserve hope, Walter Benjamin used to say. I will add that as artists, writers, and [social] scientists, we too can justify solidarity as long as we aspire to emancipation, or at least as long as we hold on to the premise that emancipation and the renewal of the real also constitute part of social life: utopia, in other words.

Postmodern thought provoked us during the 1970s and 1980s to free ourselves from the illusions of metanarratives that augured totalizing or totalitarian emancipations. Perhaps it is time to emancipate ourselves from this disenchantment. Although the description of social life given by the social sciences offers us hard data to prove that Latin America is in decay, we should also take heart from sociocultural changes that offer signs of hope. But it is not easy to find hope in prevailing monotonous cultural policies or regressive social policies. Perhaps our disagreement will prove to be an inducement to rediscover the role of intellectuals vis-à-vis the state and civil society.

Allow me to characterize this challenge by stating that we are not obliged to believe ingenuously in civil society, nor to take a calculating concern for the limits of governability and the realism of power. "Intellectuals speak as if they were ministers," observes Ricardo Piglia, and "politics has become a practice that decides what a society *cannot* do. The politicians are the new philosophers: they decree what should be taken as real, what is possible, what are the limits of truth."[11] It occurs to me that our first responsibility is to salvage these tasks that are properly *cultural* from their dissolution in the market or in politics; that is, to rethink the real together with the possible, to distinguish globalization from selective modernization, to reconstruct a democratic multiculturalism from its foundation in civil society and with the participation of the state.

Notes

Translator's Introduction

    1. Néstor García Canclini, *Cortázar, una antropología poética* (Buenos Aires: Nova, 1968); idem, *La producción simbólica* (Mexico City: Siglo XXI, 1979). [The "Boom" is an expression used to characterize the rapid emergence to worldwide recognition of a generation of writers in the 1960s. These included Julio Cortázar, Carlos Fuentes, Gabriel García Márquez, and Mario Vargas Llosa, among others. See Doris Sommer and George Yúdice, "Latin American Literature from the Boom On," in *Postmodern Literature,* ed. Lawrence McCaffery (Westport, Conn.: Greenwood Press, 1986).—*Trans.*]

    2. In Latin America, as in certain European countries (e.g., Italy), *popular* refers to the culture and practices of the peasantry and the working classes. This is why the Gramscian account of the struggle for hegemony, as reviewed later in this Introduction, is significant in Latin America, where these classes predominate over the small middle class and the tiny *alta burguesía.* In the United States, although *popular* does refer etymologically to "the people," it has become a synonym for mass culture. This may be a result of the pervasiveness of the mass media and consumer industries early on in the United States. It also stems from the lack of a universal populism that incorporates all subaltern classes. Although there have been populist moments, especially in the 1890s and during the 1930s, these did not draw their definition of national identity from an equivalent miscegenated imaginary as

in almost all Latin American countries. The failure to incorporate blacks, especially in working-class struggles, meant that populism could only be partial rather than a national universal. One might say that apartheid has undermined any possibility of a national-popular identity, and now that neoliberal postmodernity foments the multiplication of differences, this possibility is foreclosed. The national-popular requires generalization across differences in region, politics, and race.

3. Néstor García Canclini, *Las culturas populares en el capitalismo* (Mexico City: Nueva Imagen, 1982); idem, *Transforming Modernity Popular Culture in Mexico* (Austin: University of Texas Press, 1993). In Latin America, serious critical studies were (and to some degree still are) characterized as "essays," in the tradition of the most important critical thinking in the region: Andrés Bello, Domingo Faustino Sarmiento, Sílvio Romero, José Enrique Rodó, José Carlos Mariátegui, José Vasconcelos, Mário de Andrade, Gilberto Freyre, Sérgio Buarque de Holanda, Alfonso Reyes, José Lezama Lima, Fernando Ortiz, Octavio Paz, Ángel Rama, Roberto Fernández Retamar, and many others. The reason for this is that most of these writers were not incorporated into the academic world in which writing is a much more professional endeavor. Some were journalists, others had diplomatic posts or other state-related positions. Intellectuals are increasingly being integrated, as in the United States, into university systems, but these are fragile in many countries of the region, a factor that forces many to remain "independent" of the academy (although not necessarily of other institutions).

4. Néstor García Canclini, *Culturas híbridas: estrategias para entrar y salir de la modernidad* (Mexico City: Grijalbo/Consejo Nacional para la Cultura y las Artes, 1990) [English translation: *Hybrid Cultures: Strategies for Entering and Leaving Modernity,* trans. Christopher L. Chiappari and Silvia L. López (Minneapolis: University of Minnesota Press, 1995)].

5. Néstor García Canclini, *Consumidores y ciudadanos: conflictos multiculturales de la globalización* (Mexico City: Grijalbo, 1995).

6. Néstor García Canclini, ed., *La ciudad de los viajeros* (Mexico City: Grijalbo/UAM, 1997); idem, *Cultura y comunicación en la ciudad de México* (Mexico City: Grijalbo/UAM, 1998).

7. Néstor García Canclini, *Las industrias culturales en la integración latinoamericana* (Buenos Aires: Eudeba/SELA, 1999).

8. Néstor García Canclini, *La globalización imaginada* (Mexico City and Buenos Aires: Paidós, 1999).

9. García Canclini, *Hybrid Cultures,* 261.

10. *Social Text* 31/32 (1992). Some of the essays in this volume were incorporated into Anne McClintock, Aamir Mufti, and Ella Shohat, eds., *Dangerous Liaisons: Gender, Narration, and Postcolonial Perspectives* (Minneapolis: University of Minnesota Press, 1997).

11. Fredric Jameson, "Third-World Literature in the Era of Multinational Capitalism," *Social Text* 15 (fall 1986): 65–88.

12. [George] Y[údice]. Espínola, "Introduction to Special Section on Contemporary Cuban Culture," *Social Text* 15 (fall 1986): iii–xii.

13. Aijaz Ahmad, "Jameson's Rhetoric of Otherness and the 'National Allegory,'" *Social Text* 17 (fall 1987): 3–25. Madhava Prasad counters, however, that Ahmad does not adequately account for the nationalist framework that he criticizes. The national is not liquidated by global capitalism but reconverted as part of its strategies. Madhava Prasad, "On the Question of a Theory of (Third) World Literature," *Social Text* 31/32 (1992): 57–83; McClintock, Mufti, and Shohat, *Dangerous Liaisons*, 141–62.

14. Homi K. Bhabha, "DissemiNation: Time, Narrative, and the Margins of the Modern Nation," in *Nation and Narration*, ed. Homi K. Bhabha (New York: Routledge, 1990), 314.

15. García Canclini, *Hybrid Cultures*, 261.

16. Ibid., 259.

17. For an extended critique of this argument, see George Yúdice, "Postmodernity and Transnational Capitalism in Latin America," in *On Edge: The Crisis of Contemporary Latin American Culture*, ed. George Yúdice, Jean Franco, and Juan Flores (Minneapolis: University of Minnesota Press, 1992), 1–28.

18. Bhabha, "DissemiNation," 317.

19. Ibid., 318.

20. Ibid., 319.

21. Homi K. Bhabha, "Beyond the Pale: Art in the Age of Multicultural Translation," in *1993 Biennial Exhibition* (New York: Whitney Museum of American Art/Abrams, 1993), 66.

22. Homi K. Bhabha, "Introduction: Locations of Culture," in *The Location of Culture* (New York: Routledge, 1994), 6.

23. Homi K. Bhabha, "The World and the Home," *Social Text* 10:2/3 (1992): 143.

24. Homi K. Bhabha, "Signs Taken for Wonders: Questions of Ambivalence and Authority under a Tree Outside Delhi, May 1817" [1985], in *The Location of Culture*, 112.

25. Donna J. Haraway, "Manifesto for Cyborgs: Science, Technology, and Socialist Feminism in the 1980s," *Socialist Review* 80 (1985): 65–108; reprinted as "A Cyborg Manifesto: Science, Technology, and Socialist-Feminism in the Late Twentieth Century," in *Simians, Cyborgs, and Women: The Reinvention of Nature* (New York: Routledge, 1991), 149–81. Subsequent references are given in the text.

26. García Canclini, *Hybrid Cultures*, 248, 249.

27. Ibid., 239.

28. Ibid., 244.

29. Néstor García Canclini, "Too Much Determinism or Too Much Hybridization?" *Travesía: Journal of Latin American Cultural Studies* 1:2 (1992): 167.

30. John Beverley, "Sobre la situación actual de los estudios culturales," unpublished manuscript. Part of the essay, dealing with the crisis of cultural studies, was published in *Siglo XX*.

31. José Enrique Rodó's *Ariel* (Cambridge: Cambridge University Press, 1967), originally published in 1900, is a call to Latin American intellectuals to eschew the

allure of U.S. utilitarian culture and instead model their politics on a quasi-Kantian, disinterested aesthetics. Were Rodó to have taken an activist role in educational policy, it would be possible to see in him an analogue of Matthew Arnold, in whose *Culture and Anarchy* (1869) (Cambridge: Cambridge University Press, 1961) culture is characterized as the atmosphere in which an aesthetic technocracy would rule more effectively than the aristocratic or capitalist classes.

32. John Beverley and James Sanders, "Negotiating with the Disciplines: A Conversation on Latin American Subaltern Studies," *Travesía: Journal of Latin American Cultural Studies* 6:2 (November 1997): 255.

33. García Canclini, *Transforming Modernity*, 26; *Las culturas populares*, 54–55. The very able translator of this book rendered "impugnadoras" as "challenging." In this case, I think "contestatory" fits the context better.

34. García Canclini, *Hybrid Cultures*, 199.

35. Raymond Williams, *Marxism and Literature* (Oxford: Oxford University Press, 1977), 95–100, 121–27; Stuart Hall, "Culture, the Media, and the 'Ideological Effect,'" in *Mass Communication and Society*, ed. James Curran, Michael Gurevitch, and Janet Woollacott (London: Edward Arnold, 1977), 315–48; Ernesto Laclau, *Politics and Ideology in Marxist Theory* (London: NLB, 1977), 164.

36. According to Gramsci, every social group that plays a role in economic production "creates together with itself, organically, one or more strata of intellectuals which give it homogeneity and an awareness of its own function not only in the economic but also in the social and political fields." Such unified awareness requires "cultural battle," not only to create a class consciousness but also to generalize that consciousness to other classes to achieve hegemony, which is a historical act. "An historical act can only be performed by 'collective man,' and this presupposes the attainment of a 'cultural-social' unity through which a multiplicity of dispersed wills, with heterogeneous aims, are welded together with a single aim, on the basis of an equal and common conception of the world.... [G]reat importance is assumed by the general question of language, that is, the question of collectively attaining a single cultural 'climate.'" This broadening of the sphere of intellectual action leads Gramsci to declare that "all men are intellectuals" insofar as they "participate in a particular conception of the world,...and therefore contribute to sustain a conception of the world or to modify it, that is, to bring into being new modes of thought" (Antonio Gramsci, *Selections from the Prison Notebooks*, ed. and trans. Quintin Hoare and Geoffrey Nowell Smith [New York: International Publishers, 1971], 3, 348–49, 9). Subsequent references are given in the text.

37. Juan Carlos Portantiero, *Los usos de Gramsci* (Mexico City: Folios Ediciones, 1981).

38. Gramsci, *Selections from the Prison Notebooks*, 219–20.

39. One thinks, for example, of José Vasconcelos's and Gilberto Freyre's aesthetics of *mestizaje* and *mestiçagem* in the respective contexts of Mexico and Brazil; Fernando Ortiz's notion of transculturation to characterize the reciprocal condi-

tionings of various races in Cuba; Alejo Carpentier's and José Lezama Lima's re-flections on marvelous realism and the baroque character of the (Latin) American continent; Gabriel García Márquez's magical realist *Macondismo*; and many other similar expressions that draw on the ways in which popular beliefs, traditions, and practices intersected the attempts at modernization in the many regions of the hemi-sphere. With hindsight, many critics now see these as the supportive yet fetishized metaphorical renderings by artists and intellectuals of the syncretisms and often conflictive social and cultural patchworks ensuing from the encounter of peasants and workers with the industrializing and commercial bourgeoisie and landed cre-ole elites.

40. Renato Ortiz, *A moderna tradição brasileira* (São Paulo: Editora Brasiliense, 1988), 65.

41. Alison Raphael, "Samba and Social Control: Popular Culture and Racial Democracy in Rio de Janeiro," Ph.D. diss., Columbia University, 1980; Hermano Vianna, *O Mistério do Samba* (Rio de Janeiro: Jorge Zahar, 1995).

42. George Yúdice, "The Globalization of Culture and the New Civil Soci-ety," in *Cultures of Politics/Politics of Cultures: Re-Visioning Latin American Social Movements,* ed. Sonia E. Alvarez, Evelina Dagnino, and Arturo Escobar (Boulder, Colo.: Westview Press, 1998), 372.

43. Carlos Monsiváis, *Entrada libre: crónicas de la sociedad que se organiza* (Mexico City: Ediciones Era, 1987).

44. José Joaquín Brunner, "Seis Preguntas a José Joaquín Brunner," *Revista de Crítica Cultural* 1:1 (May 1990): 21.

45. Ibid.

46. Gilbert M. Joseph and Daniel Nugent, "Popular Culture and State For-mation in Revolutionary Mexico," in *Everyday Forms of State Formation: Revolu-tion and the Negotiation of Rule in Modern Mexico,* ed. Gilbert M. Joseph and Daniel Nugent (Durham, N.C.: Duke University Press, 1994), 5–6.

47. Ibid., 11–12.

48. Florencia Mallon, *Peasant and Nation: The Making of Postcolonial Mexico and Peru* (Berkeley: University of California Press, 1995).

49. Beverley and Sanders, "Negotiating with the Disciplines," 242.

50. Mallon, *Peasant and Nation,* 319.

51. García Canclini, *Transforming Modernity,* 31, 38.

52. Ibid., 91.

53. García Canclini, *Hybrid Cultures,* 156.

54. Mallon, *Peasant and Nation,* 19.

55. García Canclini, *Transforming Modernity,* 84.

56. Ibid.

57. Néstor García Canclini, "Cultural Reconversion," in *On Edge,* 31, and *Hybrid Cultures,* 155.

58. García Canclini, *Hybrid Cultures,* 230. García Canclini borrows the phrase from Renato Ortiz, who in *A moderna tradição brasileira* uses it to refer to the in-

tegration of Brazil into an international order of mass media that requires certain standards of production. The fact that Brazil is one of the largest producers of television programs for export has been internalized into the styles of popular consumption and in ways that do not correspond to the cultural imperialism hypothesis ("Do popular-nacional ao internacional-popular?" 182–206). Of course, this sleight of phrase does not carry with it the Gramscian assumptions about the ability of popular groups to influence the "leading" groups, which in any case have been internationalized.

59. Renato Ortiz, "Uma cultura internacional-popular," in *Mundialização e cultura* (São Paulo: Editora Brasiliense, 1994), 139.

60. Arjun Appadurai, "Disjuncture and Difference in the Global Cultural Economy," in *Modernity at Large: Cultural Dimensions of Globalization* (Minneapolis: University of Minnesota Press, 1996), 38.

61. David Ronfeldt, "The Battle for the Mind of Mexico," Rand Corporation, June 1995. Electronic posting: chiapas@mundo.eco.utexas.edu.

62. Gramsci, *Selections from the Prison Notebooks,* 56 n. 5.

63. Ibid.

64. Michel Foucault, *Il faut défendre la société* (Paris: Gallimard/Seuil, 1997), 170, 219.

65. George Yúdice, "The Expediency of Culture," unpublished manuscript.

66. Beverley, "Sobre la situación actual de los estudios culturales," 16.

67. These questions and problems are addressed in some of the contributions to *The Real Thing: Testimonial Discourse and Latin America,* ed. Georg M. Gugelberger (Durham, N.C.: Duke University Press, 1996). Furthermore, the debate over the truth of Rigoberta Menchú's *testimonio* only provided more fuel for the questioning about the subaltern. See the essays by John Beverley and David Stoll in *The Real Thing* and Stoll's book, *Rigoberta Menchú and the Story of All Poor Guatemalans* (Boulder, Colo.: Westview Press, 1999). Rigoberta Menchú's *testimonio* was published in English as *I, Rigoberta Menchú: An Indian Woman in Guatemala,* ed. and introd. Elisabeth Burgos-Debray, trans. Ann Wright (London: Verso, 1984).

68. Ranajit Guha, "On Some Aspects of the Historiography of Colonial India," in Ranajit Guha, ed., *Subaltern Studies II* (Delhi: Oxford University Press, 1982), 7.

69. Beverley, "Sobre la situación actual de los estudios culturales," 28.

70. Beverley and Sanders, "Negotiating with the Disciplines," 241.

71. Ibid., 242.

72. Ibid., 249.

73. Bernd Magnus, Stanley Stewart, and Jean-Pierre Mileur, *Nietzsche's Case: Philosophy as/and Literature* (New York: Routledge, 1993), 25.

74. Alberto Moreiras, "La exterioridad de la no liberación: Subalternismo y práctica teórica," 18. Unpublished manuscript.

75. Alberto Moreiras, "Totalization and the Politics of Theory," 27. Unpublished manuscript.

76. Moreiras, "La exterioridad," 20.

77. Ibid., 22. Moreiras quotes the following passage from Žižek: "The crucial point here, however, is that this ['ethnicization of the national' or] 'regression' from secondary to 'primordial' forms of identification with 'organic' communities is already 'mediated': it is a *reaction* to the universal dimension of the world market—as such, it occurs on its terrain, against its background. For that reason, what we are dealing with in these phenomena is not a 'regression' but rather the form of appearance of its exact opposite: in a kind of 'negation of negation,' *this very reassertion of 'primordial' identification signals that the loss of organic-substantial unity is fully consummated*" (Slavoj Žižek, "Multiculturalism, or, the Cultural Logic of Multinational Capitalism," *New Left Review* 225 [1997]: 42).

78. Mikhail Bakhtin, "Discourse in the Novel," in *The Dialogic Imagination: Four Essays by M. M. Bakhtin,* ed. Michael Holquist, trans. Caryl Emerson and Michael Holquist (Austin: University of Texas Press, 1981), 294.

79. Here he is drawing on Rita Laura Segato, "Alteridades históricas/identidades políticas: una crítica a las certezas del pluralismo global," Antropología working paper series, no. 234, Anthropology Department, University of Brasília, 1998, 14.

Author's Preface

I would like to thank Hugo Achugar, John Beverley, Román de la Campa, Sandra Lorenzano, Jesús Martín Barbero, Walter Mignolo, Bernardo Subercaseaux, and George Yúdice for their comments on this book, which stimulated me to think what I now add in this Preface. See also John Beverley, "Estudios culturales y vocación política," *Revista de Crítica Cultural* 12 (July 1996); Román de la Campa, "Latinoamérica y sus nuevos cartógrafos: discurso poscolonial, diásporas intelectuales y enunciación fronteriza," *Revista Iberoamericana* 62:176–77 (July–December 1996): 697–717; Jesús Martín Barbero, "Reseña al libro *Consumidores y ciudadanos,*" *Magazin Dominical de El Espectador* 654 (November 1995, 26b); Bernardo Subercaseaux, "Comentario a *Consumidores y ciudadanos,*" *Revista de Crítica Cultural* 12 (July 1996); George Yúdice, "Tradiciones comparativas de estudios culturales: América Latina y los Estados Unidos," *Alteridades* 5 (Mexico City, 1993), and "Civil Society, Consumption, and Governmentality in an Age of Global Restructuring: An Introduction," *Social Text* 45 (winter 1995).

1. James Holston and Arjun Appadurai, "Cities and Citizenship," *Public Culture* 2:2 (1996): 187–204.

2. [García Canclini has opted to distinguish between the Anglo-American and Latin American cultural studies traditions by referring *in English* to the first as "cultural studies" and to the second as "estudios culturales" or "estudios de la cultura." The difference, to a great but not exclusive degree, hinges on the preference of the former for theoretically driven discursive analysis within the humanities, and the prevalence of social-science research within the latter. See Nelly Richard,

La insubordinación de los signos (Santiago: Editorial Cuarto Propio, 1994), for a critique of the latter in the Chilean context.—*Trans.*]

3. [*Testimonios* are discourses of witnessing, usually told by individuals belonging to subaltern groups to an ethnographer, journalist, or academic, who transcribes and edits the text, which then circulates in academic and political networks that provide solidarity for the plight of the witnesses. This plight might be political repression, economic oppression, gender or race discrimination, and natural catastophes. *Testimonios* were recognized as a genre in the early 1970s by the Cuban cultural center Casa de las Américas as a way of legitimizing the expression and representation of subaltern or "popular" groups. Since the early 1990s, in the wake of the implosion of communism and the "triumph" of neoliberalism, many critics have begun to question the representativity of this genre as well as its political effectivity. See *The Real Thing: Testimonial Discourse and Latin America,* ed. Georg M. Gugelberger (Durham, N.C.: Duke University Press, 1996).—*Trans.*]

4. See Lawrence Grossberg, Cary Nelson, and Paula Treichler, eds., *Cultural Studies* (New York: Routledge, 1992).

5. Lawrence Grossberg, *We Gotta Get Out of This Place: Popular Conservatism and Postmodern Culture* (New York: Routledge, 1992).

6. Martín Barbero, "Reseña al libro *Consumidores y ciudadanos*"; Renato Ortiz, *Mundialização e cultura* (São Paulo: Editora Brasiliense, 1994); Beatriz Sarlo, *Escenas de la vida posmoderna. Intelectuales, ante y videocultura en la Argentina* (Buenos Aires: Ariel, 1994).

7. See my "Hybrid Cultures and Communicative Strategies," *Media Development* 44:1 (1997): 22–29.

8. Robert Hughes, *Culture of Complaint: The Fraying of America* (New York: Oxford University Press, 1993); Charles Taylor, "The Politics of Recognition," in David Theo Goldberg, ed., *Multiculturalism: A Critical Reader* (Oxford: Blackwell, 1994), 75–106; Michael Walzer, "Individus et communautés: les deux pluralismes," *Esprit* (Paris, June 1995).

9. Walzer, "Individus et communantés," 109, 105.

10. Heloísa Buarque de Hollanda, "O estranho horizonte da crítica feminista no Brasil," in Carlos Rincón and Petra Shumn, eds., *Nuevo Texto Crítico* 14–15 (1995): 259–69; Nelly Richard, "Signos culturales y mediaciones académicas," in Beatriz González Stephan, *Cultura y tercer mundo* (Caracas: Nueva Sociedad, 1996).

11. Paul Ricoeur, *La critique et la conviction: Entretien avec François Azouvi et Marc de Launay* (Paris: Calamann-Lévy, 1995), 96.

Introduction

1. Jürgen Habermas, "L'espace publique, 30 ans après," *Quaderni* 18 (Paris, autumn 1992).

2. See Richard Flores et al., "Concept Paper on Cultural Citizenship," working paper of the Working Group on Cultural Studies of the Interuniversity Program, and Renato Rosaldo, "Cultural Citizenship in San Jose, California," paper

presented in the session "Contested Citizenship," Annual Meeting of the Anthropological Association of America, Washington, D.C., November 1993. [See also William V. Flores and Rina Benmayer, eds., *Latino Cultural Citizenship: Claiming Identity, Space, and Rights* (Boston: Beacon Press, 1997).— *Trans.*]

3. Vera da Silva Telles, "Sociedade civil e construção de espaços públicos," in *Anos 90. Política e sociedade no Brasil*, ed. Evelina Dagnino (São Paulo: Editora Brasiliense, 1994), 91–92.

4. Evelina Dagnino, "Os movimentos sociais e a emergência de uma nova noção de cidadania," in *Anos 90*, 103–15.

5. This disseminated perspective on citizenship is noticeable in recent books like that of Bart van Steenbergen, ed., *The Condition of Citizenship* (London, Thousand Oaks, and New Delhi: Sage, 1994), in which the contributors offer perspectives on each of the modalities mentioned.

6. Günther Lottes, *Politische Aufklärung und Plebejisches Publikeum* (Munich: Oldenbourg, 1979), 110, quoted in Habermas, "L'espace publique, 30 ans après."

7. Some groundbreaking texts that go beyond the populist model are Jesús Martín Barbero, *De los medios a las mediaciones* (Mexico City: Gustavo Gili, 1987) [English translation: *Communication, Culture and Hegemony: From the Media to Mediations* (London and Newbury Park, Calif.: Sage Publications, 1993)]; Beatriz Sarlo, *Escenas de la vida posmoderna. Intelectuales, arte y videocultura en la Argentina* (Buenos Aires: Ariel, 1994); Aníbal Ford, *Navegaciones. Comunicación, cultura y crisis* (Buenos Aires: Amorrortu, 1994); Renato Ortiz, *Mundialização e cultura* (São Paulo: Editora Brasiliense, 1994).

8. Sarlo, *Escenas de la vida posmoderna*, 83.

9. Martín Barbero, *Communication, Culture and Hegemony*, Part 2.

10. According to the World Communications Report, published by UNESCO in 1990; quoted in Rafael Roncagliolo, "La integración audiovisual en América Latina: Estados, empresas y productores independientes," paper presented at the symposium on Cultural Policies in Processes of Supranational Integration, Mexico City, 3–5 October 1994.

11. Jean-Marc Ferry, "Las transformaciones de la publicidad política," in *El nuevo espacio público*, ed. Jean-Marc Ferry, Dominique Wolton, et al. (Barcelona: Gedisa, 1992), 19.

12. Benedict Anderson, *Imagined Communities: Reflections on the Origin and Spread of Nationalism* (London: Verso, 1983).

13. [In Spanish, as in other Romance languages, all nouns are gendered. *Society* is feminine, hence the puns on "her" gender.— *Trans.*]

14. Soledad Loaeza, "La sociedad civil me da miedo," *Cuadernos de Nexos* 69 (March 1994): v–vi.

15. Jean L. Cohen and Andrew Arato, *Civil Society and Political Theory* (Cambridge: MIT Press, 1994), ix.

16. As I argue earlier, I do not consider that modern and postmodern identities should be analytically differentiated in any absolute way. I conceive of postmodernity not as a different stage nor one that substitutes for modernity. It is,

rather, the development of modern tendencies that are reworked in the multicultural conflicts of globalization. I have elaborated on this position in my book *Culturas híbridas: Estrategias para entrar y salir de la modernidad* (Mexico City: Grijablo, 1990) [English translation: *Hybrid Cultures: Strategies for Entering and Leaving Modernity,* trans. Christopher L. Chiappari and Silvia L. López (Minneapolis: University of Minnesota Press, 1995)].

17. Roberto Alejandro, *Hermeneutics, Citizenship, and the Public Sphere* (Albany: State University of New York Press, 1993), 6–7.

18. I take the expression "institutional configurations" from Peter Dahlgren, "Introduction," in *Communication and Citizenship,* ed. Peter Dahlgren and Colin Sparks (London: Routledge, 1993).

19. Pierre-Yves Pétillon, "O! Chicago: images de la ville en chantier," in Jean Baudrillard et al., *Citoyenneté et urbanité* (Paris: Éditions Esprit, 1991), 144.

20. The results of these research projects are provided in the following works: Néstor García Canclini, ed., *El consumo cultural en México* (Mexico City: Consejo Nacional para la Cultura y las Artes, 1993); and Néstor García Canclini, Julio Gullco, María Eugenia Módena, Eduardo Nivón, Mabel Piccini, Ana María Rosas, and Graciela Schmilchuk, *Públicos de arte y política cultural: un estudio del II Festival de la ciudad de México* (Mexico City: DDF, INAH, UAM, 1991).

21. See Néstor García Canclini, ed., *Los nuevos espectadores. Cine, televisión y video en México* (Mexico City: Imcine-CNCA, 1994).

1. Consumption Is Good for Thinking

This chapter is an expanded version of an article of the same title that I published in *Diálogos de la Comunicación* 30 (Lima, June 1991).

1. See, for example, James Lull, ed., *World Families Watch Television* (Newbury Park, Calif.: Sage, 1988); Jesús Martín Barbero, *Communication, Culture and Hegemony: From the Media to Mediations* (New York: Sage, 1993); and Guillermo Orozco, ed., *Hablan los televidentes. Estudios de recepción en varios países* (Mexico City: Universidad Iberoamericana, 1992).

2. See, for example, Jean-Pierre Terrail, Desmond Préteceille, and Patrice Grevet, *Capitalism, Consumption, and Needs* (New York: Blackwell, 1985).

3. Manuel Castells, *The Urban Question: A Marxist Approach* (Cambridge: MIT Press, 1977), Appendix.

4. Pierre Bourdieu, *Distinction: A Social Critique of the Judgement of Taste* (Cambridge: Harvard University Press, 1987); Arjun Appadurai, ed., *The Social Life of Things: Commodities in Cultural Perspective* (New York: Cambridge University Press, 1986); Stuart Ewen, *All Consuming Images: The Politics of Style in Contemporary Culture* (New York: Basic Books, 1988).

5. Mary Douglas and Baron Isherwood, *The World of Goods* (New York: Basic Books, 1979), 65.

6. Ibid., 62.

7. Alfred Gell, "Newcomers to the World of Goods: Consumption among the Muria Gonds," in Appadurai, *The Social Life of Things*, 110–37.

8. Ibid., 47.

9. Renato Ortiz, *Mundialização e cultura* (São Paulo: Editora Brasiliense, 1994), chapter 4.

10. Néstor García Canclini and Mabel Piccini, "Culturas de la ciudad de México: símbolos colectivos y usos del espacio urbana," in Néstor García Canclini, ed., *El consumo cultural en México* (Mexico City: Consejo Nacional para la Cultura y las Artes, 1993).

11. Appadurai, *The Social Life of Things*, 29.

12. Ibid., 57.

2. Mexico

This chapter appeared in *Ciudades* 20 (Mexico City, December 1993).

1. This is a well-established distinction, still held to by some anthropologists. See, for example, Clifford Geertz, *The Interpretation of Cultures* (New York: Basic Books, 1973).

2. The most consistent attempts to convert the city from a place in which one studies into an object of study can be found in Brazilian anthropology. See Eunice Ribeiro Durham, "A pesquisa antropológica com populações urbanas: problemas e perspectivas," in Ruth Cardoso, ed., *A aventura antropológica* (Rio de Janeiro: Paz e Terra, 1986), and "A sociedade vista da periferia," *Revista Brasileira de Ciências Sociais* 1 (June 1986): 85–99.

3. Oscar Lewis, *Tepoztlán* (New York: Holt, 1960); Robert Redfield, *Tepoztlán: A Mexican Village* (Chicago: University of Chicago Press, 1973 [1930]); Clifford Geertz, *Works and Lives: The Anthropologist as Author* (Stanford, Calif.: Stanford University Press, 1987).

4. For a summary of these developments, see George E. Marcus and Michael M. J. Fischer, *Anthropology as Cultural Critique* (Chicago: University of Chicago Press, 1986). See especially the chapter titled "Taking Account of the World Historical Political Economy: Knowable Communities in Larger Systems."

5. See Marjorie Thacker and Sylvia Bazua, *Indígenas urbanos de la ciudad de México, proyectos de vida y estrategias* (Mexico City: Instituto Nacional Indigenista, 1992). As in the entire country, statistics on the size of the indigenous population are the source of many debates, as are statistics on any matter in Mexico. Thacker and Bazua's estimate is based on the Eleventh Population and Housing Census of 1990 and includes children less than five years of age and those who do not speak indigenous languages yet belong to an indigenous family despite having been born and raised in the capital.

6. Jerome Monet, "El centro histórico de la ciudad de México," in *Sábado*, Literary Supplement for *Unomásuno* (Mexico City, 26 August 1989): 1–2.

7. See Néstor García Canclini and Mabel Piccini, "Culturas de la ciudad de México: símbolos colectivos y usos del espacio urbano," in *El consumo cultural en México*, ed. Néstor García Candini (Mexico City: Consejo Nacional para la Cultura y las Artes, 1993), and Néstor García Canclini, Eduardo Nivón, and Patricia Safa, "Il consumo culturale a Città del Messico," *La Ricerca Folklorica* 28 (October 1993): 41–47.

8. Juan R. Gil Elizondo, "El futuro de la ciudad de México. Metrópoli controlada," in *Atlas de la ciudad de México* (Mexico City: Departamento del Distrito Federal y El Colegio de México, 1987), 418.

9. Eduardo Nivón, "El consumo cultural y los movimientos sociales"; Patricia Safa, "Espacio urbano, sectores sociales y consumo cultural en Coyoacán"; Ana María Rosas Mantecón, "La puesta en escena del patrimonio mexica y su apropiación por los públicos del Museo del Templo Mayor"; and Maya Lorena Pérez Ruiz, "El Museo Nacional de Culturas Populares: espacio de expresión o recreación de la cultura popular," in García Canclini, *El consumo cultural en México*.

10. Néstor García Canclini, Julio Gullco, María Eugenia Módena, Eduardo Nivón, Mabel Piccini, Ana María Rosas, and Graciela Schmilchuk, *Públicos de arte y política cultural. Un estudio del II Festival de la ciudad de México* (Mexico City: DDF, INAH, UAM, 1991).

11. To obtain this information we employed four techniques: *(a)* audience surveys, *(b)* field observation and open-ended interviews of audiences, *(c)* interviews of officials of the organizing institutions, of participating artists, and of critics, *(d)* systematic analysis of press coverage and criticism of the festival.

12. See Nivón, "El consumo cultural y los movimientos sociales."

13. It should be pointed out that the ecological view of the city is encompassing only in *territorial* terms. Otherwise, it gives little consideration to the economic and political dimensions of sociability.

14. Aldo Bonomi, "La machina metrópoli," paper presented at the symposium "The Rebirth of the City in Europe," Florence, 6–8 December 1992.

15. María Ana Portal Ariosa, "Religiosidad popular e identidad urbana. El caso de San Andrés Totoltepec, Tlalpan, D.F.," Ph.D. diss., Anthropology Department, Universidad Nacional Autónoma de México, 1994, chapter 3.

16. Guillermo de la Peña and René de la Torre, "Identidades urbanas al fin del milenio," *Ciudades* 22 (Mexico City, April–June 1994).

17. See Armand Mattelart's analysis of entrepreneurial culture in *La communication-monde* (Paris: Éditions La Découverte, 1991), 260–62.

18. Saskia Sassen, *The Global City: New York, London, Tokyo* (Princeton, N.J.: Princeton University Press, 1991).

19. Manuel Castells, "Estrategias de desarrollo metropolitano en las grandes ciudades españolas: la articulación entre crecimiento económico y calidad de vida," in *Las grandes ciudades en la década de los noventa*, ed. Jordi Borja et al. (Madrid: Editorial Sistema, 1990).

20. Raúl Monge, "Los grandes proyectos: Centro Histórico, Alameda, Polanco, Santa Fe y Xochimilco," *Proceso* 750 (18 March 1991): 10–13.

21. Ricardo Camargo, "La ciudad de México como escenario," *El Nacional* (Mexico City), 9 March 1993, 20.

22. See the symposium cited earlier, "The Rebirth of the City in Europe," and the articles by Manuel Castells and Guido Martinotti in *Las grandes ciudades en la década de los noventa.*

23. José Emilio Pacheco, *Las batallas en el desierto* (Mexico City: Ediciones Era, 1981), 67–68 [English translation: *Battles in the Desert and Other Stories,* trans. Katherine Silver (New York: New Directions, 1987).]

24. Efraín Huerta, "Declaración de odios," in *Poesía completa,* ed. Martí Soler (Mexico City: Fondo de Cultura Económica, 1988 [1944]), 102–5.

3. Urban Cultural Policies in Latin America

1. [*Chilango, paulista,* and *porteño* are the names given to the inhabitants of, respectively, Mexico City, São Paulo, and Buenos Aires.— *Trans.*]

2. [*Cariocas* are the inhabitants of Rio de Janeiro.— *Trans.*]

3. Among the studies that have dealt with this imaginary construction of national identities, see Adolfo Prieto, *El discurso criollista en la formación de la Argentina moderna* (Buenos Aires: Sudamericana, 1988); Beatriz Sarlo, *Una modernidad periférica: Buenos Aires 1920 y 1930* (Buenos Aires: Nueva Visión, 1988); Renato Ortiz, *Cultura brasileira & identidade nacional* (São Paulo: Editora Brasiliense, 1985); Roberto Schwartz, "Nacional por substração," in *Que horas são* (São Paulo: Companhia das Letras, 1987); Roger Bartra, *La jaula de la melancolía. Identidad y metamorfosis del mexicano* (Mexico City: Grijalbo, 1987) [English translation: *The Cage of Melancholy: Identity and Metamorphosis in the Mexican Character,* trans. Christopher J. Hall (New Brunswick, N.J.: Rutgers University Press, 1992)]; Claudio Lomnitz-Adler, *Exits from the Labyrinth: Culture and Ideology in the Mexican National Space* (Berkeley: University of California Press, 1992).

4. Antônio Augusto Arantes, "Horas furtadas. Dois ensaios sobre consumo e lazer," unpublished manuscript.

5. Eunice Ribeiro Durham, "A sociedade vista da periferia," *Revista Brasileira de Ciências Sociais* 1:1 (June 1996): 84–99.

6. See Oscar Landi, A. Vacchieri, and L. A. Quevedo, *Públicos y consumos culturales en Buenos Aires* (Buenos Aires: CEDES, 1990); the articles by Néstor García Canclini, Mabel Piccini, Patricia Safa, Eduardo Nivón, Ana Rosas, and Maya Lorena Pérez in *El consumo cultural en México,* ed. Néstor García Canclini (Mexico City: Consejo Nacional para la Cultura y las Artes, 1993); Carlos Catalán and Guillermo Sunkel, *Consumo cultural en Chile: la élite, lo masivo y lo popular* (Santiago: FLACSO, 1990); and Arantes, *Horas furtadas.*

7. See Eduardo Nivón, "El consumo cultural y los movimientos sociales," in García Canclini, *El consumo cultural en México.*

8. See Héctor Castillo Berthier, Sergio Zermeño, and Alicia Ziccardi, "La cultura de las bandas," in *Cultura y postpolítica,* ed. Néstor García Canclini (Mexico City: Consejo Nacional para la Cultura y las Artes, 1995).

9. For those unfamiliar with Mexico City, Las Lomas is one of the traditional elegant neighborhoods.

10. "Nacos" is the pejorative name given in Mexico to Indians and members
of popular groups, especially those who live in cities.

11. Carlos Monsiváis, *Entrada libre. Crónicas de la sociedad que se organiza*
(Mexico City: Era, 1987), 144–50.

12. Antônio Flávio Pierucci, "Linguagens autoritárias, voto popular," in *Anos
90. Política e sociedade no Brasil,* ed. Evelina Dagnino (São Paulo: Editora Brasiliense,
1994), 137–49.

13. Armando Silva, *Imaginarios urbanos. Bogotá y São Paulo: cultura y comunicación urbana en América Latina* (Bogotá: Tercer Mundo Editores, 1992), 205–8,
272–75.

14. Marc Augé, *Los "no lugares." Espacios del anonimato: Una antropología de
la sobremodernidad* (Barcelona: Gedisa, 1993), 41 [English translation: *Non-places:
Introduction to an Anthropology of Supermodernity,* trans. John Howe (New York:
Verso, 1995)].

15. Sarlo, *Una modernidad periférica,* 15–19.

4. Narrating the Multicultural

A first version of this chapter was presented in the symposium "La literatura
latinoamericana: encrucijada de lenguas y culturas," University of California, Berkeley, April 1994.

1. In these introductory paragraphs I rehearse, with certain changes, the theoretical discussion that I presented on these issues in *Hybrid Cultures: Strategies for
Entering and Leaving Modernity* (Minneapolis: University of Minnesota Press, 1995).

2. [*Criollismo* refers to a regionally defined literature that draws on the customs of popular classes to depict a nativist world distinguished from the European
and the North American.— *Trans.*] On the *gaucho* genre, see Josefina Ludmer, *El
género gauchesco. Un tratado sobre la patria* (Buenos Aires: Sudamericana, 1988).

3. Antonio Cornejo Polar, "Literatura peruana: totalidad contradictoria," *Revista de crítica literaria latinoamericana,* 9:18 (Lima, 1983): 31–50.

4. The dangers of this homogenization of Latin America for metropolitan
consumption are pointed out by literary and art critics. See Carlos Dámaso
Martínez's interview, "Jean Franco: el multiculturalismo y el poder del centro,"
Espacios 12 (Buenos Aires, June–July 1993): 37–40; Mari Carmen Ramírez, "Imagen
e identidad en el arte latino de Estados Unidos," *La Jornada Semanal* 228 (Mexico
City, 24 October 1993): 18–25; and George Yúdice, "Globalización y nuevas formas
de intermediación cultural," in Hugo Achugar y Gerardo Caetano, eds., *Mundo,
Región, Aldea: Identidades, políticas culturales e integración regional* (Montevideo:
FESUR, 1994), 134–57.

5. Wim Wenders, "Historias para soportar la vida," *La Jornada Semanal* (Mexico City, 18 January 1987): 6–7.

6. Manuel Rivera Cambas, *México pintorsco, artístico y monumental,* vol. 2 (Mexico City: Editora Nacional, 1967), 198.

7. Julio Ramos, *Desencuentros de la modernidad en América Latina. Literatura y política en el siglo XIX* (Mexico City: Fondo de Cultural Económica, 1989), 128.

8. Edward W. Soja, *Postmodern Geographies: The Reassertion of Space in Critical Social Theory* (London and New York: Verso, 1989), 222–23.

9. Carlos Monsiváis, "Nueva guía de pecadores y anexas," Introduction to "Guía del pleno disfrute de la ciudad de México," *La Jornada* (Mexico City), 18 December 1994, 27.

5. Identities as a Multimedia Spectacle

1. Jesús Martín Barbero, *Communication, Culture and Hegemony: From the Media to Mediations* (New York: Sage, 1993).

2. I borrow this expression from *Art from Latin America: La cita transcultural,* the catalog for the exhibition curated by Nelly Richard in the Museum of Contemporary Art in Sydney, 10 March–13 June 1993.

3. This formula was coined by Achille Bonito Oliva, curator of the Biennale. Cited in Lelia Driben, "La XLV Bienal de Venecia, los puntos cardinales del arte nómada de 56 países," *La Jornada* (Mexico City), 23 August 1993, 23.

4. Charles-Albert Michelet, "Réflexion sur le drôle de drame du cinéma mondial," *CinémAction* (1988): 156–61.

5. [García Canclini employs the notion of *mestizaje* (race mixing) to refer to certain types of hybrid consumer commodities. The neologism *mesticize* is preferable to the idiomatic *miscegenated,* which in English has a pejorative connotation.— *Trans.*]

6. Renato Ortiz, *Mundialização e cultura,* (São Paulo: Editora Brasiliense, 1994), chapter 5. See also Armand Mattelart, *La communication-monde* (Paris: La Découverte, 1992); Stuart Hall, "The Local and the Global: Globalization and Ethnicity," in *Culture, Globalization, and the World System* (Binghamton: State University of New York at Binghamton, 1991).

7. Gideón Kunda, *Engineering Culture: Control and Commitment in a High-Tech Corporation* (Philadelphia: Temple University Press, 1992). I review here certain lines of research that are being adopted and elaborated in Mexican industrial anthropology, particularly on *maquiladora* production. See Luis Reygadas, "Estructuración de la cultura del trabajo en las maquiladoras," project proposal submitted to the Doctoral Program in Anthropology at the Universidad Autónoma Metropolitana-Iztapalapa, 1993.

6. Latin America and Europe as Suburbs of Hollywood

This chapter is a revised version of a lecture given at the Forum "Visión Iberoamericana 2000," sponsored by UNESCO in Cartagena de Indias, Colombia, 16–18 March 1994.

1. "Un negocio de más de 500 000 millones de pesetas," *El País* (Madrid), 11 December 1993, 35.

2. "Entrevista a Edouard Balladur, primer ministro francés. ¿Qué es lo que quiere EU . . . la desaparición del cine europeo?" *El Nacional* (Mexico City), 23 October 1993, 27.

3. *Variety,* 28 June 1993; cited in Deborah Holtz, "Los públicos de video," in *Los nuevos espectadores. Cine, televisión y video en México,* Néstor García Canclini (Mexico City: Imcine-CNCA, 1994).

4. Pierre Musso, "Audiovisuel et télécommunications en Europe: quelle recompositions?" *Quaderni. La revue de la communication* 19 (Paris, winter 1993): 13.

5. Joëlle Farchy, *Le cinéma déchaîné. Mutation d'une industrie* (Paris: Presses du CNRS, 1992), 37–38.

6. Statistics obtained from the Instituto Mexicano de Cinematografía.

7. I analyze this shift in audience in the next chapter.

8. *El País,* 11 December 1993, 35.

9. Eduardo Haro Tecglen, "Cine agónico," *El País,* 11 December 1993, 57.

10. Bernard Miége, "Les mouvements de longue durée de la communication en Europe de l'ouest," *Quaderni. La revue de la communication* 19 (Paris, winter 1993).

11. *El País,* 11 December 1993, 35.

12. Régis Debray, "Respuesta a Mario Vargas Llosa," *El País,* 4 November 1993.

13. Mario Vargas Llosa, "La tribu y el mercado," *El País,* 21 November 1993.

14. Marco Vinicio González, "Cine mexicano en Nueva York," *La Jornada Semanal* 230 (7 November 1993): 46.

15. Vargas Llosa, "La tribu y el mercado."

16. André Lange, "Descartes, c'est la Hollande. La communauté Europeénne: culture et audiovisuel," *Quaderni. La revue de la communication* 19 (Paris, winter 1993): 98.

17. Antonio Pasquali, "Bienvenida global village," *Intermedios* 8 (Mexico City, August 1993): 14.

18. Alain Touraine, "La excepción cultural," *El País,* 11 December 1993.

7. From the Public to the Private

1. Information from the Argentine Subsecretariat of Culture.

2. The study *Los nuevos espectadores. Cine, televisión y video en México* (Mexico City: Imcine-CNCA, 1994) was edited by Néstor García Canclini and carried out with the participation of Déborah Holtz, Javier Lozano Espinosa, María Eugenia Módena, Ella Fany Quintal, Guadalupe Reyes Domínguez, Ana Rosas Mantecón, Enrique Sánchez Ruiz, and José Manuel Valenzuela. It is based on surveys of film and video spectators in Mexico City, Tijuana, and Mérida between 1990 and 1993.

3. This is how Félix Mesquich tells the story of the 1896 projection of *L'Arivée d'un train en gare de La Ciotat* in his *Tour de manivelle. Souvenirs d'un chasseur d'images* (Paris: Grasset, 1933), 5–6; quoted in André Gaudreault and Germain Lacasse, "Premier regard, les 'néo-spectateurs' du Canada Français," *Vertigo* 10 (Paris: 1993): 19.

4. Ana Rosas Mantecón, "Los públicos de cine," in García Canclini, *Los nuevos espectadores.*

5. Carlos Monsiváis, "Notas sobre el Estado, la cultura nacional y las culturas populares," *Cuadernos políticos* 30 (Mexico City, 1984).

6. Ignacio Durán Loera, "El cine mexicano y sus perspectivas, *Intermedios* 4 (October 1992). See also Emilio García Riera, *Historia documental del cine mexicano* (Guadalajara: CNCA, Gobierno de Jalisco, Imcine, 1992), especially vol. 3.

7. See, for example, García Riera, *Historia documental del cine mexicano,* vols. 4 and 5; and Hugo Vargas, "El cine mexicano: la eterna crisis y la nueva generación," *La Jornada Semanal* 87 (29 February 1991).

8. Déborah Holtz, "Los públicos de video," in García Canclini, *Los nuevos espectadores.*

9. Ella Fany Quintal and Guadalupe Reyes Domínguez, "Mérida: ver cine en una ciudad de provincia," in García Canclini, *Los nuevos espectadores.*

10. Renato Janine Ribeiro, "A política como espetáculo," in Evelina Dagnino, ed., *Anos 90. Política e sociedade no Brasil.* (São Paulo: Editora Brasiliense, 1994).

11. Ibid.

12. Raúl Becerro, "El cine por venir," *Punto de vista* 47 (Buenos Aires, December 1993): 8.

8. Multicultural Policies and Integration via the Market

This chapter is a reworking and expansion of a paper presented at the Forum "Visión Iberoamericana 2000," sponsored by UNESCO in Cartagena de Indias, Colombia, 16–18 March 1994. The meeting was for the purpose of preparing a dossier of documents for the summit of Iberoamerican presidents, which was held in June of the same year, in Cartagena de Indias.

1. Lourdes Arizpe, "Pluralismo cultural y desarrollo social en América Latina: elementos para una discusión," *Estudios Sociológicos* 2:4 (Mexico City, January–April 1984); Rodolfo Stavenhagen and Margarita Nolasco, *Política cultural para un país multiétnico* (Mexico City: Universidad de las Naciones Unidas, 1988).

2. [In Latin America, and especially in Mexico, Central America, and the Andean countries, *indigenismo* is the name for a literary and artistic style that represents the circumstances and struggles of indigenous peoples. It is also the name for political movements and state policies regarding indigenous peoples.— *Trans.*]

3. Guillermo Bonfil Batalla, ed., *Hacia nuevos modelos de relaciones interculturales* (Mexico City: Consejo Nacional para la Cultura y las Artes, 1993).

4. On these topics, see José Jorge de Carvalho, *O lugar da cultura tradicional na sociedade moderna* in *Seminário folclore e cultura popular. As várias faces de um debate* (Rio de Janeiro: INF Coordenadoria de Estudos y Pesquisas/IBAC 1992), 23–38 [Spanish translation: "Las dos caras de la tradición: Lo clásico y lo popular en la modernidad latinoamericana," in *Cultura y pospolítica,* ed. Néstor García Canclini (Mexico City: Consejo Nacional para la Cultura y las Artes, 1995), 125–65]; and Roger Bartra, *Oficio mexicano* (Mexico City: Grijalbo, 1993).

5. Emile McAnany and Antonio C. La Pastina, "Telenovela Audiences: A Review and Methodological Critique of Latin American Research," paper presented at the Eighteenth Convention of the Latin American Studies Association (LASA), Atlanta, March 1994. See also Joseph D. Straubhaar, "Más allá del imperialismo de los medios. Interdependencia asimétrica y proximidad cultural," *Comunicación y sociedad* 18–19 (Guadalajara, May–December 1993).

6. Fernando Calderón and Martín Hopenhayn, "Educación y desarrollo en América Latina y el Caribe: tendencias emergentes y líneas estratégicas de acción," Third Meeting of the World Commission on Culture and Development, San José, Costa Rica, 22–26 February 1994.

7. See Carlos Catalán and Guillermo Sunkel, *Consumo cultural en Chile: la élite, lo masivo y lo popular* (Santiago: CLACSO, 1990); Néstor García Canclini, ed., *El consumo cultural en México* (Mexico City: Consejo Nacional para la Cultura y las Artes, 1993); and Oscar Landi, A. Vacchieri, and L. A. Quevedo, *Públicos y consumos culturales de Buenos Aires* (Buenos Aires: CEDES, 1990).

8. The Economic Commission for Latin America (CEPAL) is one of the few international organizations of the region that has begun to deal with these questions. See *La industria cultural en la dinámica del desarrollo y la modernidad: nuevas lecturas para América Latina y el Caribe,* LC/G. 1823 (14 June 1994).

9. Ibid., 47.

10. Manuel A. Garretón, "Políticas, financiamiento e industrias culturales en América Latina y el Caribe," Third Meeting of the World Commission on Culture and Development, San José, Costa Rica, 22–26 February 1994.

11. Rafael Roncagliolo, "La integración audiovisual en América Latina: Estados, empresas y productores independientes," paper presented at the symposium on Cultural Policies in Processes of Supranational Integration, Mexico City, 3–5 October 1994.

9. Negotiation of Identity in Popular Classes?

This chapter is based on a paper presented at the seminar "Entre el acontecimiento y la significación: el discurso sobre la cultura en el nuevo mundo," Trujillo, Spain, December 1992.

1. For a more encompassing review of popular culture studies, see Chandra Mukerji and Michael Schudson, eds., *Rethinking Popular Culture: Contemporary Perspectives in Cultural Studies* (Berkeley: University of California Press, 1991); Claude

Grignon and Jean-Claude Passeron, *Lo culto y lo popular. Miserabilismo y populismo en sociología y literatura* (Buenos Aires: Nueva Visión, 1991) [translation of *Le savant et le populaire: misérabilisme et populisme sociologie et en littérature* (Paris: Gallimard/Seuil, 1989)].

2. Arjun Appadurai, "Disjuncture and Difference in the Global Cultural Economy," in *Global Culture, Nationalism, Globalization and Modernity,* ed. Mike Featherstone (London/Newbury Park/New Delhi: Sage, 1990). See also Daniel Mato, ed., *Teoría y política de la construcción de identidades y diferencias en América Latina y el Caribe* (Caracas: UNESCO-Nueva Sociedad, 1994).

3. Néstor García Canclini, *Culturas híbridas: estrategias para entrar y salir de la modernidad* (Mexico City: Grijalbo/Consejo Nacional para la Cultura y las Artes, 1990), chapter 5 [English translation: *Hybrid Cultures: Strategies for Entering and Leaving Modernity,* trans. Christopher L. Chiappari and Silvia L. López (Minneapolis: University of Minnesota Press, 1995)].

4. Eduardo Menéndez, *Poder, estratificación y salud* (Mexico City: Ediciones de la Casa Chata, 1981), 316–86.

5. Friedrich Barth, *Los grupos étnicos y sus fronteras* (Mexico City: Fondo de Cultura Económica, 1976); R. C. Harman, *Cambios médicos y sociales en una comunidad maya tzeltal* (Mexico City: Instituto Nacional Indigenista, 1974) [original English version: "Medical and Social Changes in a Tzeltal Mayan Community," Ph.D. diss., University of Arizona, 1969].

6. Alberto M. Cirese, *Ensayos sobre las culturas subalternas* (Mexico City: Centro de Investigaciones y Estudios Superiores en Antropología Social, 1979), 53–54.

7. See, for example, Michel Foucault, *Historia de la sexualidad I: La voluntad de saber* (Mexico City: Siglo XXI, 1977). [English: *The History of Sexuality* (New York: Pantheon, 1978)].

8. Cécile Gouy-Gilbert, *Ocumicho y Patamban: dos maneras de ser artesano* (Mexico City: Centre d'Études Mexicaines et Centraméricaines, 1987).

9. I take the phrase from Anselm Strauss, *Negotiations: Contexts, Processes and Social Order* (San Francisco, Washington, and London: Jossey-Bass Publishers, 1978). For a recent discussion of the contributions of this writer and his followers, see the collection compiled by Isabelle Baszanger and her introduction, "Les chantiers d'un interaccionisme américaine," in Anselm Strauss, *La trame de la négotiation. Sociologie qualitative et interactionisme* (Paris: L'Harmattan, 1992).

10. Néstor García Canclini, Jennifer Metcalfe, and Patricia Safa, "Politicas culturales y necesidades socioculturales en la frontera norte," mimeo, 1989.

11. Rosalía Winocur, "Políticas culturales y participación popular en la Argentina. Evaluación del Programa Cultural en Barrios," thesis presented in the Facultad Latinoamericana de Ciencias Sociales (FLACSO), Mexico City, 1992.

12. Jesús Martín Barbero and Sonia Muñoz, *Televisión y melodrama* (Bogotá: Tercer Mundo Editores, 1992), 26–29.

13. Beatriz Sarlo, "Cultura y pospolítica: un recorrido de Fujimori a la guerra del Golfo," in *Cultura y pospolítica,* ed. Néstor García Canclini (Mexico City: Consejo Nacional para la Cultura y las Artes, 1995).

14. Ibid.

10. How Civil Society Speaks Today

1. On this topic, see Renato Rosaldo, *Culture and Truth: The Remaking of Social Analysis,* especially the chapter "The Changing Chicano Narratives" (Boston: Beacon Press, 1989); and George Yúdice, Jean Franco, and Juan Flores, eds., *On Edge: The Crisis of Contemporary Latin American Culture* (Minneapolis: University of Minnesota Press, 1992).

2. For a compelling treatment of this matter, see José Jorge de Carvalho, *O lugar da cultura tradicional na sociedade moderna,* in *Seminário folclore e cultura popular. As várias faces de um debate* (Rio de Janeiro: INF Coordenadoria de Estudos y Pesquisas/IBAC, 1992).

3. Robert Hughes, *Nothing if Not Critical: Selected Essays on Art and Artists* (New York: Knopf, 1990).

4. Robert Hughes, *The Culture of Complaint* (New York: Oxford University Press, 1993).

5. Roberto Alejandro, *Hermeneutics, Citizenship, and the Public Sphere* (Albany: State University of New York Press, 1993).

6. See Renato Ortiz, *Mundialização e cultura,* (São Paulo: Editora Brasiliense, 1994), chapters 4 and 5.

7. Jean-Marc Ferry, "Las transformaciones de la publicidad política," in *El nuevo espacio público,* Jean-Marc Ferry, Dominique Wolton, et al. (Barcelona: Gedisa, 1992), 18–20.

8. See Jürgen Habermas, "Citizenship and National Identity," and Richard Falk, "The Making of Global Citizenship," in *The Condition of Citizenship,* ed. Bart van Steenbergen (London, Thousand Oaks, and New Delhi: Sage Publications, 1994).

9. Norbert Lechner, "La búsqueda de la comunidad perdida. Los retos de la democracia en América Latina," *Sociológica* 7:19 (Mexico City, UAM-Azcapotzalco, May–August 1992).

10. Diamela Eltit, *El padre mío* (Santiago: Francisco Zegers Editor, 1989), 17.

11. Ricardo Piglia, *Crítica y ficción* (Buenos Aures: Siglo Veinte, 1990), 177.

Index

Identity *(continued)*, class/class struggle and, 141, 142; classic, 5–6; as coproduction, xxxv, 94–96; crisis of, 137; ethnic, 11; formation of, xxxiv, xxxviii, 16, 17, 29, 33, 60, 67, 77, 91, 137, 138, 142; fundamentalist fixation of, 80; generational conflicts and, 16; history and, 93; homogenous, 70; internationalization and, 93; Latin American/U.S., xxxvi–xxxviii; local, 96; loss of, 30; media and, 94–96; Mesoamerican/Mexican, 143; modern, xi, 29, 171n16; monadic, 68–72; multinational, 30; multiple, 133; as narrated construct, 89; national, xxv, 89, 95–96, 100, 163n2, 164n3; negation of, 138; performance/action and, 96; politics of, 13, 28; popular, 137; postmodern, 29, 171n16; as processes of negotiation, 96; reformulation of, 24, 29, 31, 94, 96, 124; regional, 79, 91, 95–96; shared, 159; sociospatial definition of, 29; struggle for, 148–49; symbols, xxv, 101; theater/politics and, 96; Western, xv

Identity narratives, 90; citizenship and, 89; radio/film, 89

Identity politics, xxxvi; cultural parallax for, xxxvii–xxxviii

Ideology, 3; developmentalist, 90

Ideoscapes, 138

Iglesias, Julio, 45

Imperialism, 4; opposition to, xxii

Import substitution, xxi, 90

Indigenous peoples, x, xxv, 11, 139, 173n5; circumstances/struggles of, 179n2; globalization and, 125–27; modernization among, 126

Industrialization, 16, 53, 72; homogeneity imposed by, 17; urban expansion and, 58

Inequality, 13, 44, 130, 160

Infante, Pedro, 72, 112

Informal economy, 19

Informatics, 152

Information: consciousness-raising, 119; global distribution of, 25; international, 102; mass media and, 76; networks, 155; for NGOs, 156; processing, 22, 59, 156; production, 29; restricted systems of, 31; technologies, 96, 100; television and, 127; transnational system of, 49; U.S. hegemony over, 103

Institute for Latin America, directory by, 130

Institutionalization, xxxii, 30

Integration, 104, 130; competition and, 154; cultural, 32, 124, 131–34; economic, 124; multiethnic relations and, 125; regional, xxxiv, 30–31, 123; supranational, 33; transnational, 128; unplugging and, 154–56

Intellectuals, 148; politicians and, 161; state/civil society and, 161

Interaction, 39, 69

Intercultural relations, 78, 89, 126, 143, 160; globalization and, xi; reconceptualization of, 142

International Film Festivals, 120

Internationalization, xxi, 75, 139; and globalization compared, 18; identity and, 93; symbols of status and, 17

International organizations, cultural actions of, 128–29

Invisible Cities (Calvino), 60

Irrationalism, exaltation of, 80

Isherwood, Baron: on rituals, 41–42

Italian Futurism, 79

Jacobin individualism, 11

Jameson, Fredric, xi

Jarman, Derek, 121

Jarmusch, Jim, 121
Jencks, Charles, 152
Joseph, Gilbert, xxiii
Journal of Consumer Marketing, 93
Jurassic Park (film), 92; Spanish/French premieres of, 98

Kaliman, 84

Labor force, reproduction of, 38–39
Labor regulation, 123, 126
Labor unions, 4, 15, 138, 148, 156; negotiation/confrontation and, 159
La ciudad ausente (Piglia), 83
La ciudad de los viajeros (García Canclini), x
Laclau, xvii, xxxiii
La globalización imaginada (García Canclini), xi, xxxvi
La mujer de Benjamín (film), 93, 114
Lang, Jack: on culture, 151
Lange, André: on horticulture of creation, 104
Languages: crisis in, 160; multiplicity of, 70
La producción simbólica (García Canclini), ix
Las batallas en el desierto (Pacheco), 65
Las culturas populares en el capitalismo (García Canclini), x
Las industrias culturales en la integración latinoamericana (García Canclini), x
Las Lomas, 71, 176n9
La Tarea (film), 93, 114
Latin America: invention of, 4; multicultural realities in, 11
Latin American Association for Integration (ALADI), 133–34
Latin American Culture House, 129
Latin American Economic System (SELA), 133
Latin American Free Trade Association (ALALC), 124

Latin American Fund for Audiovisual Production and Diffusion, 132
Latin American Fund for Cultural Development, 129
Latin American Fund for the Arts, 129
Latinamericanism, 79
Latin American Subaltern Studies Group, xiv
Lechner, Norbert, 158, 159
Left, popular masses and, xix
Legitimation strategy, xv
Leisure time, in Mexico City, 52
Lévi-Strauss, Claude, 92
Lewis, Oscar: Tepoztlán and, 51
Lezama Lima, José, 164n3, 167n39
Lifestyles, multiplicity of, 70
Like Water for Chocolate (film), 93, 103, 114, 120
Liminality, xiii, xiv
Literacy, 7; Spanish/Portuguese, 123
Literary theory, xiv
Local, globalization and, 3, 58–60, 154
Local cultures, 19, 29, 74, 90, 146; displacement of, 68; participation in, 61, 75
Lottes, Günther: on bourgeois public sphere, 22–23
Lucas, George, 92, 101
Ludmer, Josefina, 79
Lumière, 110
Lyotard, Jean-François, 41

Macondismo, xxvi, 79, 167n39
Macunaíma (film), 93
Maldita Vecindad, 85
Malinowski, Bronislaw, 51
Mallon, Florencia, xxiii, xxiv; on embedded memory/practice, xxv
Maluf, Paulo, 72
Mapplethorpe, Robert, 153
Mapuches, population of, 125
Maquiladoras, xv, 177n7
Marginalization, 126, 127

Néstor García Canclini received his doctorate in philosophy from the University of Paris. He lived in Argentina until 1976, and since then has resided in Mexico. He currently directs the program of studies on urban culture at the Universidad Autónoma Metropolitana in Mexico City. He has published twenty books on cultural studies, globalization, and the urban imagination; his book *Hybrid Cultures* (Minnesota, 1995) was chosen by the Latin American Association to receive the first Ibero-American Book Award for the best book about Latin America.

George Yúdice teaches in the American Studies program and in the Department of Spanish and Portuguese at New York University. He is the coeditor of *On Edge: The Crisis of Contemporary Latin American Culture* (Minnesota, 1992).